LEAVING MONEY
WISELY

ALSO BY DAVID W. BELIN

November 22, 1963: You Are the Jury

*Final Disclosure: The Full Truth About the
Assassination of President Kennedy*

LEAVING MONEY WISELY

*Creative Estate Planning
for Middle- and
Upper-Income Americans
for the 1990s*

David W. Belin

CHARLES SCRIBNER'S SONS
New York

Collier Macmillan Canada
Toronto

Maxwell Macmillan International
New York Oxford Singapore Sydney

Charles Scribner's Sons
Macmillan Publishing Company
866 Third Avenue
New York, NY 10022

Collier Macmillan Canada, Inc.
1200 Eglinton Avenue East, Suite 200
Don Mills, Ontario M3C 3N1

Library of Congress Cataloging-in-Publication Data
Belin, David W.
Leaving money wisely: creative estate planning for middle- and upper-income Americans for the 1990s/by David W. Belin.
p.   cm.
ISBN 0-684-19227-6
1. Estate Planning—United States—Popular works.   I. Title.
KF750.Z9B43   1990
346.7305'2—dc20   90-8502
[347.30652]

Macmillan books are available at special discounts for bulk purchases for sales promotions, premiums, fund-raising, or educational use. For details, contact:

Special Sales Director
Macmillan Publishing Company
866 Third Avenue
New York, NY 10022

Designed by Nancy Sugihara
10 9 8 7 6 5 4 3 2 1

Printed in the United States of America

*To Jon, Jim, Joy, Tom, and Laurie, my
wonderful children, who have given so much
in so many ways to me*

Contents

PART IV

Special Opportunities for People of Great Wealth

PART V

Potpourri

Preface

The Challenge of Leaving Money Wisely

Life is filled with paradoxes, many of which involve money. From my perspective as a counselor to people of moderate means as well as to the very rich, I have been astounded at how many women and men spend lifetimes accumulating money but yet spend so little time in deciding what the fate of their property will be once they are gone. People will spend more thought and effort on purchasing an automobile than they will spend on planning their estates.

Why does this happen? The primary reason is probably that individuals do not like to think about their own deaths. But there are other reasons, including the fact that preparing a will involves far more than legal doctrines and tax considerations. There is a core of fundamental psychological and emotional dilemmas to resolve. In the words of one of the most sophisticated and highly respected young business leaders in New York City, "The fact is that wills and trusts bring up a lot of stuff. They bring up issues of control, issues of people's relationship with money, people's relationship with their kids. These issues are so psychologically glaring, and so psychologically invested, it's really difficult to get people to focus on them, to unbundle them, to really confront them. As a lawyer who has dealt with this both in New York, on a very sophisticated level, and in Des Moines, at a very human level, in ways big firms can't, you have had the privilege of sitting in on theater that's better than the great playwrights could write because you've seen families work through very fundamental questions and relationships—fundamental parts of life. You are like the traditional country doctor who is also a family counselor."

He is right in his recognition of the psychological and emotional aspects of these problems (and I am sure that he would agree with me that they take place at a very human level in New York as well as in Des Moines and at a sophisticated level in Des Moines as well as in New York). When people come to me to explore in depth the planning of their estates, they go through great soul searching, and the questions they raise are the same no matter what their walk of life:

How much should I leave my spouse and how much should I leave my children? Should I leave it outright or in trust? What can I do to protect my family if the trustee is too inflexible or does a poor job of managing assets?

If I have children, should I leave anything to them as long as my spouse is living? What if she or he lives past ninety?

Should I treat all children "equally"—equally in the amount I leave them and equally in the form in which I leave the property?

What if one child is a wealthy surgeon and the other child is a schoolteacher? What if one child knows how to handle money and the other child doesn't? What if one child is unmarried and will not likely ever be married and another child is married with one or more children? What about the possibility that one or more of my children will be divorced?

What happens if I leave my children too much money? What happens if I leave my children too little money? What happens if I leave the money in trust and the trustee is too restrictive? or too expensive? or too bureaucratic?

What should I leave grandchildren? How should I leave it?

What about sons-in-law or daughters-in-law? Should I leave any money to them? Should it be conditioned on their staying married to my children?

Should I leave anything to brothers, sisters, nieces, nephews, cousins, close friends? If my parents are living, how much should I leave them and where should the property go on their death?

Should I leave any money to dear friends? How much and how?

If I am single with no children, how should I leave my money? Should I treat my collateral relatives—brothers and sisters, nieces and nephews—equally?

How much should I leave to charity? What is the best way to leave money to a charity? If I am wealthy, should I consider setting up a private foundation in my memory?

What about taxes? How bad will the tax bite be? How can I reduce taxes? What about the "generation-skipping tax" exemption?

What about the ownership of assets? If I am married, should I transfer substantial assets to my husband? to my wife? to my children?

What about gifts? What happens if I make gifts to avoid estate taxes? How much tax should I be willing to pay? How much should I retain to make sure I have enough left for me? What should women and men of great financial means do in giving their assets away to individuals and to charities?

Are there ways in which I can give other people the power to make some decisions after I am dead? What kind of powers can I give my children? or trusted friend?

What about life insurance? Who should own it? Who should the beneficiary be?

Is there any way to minimize the problems, complications, lawyers' fees and other expenses that come with probating a will? How can I best avoid probate, if I so choose?

Although most estate-planning situations involve either couples or unmarried people with children, I have also seen single people without children struggle with these problems, as they vacillate about alternative solutions.

One thing is clear: Every individual, no matter how wealthy or sophisticated, feels a lot of uncertainty about the wisest way to leave his or her money, uncertainty that is also affected by the impact of taxes. One does not have to be a multimillionaire to be affected by the federal estate tax laws. Today, anyone with more than $600,000 in assets—including the value of a home, life insurance policy proceeds, and retirement plans—is affected by these laws, and millions of Americans fall into this category.

To help you understand how to integrate tax planning with your personal estate planning, I will summarize in nontechnical language key tax considerations. I will show how those of you whose net worth exceeds $600,000 and who are not familiar with federal estate tax laws can save tens of thousands—and in the case of moderately wealthy and very wealthy taxpayers, hundreds of thousands and millions—of dollars in taxes over the years.

Many of you may have already consulted estate-planning experts who supposedly possess the technical expertise to maximize the savings of taxes. Unfortunately, some of these "experts" do not give sufficient attention to the unique family and philosophical considerations of their clients, which in the long run are even more important than tax savings. These personal considerations are often lost in the technical discussions of how best to minimize the impact of estate taxes—a classic case of missing the forest for the trees.

The perspective that I bring is unique to the extent that my early years of legal experience were in the general practice of law, primarily as an Iowa trial lawyer dealing with problems that touched all aspects of life. My trial work ranged from business and personal injury litigation to lawsuits involving constitutional issues, will contests, tax claims, and divorce and child custody controversies. One learns a lot about people when trying lawsuits in cities and towns, working with clients and witnesses, arguing before judges and juries, and dealing with the whole range of human emotion.

Over the years, my practice has evolved so that I now spend the majority of my time in the broad spectrum of the business world, with all of its related aspects—including business and estate planning for corporate executives and families of wealth. My work in this area has been helped by practical business and investment experience as well as by my educational background, which includes a graduate degree in business administration. Deliberately, I have included in my practice people from varying social and economic backgrounds, because I believe this helps keep me in touch with reality and makes me a better lawyer and counselor. In working with people to help solve their problems, there is much that I myself have learned.

Today I divide my time between Des Moines and New York, with occasional time in other major metropolitan areas. Some people think Des Moines and New York are two worlds apart, but I know from experience that there are common problems that many people face—no matter where they live—and I have focused the greater portion of this book on some of the most salient of these. Because of concern for confidentiality, the names I have used in discussing specific problems are not the actual names of the people involved, and at times the examples given are somewhat modified from the actual circumstances.

This book is in no way intended to be a substitute for the independent judgment and counsel of your own lawyer. Probate and trust laws vary from state to state. Moreover, federal estate and gift tax laws as well as state inheritance tax laws can change rapidly. Therefore, it is important to retain competent counsel to advise you of the laws in your state and, if you have potential tax problems, to keep abreast of federal and state tax law changes.

The book is divided into five major sections. Part I addresses some of the most important family questions that almost all people face when they think about how best to leave their property, and Part II addresses several special estate-planning problems.

Part III looks at important additional issues commonly faced by people of wealth or potential wealth, and Part IV offers some special opportunities for the very wealthy. The final section, which I call "Potpourri," includes chapters on the living will and statements of custody.

One thing I can guarantee: Whether you are rich or poor, old or young, married or unmarried, you will probably be making a big mistake if you do not have a will or living trust. If that is the course you choose, the state will write your will for you. In some states, here is the kind of a will the law will provide if you have no will or living trust of your own:

If I am married and have children, I leave my surviving spouse one-third of my property and my children two-thirds of my property. If I don't have a surviving spouse or children, I will leave my property to my parents, and if neither parent is living, I will leave it to my brothers and sisters.

I understand that if I have children and they are under twenty-one, guardians will have to be appointed who will manage the property for my children through a guardianship court proceeding until a child reaches age twenty-one, when he or she will get all of his share of the property outright.

In Iowa, if you die without a will and are married and either have no children or have children who are also children of your surviving spouse, new legislation directs that everything will go to your surviving spouse (and nothing will go to your children).

If you want your spouse to get more or less than one third of your property, if you want your children to have property held in a way to avoid cumbersome and expensive guardianship or conservatorship proceedings, if you don't want children to get a big lump sum of cash when they reach the age of twenty-one because you are concerned about whether they can handle it properly, then you had better prepare a will promptly. If not, and you die without a will, the laws of the state in which you live will determine where your property goes.

At the very least, I hope this book will convince you that it is important for you to take some time and think about how you want to leave your assets, and then act upon your decisions by either executing a will or a living trust.

I do not purport to ask all of the questions, nor do I attempt to provide all of the answers. Rather, my goal is to help open the door for you, broaden your perspective, challenge you to give thoughtful consideration to some important issues, and offer some suggestions and perspectives of my own to help you address the many-faceted problem of leaving money wisely to those for whom you care.

Acknowledgments

Most acknowledgments are to individuals who directly and indirectly help contribute to a book. However, from my perspective, my primary acknowledgment is to an institution—the University of Michigan, and in particular the Literary College, Graduate School of Business Administration, and Law School, where the education I received was a wonderful foundation for my professional career.

My children, who fortunately have no hesitancy to offer constructive criticism to their father, reviewed the penultimate draft and provided invaluable suggestions, as did my brother Daniel and my uncle, Marvin Klass, both superb attorneys (in Los Angeles and Sioux City, Iowa, respectively).

Michael Gartner, one of the most gifted persons I know, graciously took the time to edit my manuscript, despite the tremendous demands on his work schedule. Tom Tisch, a man of many talents and much wisdom, provided keen insights that were of great help. My brother-in-law and sister-in-law, Leonard Newman and Eileen Newman, were also of great help in their constructive comments, as was Catherine Sheridan, my secretary and assistant for more than twenty-seven years. She also patiently and capably typed and retyped again and again to enable me to meet all deadlines. Edward T. Chase, Senior Editor of Scribners, was also very helpful and supportive, and I want to express special appreciation to Kristine Dahl of International Creative Management for having confidence in my initial work and for providing me with sound counsel and advice.

Charles Harris, Jon Staudt, and Steven Zumbach—each of them an outstanding lawyer in his own right—also made important suggestions. I owe a great deal not only to them but to all of my other law partners at Belin Harris Helmick Lamson McCormick who have understood my desire to undertake many outside endeavors, ranging from the writing of my books to my activities in support of education and the arts.

Many of my close friends—both in Des Moines and in New York—have also been of great help in sharing insights with me about problems I discuss in this book. They have reinforced my conviction that the most important considerations in giving sound advice are not the academic or professional background and achievements of a person but rather basic common sense and good judgment. The critical importance of these qualities is not limited to the legal profession. They make the ultimate difference in almost every aspect of life.

LEAVING MONEY
WISELY

Introduction

*Choosing Your Financial Destiny
—Everybody's Problem*

Making lots of money is very hard. But leaving money wisely can be even harder.

I have counseled people whose only tangible assets are their home, plus some life insurance and a few thousand dollars in bank savings. I have counseled millionaires and multimillionaires. No matter the size of the pocketbook, as women and men look to the future and the inevitability of death—and, for wealthy people, death taxes—they face a common uncertainty about how best to leave their money.

Choosing the way you leave your property is part of choosing your destiny. The decisions we all face are very personal and often difficult, and I want to help broaden your perspective and encourage you to start thinking about these decisions, to confront them and understand the choices that you have, and not be frightened by them, not be put off by any "legalese." This book will, hopefully, serve to provide a framework for helping you make better decisions. In many chapters I will seek to help you make wise choices by giving you options to consider and suggestions for picking a direction in which to go. I use the word "help" because of my belief that the practice of law ultimately involves helping people. Some of my most satisfying experiences as a lawyer have

1

come from helping people gain confidence in their own wisdom and common sense to address the kinds of issues that are involved in leaving money wisely.

Most of us live our lives struggling to strike a balance between what we want for ourselves and what we want for others. We seek to do well and we also seek to do good. The accumulation of property is part of our having "done well," working hard to accumulate resources for personal enjoyment and security and, for those who have families, for the enjoyment and security of loved ones.

But when it comes to deciding how to leave the property that has been accumulated, which is part of "doing good," there is often a certain amount of ambivalence, tension, and perhaps even fear or dread. The problem is compounded because many people—perhaps most—do not like to think about preparing for death. But by not planning how to leave their money wisely, they are undermining a major portion of all of their work and effort. Moreover, they may inadvertently create strains and pressures among their beneficiaries that end up hurting the very people they love, and thus undermine part of their goal of "doing good."

Even though contemplation of one's death is not a happy thought, I believe that people can ultimately find a great deal of satisfaction when they spend sufficient time and effort in determining how they want to leave their property. There are a lot of positive things we can do toward influencing our destiny and the destinies of our loved ones. We can have a substantial influence on the kind of legacy we leave.

As you read this book, think about what you want for yourself and your loved ones, what choices you would like to make in leaving your property to your heirs, and how you might communicate your goals and aspirations to them. Your choices can make a tremendous difference in their lives.

As your perspectives are broadened, you will understand that the choices you will make can not only provide great benefits but may also involve risks. As you will see in example after example in the chapters ahead, leaving money holds the promise of providing opportunities to beneficiaries, enhancing their security, imparting responsibility to them, and encouraging positive feelings toward you, toward themselves, and toward the entire family. But leaving money also carries with it the possibilities of overburdening your beneficiaries, creating an environment in which relatives maneuver or fight with one another, potentially inhibiting motivation and fostering laziness, and even creating or exacerbating feelings of anger, guilt, envy, and regret among family members. A litany of books written by unhappy children of wealthy and powerful individuals can testify to the latter.

In this book, I will discuss strategies that enhance the positive aspects of giving over the potentially negative side effects, and I will often temper these discussions with many references to human feelings and emotions. This perspective is based on my conviction that in leaving money wisely, one of the primary considerations is the effects that our decisions will have on the people who are most important in our lives.

You will find that there are many competing considerations, some of which involve questions about how much control it is appropriate to exercise in the lives of others. Issues of equality and related issues come up again and again in various contexts throughout the book. The resolution of these issues is not necessarily easy. Yet these are the types of questions that have to be addressed. Reasonable minds can differ. Givers and receivers may have starkly different ideas of fairness, both of which may be understandable and appropriate from their personal perspectives. Ultimately, the decisions are for you to make.

Often when clients turn to me for advice as they struggle to resolve these problems, I refer to what I call "Belin Basic Rules One and Two."

Belin Rule Number One: There is more than one right way.

Belin Rule Number Two: When trying to choose among two or more alternatives, consider what you would advise your best friend to do if he or she came to you for advice under similar facts and circumstances.

These rules are applicable not only to questions about how to leave money wisely but also to many decisions that confront people in their daily lives. I think you will find that they can be very helpful in dealing with a wide range of problems for which you seek solutions.

This leads to another observation. All too often I have seen spouses of wealthy people (particularly wives of wealthy men, given the patterns of ownership of property in our society) left out of major decision making in estate planning, which is not likely to lead to the best decisions. This is not just a question of equal rights; it's a question of enhancing the quality of the decision-making process. Two perspectives are better than one, especially when there is disclosure of all relevant information and good communication. And good communication includes listening, open sharing of feelings, understanding, tolerance of different views, and "give and take" on both sides.

Sometimes when I highlight major problems, I will offer you a number of alternatives to consider and give you my recommendations. However, I do not seek to substitute my views for your own judgment or the opinion of your own attorney. Rather, I hope that you will be better prepared to reach good decisions because you will be more familiar with the problems and some of the alternatives that you can consider. This may also have the additional benefit of reducing the time you will have to spend with your attorney during the course of your consultations, in part because it should reduce the number of revisions you might otherwise make.

The most important consideration, however, does not have to do with saving time and money, but rather with something I have found in almost every family planning situation in which I have been involved: When people really focus on these problems, unbundle them, confront them, deal with them psychologically and emotionally, and understand the choices they have, they will begin to find the wisdom that's inside themselves to make wise decisions.

That wisdom doesn't necessarily come from a college degree, a Phi Beta Kappa key, or a law degree. It comes from living—from life, from experience.

So my ultimate goal in writing this book is to help you focus on these issues, confront them, deal with them, and in so doing find the wisdom that's inside you to help you reach your goal of leaving money wisely. You spent a lot of time working and saving to accumulate it; you should also spend substantial effort deciding how best to leave it. And should you at times be perplexed about which alternative to choose, please remember Belin Basic Rule Number One: *There is more than one right way.*

PART I

Basic Family Issues —Some Important Considerations

1

Leaving Money Outright to a Spouse Is Not Always Best

In a first marriage, the typical will for a married couple with no estate tax problems is usually very simple. Each person leaves all of her or his property outright to the surviving partner. If the spouse does not survive, then the property will go outright to the children or, if none, to brothers and sisters or nieces or nephews. Although this is a very natural and understandable approach, it can result in major problems.

For instance, if a wife and husband (or single parent) are killed in a car accident, and there are children under legal age who survive and there is no trust, the property will generally be managed under the jurisdiction of a court. This is often a cumbersome and relatively expensive proceeding, with the added disadvantage of limited investment flexibility.

There is another potential risk associated with a child receiving her or his inheritance outright on attaining legal age. Young people often make mistakes in handling large sums of money they receive in one lump sum, mistakes they would not make if they were older and had more experience. Despite my overall disposition that free choice is a desirable state of affairs, I have seen lots of situations that suggest that young people who receive large amounts of money in one lump sum may dissipate all or a major portion in a relatively short time. Restraints on access to inherited wealth make sense in many instances.

Problems can also arise when a couple have no children. If an experienced businessman or businesswoman leaves everything to a spouse, and the spouse is not experienced in handling assets, the property could be mismanaged and conceivably be entirely dissipated. The event of remarriage poses another potential problem: property owned by an inexperienced widow or widower may become subject to the control of the second spouse, which can lead to many negative ramifications.

Related to these scenarios is the question of what happens to property owned by a couple without children when one partner leaves everything to the other. If the husband dies first and the wife receives all of the property, on her death the property might very well go to members of her family—brothers and sisters, nieces and nephews—with none to the family of the husband. Sometimes couples avoid this eventuality by having wills that state that the person who is the second to die will leave the property, half to the husband's side and half to the wife's side.

But the terms of a will are alterable, subject to a person's shifting moods. A person can make a will today and change that will tomorrow. And while a will may include a contractual provision prohibiting any change, contractual documents of this kind can result in unexpected tax consequences.

These complex problems illustrate why it is often better to consider the alternative known as a *trust,* a uniquely flexible device that is not nearly as complex as most people assume. Instead of leaving money outright, the property is left to a trust for the benefit of a particular person or persons. They are known as *beneficiaries.*

When property is placed in trust, a third person, called the *trustee,* manages the property. Income is distributed in accordance with the directions of the person who created the trust (who is known as the *settlor* or *trustor*). The settlor generally also gives directions about whether the principal of the trust can also be used, if needed, for the beneficiaries.

Sometimes the "third person" is more than one individual. It could be two co-trustees, one of whom may be a financial institution with expertise in managing assets. The other trustee may be an individual, including a beneficiary of the trust, such as the spouse or a child.*

To understand how a trust works, the starting point is the basic concept that there are two aspects to property: the earnings that the property produces, which are generally referred to as *income,* and the *principal* of the trust, which is sometimes called the *corpus.* Under the terms of many trust instruments, portions of the principal can be withdrawn, or *invaded,* from time to time if the beneficiary needs more funds than are available from the income.

To illustrate how a trust works, we can start with a simple example—a $100,000 savings account. The importance of that savings account is twofold: It produces income and it also has principal available that one can draw upon if the income is insufficient to meet current living needs. Of course, the more principal that is withdrawn, the less remaining principal there is to earn income, and gradually the income stream becomes smaller. This, in turn, may lead to increased invasion of principal, and eventually the $100,000 will be gone.

On the other hand, if the principal is not invaded, the income will go on for as long as the trust is in existence. And if the principal is invested wisely in a combination of fixed income assets (such as a savings account, a money market fund, or bonds that pay a specified rate of interest) and growth assets that can increase in value (such as sound stocks or real estate), the principal can gradually increase and eventually produce more income.

The allocation of principal and income from any particular trust is dependent upon the terms of the written instrument that creates the trust. A typical trust arrangement for a husband and wife with a relatively small estate will provide that the surviving spouse will receive all of the income from the trust and, in addition, the trustees will pay whatever is necessary out of the principal of the trust to provide for the proper care, support, and maintenance of the surviving spouse and any children.

---

*Where beneficiaries are trustees, income tax problems as well as estate tax problems can arise if there are not also independent trustees who exercise whatever discretionary power there may be in the trust instrument to distribute income and principal.

Then, on the death of the surviving spouse, the trust instrument will specifically state where the property is to go. If there are children who are to receive the property outright, the trust will state at what ages the property will be distributed. In the meantime, the trust will typically provide that income and, if needed, principal will be distributed to the beneficiaries in accordance with the terms of the trust until the time of final distribution. If there are no children, the trust instrument may very well specify that one half will go to the brothers and sisters of the husband and the other half will go to the brothers and sisters of the wife. There may also be provisions for other relatives or close friends.

For older couples, the trust offers another important advantage. It can automatically take care of the situation where the surviving spouse may not be physically or mentally competent to handle his or her own financial resources. Even if the surviving spouse is initially competent to handle the assets that have been left, the passing of years might diminish the mental capacity to handle this property. If the property is left in trust, it can readily be administered by the trustee. (If the surviving spouse was originally designated a co-trustee, the remaining trustee can readily handle the administration.)

In contrast, if the property is left outright and serious physical or mental incapacity develops, this may force the family to resort to a conservatorship—a cumbersome, expensive legal proceeding that involves far more red tape and time of lawyers and courts than most well-drawn trusts. Conservatorships also have much less flexibility in the investment and management of assets. Corporate trustees, of course, charge management fees, but most experts agree that a trust is far preferable to a conservatorship.

Another practical matter to consider relates to what might happen if the surviving spouse remarries. In many states, if there is no prenuptial agreement to the contrary, when a couple get married and subsequently one partner dies, the surviving partner can elect to receive a portion of the property, such as one-third, even though that was not the intent of the couple when they first got married. That entitlement is called a *dower interest.*

Approximately fifteen years ago, Howard, a man in his eighties, was widowed. Some years later he married Alice, a woman in her seventies, who was also widowed. They each had estates of several hundred thousand dollars. Both agreed that, in the event one of them died, the other one would not expect to receive any of the property because the property should instead go to the deceased partner's children. I urged that they put this agreement in writing, before the marriage, but they both assured me that they trusted one another and there was no need to do this.

Five years later, Howard died. The children of Alice helped persuade their mother that, even though she and her second husband had agreed neither would claim any dower interest in the other's estate, she had given him a lot of care, particularly in the year preceding his death, and it was only "fair" that she exercise her statutory rights. Indeed, this is what she did, and she received one-third of Howard's property, which, in turn, on her death went to her children instead of his.

From the standpoint of Howard's children, the problem was compounded because Howard's first wife, Virginia, left a substantial amount of property to Howard, outright. In turn, when Howard died, Alice's claim for one-third of all of his property included the property he had inherited from his first wife. If Virginia had just left the money to Howard in trust, with the provision that Howard would have all of the income during his life, and also that the trustee could spend part of the principal, if necessary, to provide for Howard's proper care, support, and maintenance, on Howard's death Alice would not have received any portion of that property and the oral understanding between Howard and Alice would have been honored as to that portion of the estate.

Similar problems can arise with younger families. Mary's husband, Bill, died in an auto accident when he was only thirty-four. His estate was over $500,000, primarily because of benefits paid under an accidental death life insurance policy. The proceeds of the policy were paid outright to Mary, rather than being placed in trust. They had one child. A number of years later Mary remarried, but she had no more children. Not too long after the second marriage, Mary died. Her second husband made a claim against her estate and received one-third of Mary's property, which in fact constituted the funds that Bill had left and that Bill (and perhaps Mary) would have wanted to go to their child. The point here is not whether it was or was not appropriate that Mary's second husband received one-third of Mary's property. Rather, the point is that people should not ignore these issues and have the matter resolved by what the law provides in the state of their residence. They should be aware of these possibilities and make conscious decisions about what they feel is appropriate.

Another common consideration concerns the possibility of divorce. Here again, trusts serve a useful purpose. When property is left outright by one spouse to another, and the surviving spouse remarries but the second marriage does not work out, that property in many states can often become entangled in divorce disputes. In contrast, if the property is left in trust, the surviving spouse is somewhat more protected from the claims of the divorcing partner.

Some people believe that, despite all of the problems that can arise when property is left outright to a spouse, the advantages of leaving money outright nevertheless outweigh the disadvantages. After all, why should the surviving spouse not have complete control of the property without bringing in a trustee?

There is one set of circumstances where for income tax reasons you may want to avoid using a testamentary trust. This involves a provision in the tax laws known as Subchapter S, which allows a small corporation to be taxed as a partnership. A Subchapter S election normally cannot be made if one of the shareholders is a trust. (However, a revocable or a living trust, which is discussed in Chapter 10, can own stock in a Subchapter S corporation.)

One other disadvantage of a trust occurs where the assets are relatively small and there is a corporate trustee. There are certain minimal costs of corporate trust management, regardless of the size of the trust, and in a small trust the amount of trustee fees can take a disproportionately large portion of the income.

Here is my overall recommendation, should you have no strong preferences of your own: Leave your property in a trust. A well-prepared trust instrument with capable trustees offers protection and flexibility for many possible problems that can arise. Consider making your surviving spouse a co-trustee. Give your spouse all of the income and give the independent trustee the additional power to use whatever principal is needed to provide for the proper care, maintenance, and support of your spouse. If your assets, including your house, life insurance, and retirement plans, total more than $200,000, consider incorporating in that trust instrument some of the added power of appointment provisions for added flexibility that will be discussed in Chapter 17.

Because the surviving spouse will receive all of the income, from an income standpoint the trust is as advantageous as if she or he owned the property outright. If there are provisions for invading principal to provide for proper care, support, and maintenance, a trust can also meet financial needs in almost the same way that would occur if the property were owned outright. The other area of concern relates to the selection and management of trust assets. By making a surviving spouse a co-trustee, he or she can participate in management decisions. This does not have any adverse tax consequences as long as it is the independent trustee who makes the decisions on the distribution of principal and on the distribution of income, if the trust instrument does not provide for mandatory distribution to the surviving spouse.

If the total assets of the trust are less than $200,000, you may want to avoid using a corporate trustee, because the fees charged might take up too large a share of income. You can investigate current schedules of trust management fees before you make any decision.

A well-prepared trust document with capable trustees has many advantages. To sum up very simply, leaving money outright to a spouse is often not best. A trust can usually provide much upside gain with little downside risk.

2

Leaving Money Outright
to Children
Is Not Always Best

In the typical will for a person with children, if there is no surviving spouse because of death or divorce, the property generally is distributed outright to the children.

In many instances this may be fine, but there are situations where this can result in difficulties. We have already discussed problems that can arise when property is left outright to children who are not of legal age. Even when the size of the estate is not large, the astute person with young children will consider putting the property in trust instead of leaving it outright to children. The trust terms can provide that the income can be used for their proper care, support, maintenance, and education, and the trustee can be given discretionary power to invade the principal, if necessary. Then, when the children reach an age when the parent thinks they can handle large sums of money, the property can be distributed outright.

There are many people who elect to leave money in trust for their children for many years after they attain the age of twenty-one, particularly in medium-size and large estates. Here is a specific example that involved a salaried, middle-tier executive and a schoolteacher who were approaching retirement age. They had accumulated a net worth of $400,000, which included the equity in their home, life insurance, and retirement plans. They had only one child, who was thirty-five years old, and they wanted him to have the rest of the property when both of them were no longer living. Although they had confidence in their son's judgment—he was not a spendthrift—they asked about alternatives to leaving the property outright.

In my consultations with this couple, I pointed out that if their $400,000 remained intact in a trust, it could be invested in a combination of bonds and stocks, giving their son a substantial annual income for the rest of his life. An average return of 6 percent would yield $24,000 a year, or $2,000 a month. On the death of their son, the property would then go to their grandchildren, and because the property was held in trust it would be distributed free of any estate or inheritance taxes.*

We then turned to the question of how their son could be protected in the event for some reason he wanted to have access to the principal. Trust instruments frequently give the independent trustee the right to use principal, if necessary, for the trust beneficiary's care, support, maintenance, and education. But many individuals are naturally concerned about whether trustees would be sufficiently generous in the event that a particular family need arose. My experience is that trustees generally respond liberally in times of need, but I suggested that, if there were any doubt, the trust terms could give the child a right each year to take out 5 percent of the principal. I then reviewed other advantages of a trust. No one can predict what future federal estate tax rates will be. By leaving assets in trust for a child, one can insulate the property from any estate taxes on his or her death so that it could go to grandchildren tax free. If the child were to die without children, the trust instrument could designate that the remaining assets go to whomever the couple desired—brothers, sisters, nieces, nephews, friends, or particular charities.

In addition, by having the property in trust, rather than being given outright, the property could be shielded from potential creditors of the child in the event the child experienced financial dif-

---

*This ignores generation-skipping taxes where more than $1 million is involved.

ficulty. A well-prepared trust instrument will contain a provision called a *spendthrift provision,* which shields the property from creditors. That provision will state that the beneficiary cannot assign her or his interest in the trust, and that a creditor of the beneficiary cannot levy or attach the beneficiary's interest in the trust to pay off a debt or judgment. (However, the creditor can levy against funds the beneficiary may have received from the trust.) The trustee will still have the discretion to pay out amounts to the beneficiary, but the distribution will be solely discretionary and will not be subject to any claims of creditors.

Another advantage to using a trust arises if a child is divorced. Property owned outright by a child generally becomes part of the property to be divided by the court. On the other hand, if property remains in trust, it is at least partially shielded from claims of the child's spouse.

There is yet another advantage to a trust: It can act as a shield from the psychological pressures exerted by a spouse or other members of a family. Early in my career I had a client who left his daughter a relatively large sum of money. Within a year after the inheritance, her husband, who was a salaried business executive at a middle level, began to pressure his wife (my client's daughter) to enable him to invest the money in a business that had all the earmarks of fabulous success.

At first she resisted, because she felt she was putting at risk her lifetime security. But her husband was very persistent—and persuasive. "Look at the opportunity we have to make all of this money for ourselves and our children." The emotional pulls became stronger, and the wife soon realized that if she did not yield to her husband, the issue would affect their marriage adversely. She turned over most of the inheritance to him. Unfortunately, the husband turned out to be a better middle-level executive than an entrepreneur, and he lost the entire sum.

This sad outcome could have been avoided if the property had been left in trust. If the husband desired to invest in a business, he could have waited several years to accumulate income from the trust. If the accumulated income had been invested in a new business, and the business fell flat on its face, the basic principal would still have been intact and would have continued to produce income. The wife would not have been subjected to pressure and potential adverse impact on her marriage because the choice would not have been hers to invest the principal. Indeed, when the husband lost all of the principal, this made the wife very angry, as one can well understand, and her marriage was adversely affected. Her parents did her no favor by leaving the money outright; she would have been better served financially, and psychologically, if the inheritance had been in a trust.

Another reason for leaving property in trust for children involves situations where the parents are divorced with unmarried children. No parent likes to think of a child predeceasing her or him, but it can occur. If a child dies who has never been married and has no children, and that child has no will, under the laws of most states, any property of that child will pass to her or his surviving parents.

Here is an example of what could occur. While Charles and Jane were married, they built a very expensive vacation house in Colorado. Marital problems subsequently developed, and they were divorced. Under the terms of the decree, Jane received title to the vacation house. When Charles remarried, Jane started to think about her will, which at the time left all of her property to her only child, Amy. Suddenly Jane realized that if she left her property to Amy and if Amy should die without a husband or children, and without a will, all of the property could go back to Charles and, on Charles's death, could end up with Charles's second wife. That scenario was not exactly number one on Jane's priority list. So she changed her will and left the property in a trust with very flexible terms. If Amy died without children, in no way would Charles ever inherit any of Jane's property.

To leave money wisely, one should understand the alternative of a trust. In most situations, a trust can be tailor-made to meet the particular needs and circumstances of each family.

One way of looking at the alternatives is to think of what it actually means to own property outright. When you put it in very basic terms, it simply means to have the right to income, the right to use the principal, and the right to manage the assets. Correspondingly, a trust directs how income is to be distributed and how principal is to be distributed. As we discussed in Chapter 1, if the trust provides for mandatory distribution of income, there really is no difference so far as access to income is concerned. And the provisions of a trust can provide for great flexibility for access to principal, including, as we shall see in Chapter 16, the possibility of giving a child direct access each year to a portion of the property, regardless of what the trustee says. A trust instrument can also direct that an adult child can be a co-trustee of the share of the trust being held for him or her and can help participate in the decisions to manage trust assets.

One of the reasons I strongly recommend that clients consider leaving property in trust is that, in the great majority of families with whom I have worked, I have seen that the advantages gained by leaving property in trust for children have far outweighed the disadvantages.

When should property be distributed outright to children? My own preference is to give a child two or three opportunities to handle a large sum. For example, if a trust were to have $75,000 of principal, instead of having a child get the entire $75,000 in one lump sum at age twenty-one, I might suggest distributing half at twenty-five and half at thirty, or one-third at twenty-five, one-third at thirty, and one-third at thirty-five. The undistributed balance can continue to be held in trust, with the income distributed each year to the child. There can also be flexible provisions to invade the principal if there are specific needs, such as medical bills, college or post-graduate education costs, a down payment for a house, the purchase of an automobile or household furniture, etc.

Should one provide that all of the income goes outright to the child until the end of the trust, or should the trustee be given discretion to distribute only as much of the income as is necessary to provide for the proper care and support of the child? This is a very personal decision and depends on many factors, including the personal characteristics of the children of the family and the amount of property involved. If the trust is not large, most people provide for mandatory distribution of income. Many people do this in large trusts as well, unless they have concern about the ability of the child to handle money. Because I have seen many situations where children made serious mistakes when they received an immediate influx of substantial income they previously did not have, and where excessive income sometimes inhibited motivation or otherwise had an adverse impact on a child, I lean toward giving the trustee some discretion. If a beneficiary has minor children, there are also potential income tax benefits by giving the trustee discretion to distribute income among family members, taking advantage of the children's lower tax brackets.

In an age when the divorce rate is relatively high, when traditional habits of thrift are often dismissed as outmoded, I strongly recommend putting property in trust for beneficiaries, rather than leaving it outright. After all, most of us grew up without any outside income of any kind and would have thought that annual distributions of substantial income from a trust would have been a wonderful blessing. To be sure, whenever property is placed in trust, instead of being distributed outright, there are psychological issues of dominance and control. But the practical experience that I have had, the real life situations I have so often seen, form the basis for my conclusion that, in most family situations, leaving money to children in trust has greater advantages than leaving money outright.

3

All Children
Are Not Equal

What do you do when you have three children—a schoolteacher earning $30,000 a year, an ophthalmologist earning $300,000 a year, and a graduate student heading toward a business career? Do you divide your property equally among all three?

If you are a multimillionaire and can leave each of your three children several million dollars, it may not make too much difference. But suppose you have $600,000 to divide. If you divide it into three equal amounts, then each of the three children will get $200,000, which, assuming an average yield of 6 percent, will produce $12,000 a year of income. To the schoolteacher, the income could make a major difference in life-style. It may even enable the teacher to purchase a home, which might otherwise not be affordable. Or if the teacher has children, the added funds could be used to help pay for a child's college education.

On the other hand, the added $12,000 a year of income to the ophthalmologist will not bring about much difference in life-style —at least as long as she or he is in good health and able to practice ophthalmology. Yet, if the ophthalmologist were to be ignored in overall estate planning, just on the basis of high earnings, she or he might feel very resentful toward parents or siblings.

When this problem was presented to me several years ago, I

developed a proposal that I called the "extra common share" approach, and my clients liked the concept. I suggested that my clients, instead of dividing their estates into equal parts for each of their three children, divide their estates into four parts. The fourth part would be a common share. The income from that share would be distributed to those children who were earning less than $75,000 a year annually, with that figure to be adjusted by inflation. If all of their children were earning above the $75,000 floor, then the income would be divided equally among all three, but if only two were earning above $75,000, then the third child would get all of the income from the fourth share.

The family liked the philosophy underlying this approach. They felt it would be the best way to take into consideration changes in earning power from year to year and yet not engender any hard feelings among their children. The trust instrument also provided that the earnings of a spouse would be taken into consideration. Eventually, the $75,000 floor was increased to $90,000.

The equal treatment dilemma is not a new one, and people have attempted to resolve it in many ways. More than twenty years ago, a retired man in his eighties scheduled annual meetings with his lawyers to change his will. He had immigrated to the United States as a young boy and raised seven children. He accumulated an estate of nearly $750,000—about $100,000 per child. The purpose of his annual lawyers' meeting was to redivide his estate among his children, according to their changing economic circumstances. If he felt that a child was very well off, or was married to someone who was very well off, that child got nothing, and the money was redistributed among the two or three who "needed it most."

When he died, there were two children who received nothing, and they were very resentful—not at those sisters and brothers who had received the extra money, but rather at their father. They felt that they should have been left some amount of property. Even if it would not have been a full share, at least it would have symbolized the fact that their father cared as much for them as he cared for his other children.

The "extra common share" approach, although it is not perfect, helps resolve such problems. It also addresses changing economic conditions that can develop from time to time.

Other circumstances may arise where treating children "equally" is not necessarily the wisest course. Some families are confronted with the problem that one of their children has a learning disability or a severe medical problem that requires substantial additional funds for care and treatment.

No absolute rules cover this area. I have generally counseled clients that in addition to looking at the actual dollars involved, they should take into consideration the proportional relationship between the enlarged share given one child as compared with the reduced shares for siblings. For instance, I once counseled a couple with four children, one of whom had a learning disability. The parents knew they did not want to divide their property equally, but they were not sure what adjustment to make. As a starting point for discussion, I suggested that they might take 3 percentage points each from the 25 percent shares of the three children without disabilities, reducing their shares to 22 percent each. The total of 9 points taken away would be added to the 25 percent share of the child with the learning disability so that his share became 34 percent. From the perspective of the three children who were not disabled, their reduction from 25 to 22 percent was not that substantial. But on a relative basis, their disadvantaged brother had 12 percentage points more than their 22 percent, or a share that was approximately 50 percent greater. The family felt that this arrangement provided appropriately for their disadvantaged child.

In a three-child family with a similar problem, I suggested in our initial conference that they consider taking away 5⅓ percentage points from each of their two children who were not disadvantaged. This reduced their share from 33⅓ percent to 28 percent. The total of 10⅔ percentage points taken away was then added to the share of the child with the learning disability, increasing her share from 33⅓ percent to 44 percent. Among the three children, the relationship of percentages was 28-28-44 instead of 33⅓ percent each. The extra 16 percentage points for the child with the learning disability was slightly more than 50 percent above the 28 percent base of the other two children.

In both of these situations, I did not try to convince the families what the exact percentage ratio should be. Rather, I wanted to propose possible guideposts to help each family arrive at what they believed to be equitable distribution for their children. Obviously, the ratios that a family decides upon are affected by the specific needs and by the actual dollars involved. It is also important to be alert to the need to make modifications promptly when circumstances change.

In situations involving a disabled child, it often helps to sit down with those children who are not faced with the physical or mental impairment and explain why you are setting aside some extra money in trust to take care of their sister or brother. Frank discussions of this kind can often lead to understanding and acceptance of the overall estate plan and even gratitude for being informed.

However, I do not necessarily recommend that differences in treatment of children or even the "extra common share" approach should always be discussed with children when the only differences are based on the question of economic earnings. That depends to a large extent upon the individuals involved. In some situations it can be very constructive, and in other situations it can result in numerous family difficulties.

When I was an eighteen-year-old Army enlistee, I remember a platoon sergeant advising me that, if I didn't know the answer to a question, I should always say, "It depends upon the situation and the terrain." When a parent or parents are considering treating children unequally in the division of property, a discussion ahead of time is not necessarily wise, even when they are mature adults. It all depends "on the situation and the terrain."

Often the question of equal treatment is more subtle and does not involve differences in the amount of property being left among children. Rather, the issue concerns whether there should be equality in the form in which property is left. Recently I was approached by a couple in New York with two daughters, one of whom, Barbara, was an employee working for a bank in New York, and the other, Jean, was living with an actor in California and was only intermittently employed. Philosophically, the parents wanted to hold the property in trust until their daughters were in their middle thirties. They then felt that Barbara's share could be distributed outright to her, but they did not want to leave any money outright to Jean because they felt she would go through her inheritance within a relatively few years. If they gave money to Barbara outright and did not do the same for Jean, they felt Jean would be resentful toward them and also perhaps toward her sister. What should they do?

After discussing several possibilities, we narrowed them to two choices. In the first scenario, the parents would sit down with Jean and discuss their concerns with her. They would let her know that whatever money they were leaving her would be left in trust, with the understanding that she would receive all of the income. The trustee would be empowered to give her principal if she really needed it for a particular purpose. Jean's parents might also tell her that, although they were firm in that decision so far as her share was concerned, they had not made any final decision on Barbara's share. Jean knew that Barbara was more experienced in dealing with money, and the parents could ask Jean if she were to have any objection if Barbara's share were to go outright to her. Jean's response might have some effect on the final decision.

The alternative approach was to keep the property in trust for both. This could not only save taxes, but it also would shield property from creditors and from the divorce courts and would offer a number of other benefits that trusts provide.

Eventually, the parents decided on a compromise approach. The mother in her will kept the property in trust for both daughters, and the father in his will kept Jean's share in trust but gave Barbara her share outright, one-half at age thirty-five and one-half at forty.

Myriad other circumstances can lead a person to treat children unequally. For instance, one college professor left his wife after twenty-five years of marriage and married a younger woman. He had three children, one of whom remained bitter about his father's divorce and became very distant. His father struggled. "On the one hand, I want to treat my children equally, but yet one has caused me such consternation that I just don't feel right about giving him a full third." He eventually decided to disinherit that son.

In another situation, a wealthy industrialist with two sons made annual outright gifts aggregating over $400,000 each. The accumulated funds were turned over to each son when he reached twenty-one and provided annual income approaching $30,000. One son was a hard-working middle manager of a small corporation. The other was unemployed, living off the income from the $400,000, and had become addicted to drugs.

His father took a very hard position: "I am not going to subsidize his drug habit even more."

"But you can't completely cut him out," said the industrialist's wife. "He's addicted—it's a sickness—with help and counsel he can get over it."

In her will, the mother divided her property equally, but she put it in trust with discretionary powers in the trustee to distribute income and principal and with a letter making the trustee aware of the drug problem. In his will, the father also left the property in trust, but he did not divide his property equally between his two sons.

These are typical examples of situations where equality of treatment is not always chosen.

There is more than one right way to divide property among your children. In making decisions about which path to take, one cardinal rule to remember is that all children are not equal, and there is no absolute requirement that all children must be treated equally under a will or living trust.

Issues of power and control are often present. If one is angry or disappointed with a child, that child can be disinherited. I have seen it happen on very few occasions, generally where either crime or total estrangement is involved. Even here I have suggested some leavening by putting a portion of the property in a trust to cover the possibilities of rehabilitation or reconciliation.

If you have no strong opinions of your own concerning questions of equality of treatment of all children, here are my overall recommendations. Those people who want to leave money wisely will at the very least consider whether in their particular family situation it is appropriate to have some variance from absolute equality. The greater the differences in circumstances, the greater the reasons for differentiation.

Where differences between children involve limitations because of mental or physical capabilities, it is often appropriate to make percentage adjustments. Where one child is financially better off and has far greater future prospects of high financial earnings, it is also often appropriate to make adjustments, with one caveat:

Those high earnings may not go on forever if health or other problems arise.

Where the differences are basically those involving economic earning power or net worth, I lean toward the "extra common share" approach because of its combination of fairness and flexibility in adapting to changing circumstances. The minimum base line can be whatever figure you choose, such as $50,000 a year, $75,000, or even more. It is very important to provide in the trust instrument that this baseline be adjusted by a Consumer Price Index* formula, so that changes in the value of distort the overall plan.

If the question of equal treatment involve leaving property outright to one child and in unless there are problems such as a medical d impairment, I would lean toward equal treatm can put the property in trust for one or more cl period of time you feel is appropriate. Howe that one of the reasons I reach this conclusion i ence that, in the great majority of circumsta for children in trust works out better than leaving money outright.

If one's children are all adults, it may be helpful to discuss these problems directly with them. In many cases, the input from the children can be helpful in reaching any final decision. But this can raise other issues, like power and control. The relationships between parents and children, the relationships between and among siblings, and the amount of money involved, all influence the decision. "It all depends on the situation and the terrain." If you are a parent, the decision is yours. It can be one of the most important financial decisions that you will ever make.

Decisions about possible inequality in treatment of one's children can be very difficult. I can almost guarantee that from time to time you will have some doubts about which way to go. If those doubts are substantial, or if they continue, then my recommendation would be to treat the children equally—both in the amounts that you give them and in the form in which you leave the property.

*The Consumer Price Index is a standard index published by the United States Government.

4

Problems of Equity
Among Grandchildren

Most people start from the premise that they want to treat their grandchildren equally. But sometimes it is difficult to determine how to measure equality. Here is a specific example.

Fred and Dorothy have two children, John and Mary. John has one child and Mary has three children, so Fred and Dorothy have four grandchildren. Under typical circumstances, when Fred and Dorothy have passed away, their property would go one-half to John and one-half to Mary. In turn, when John died, he would leave his property to his child (assuming no surviving spouse), who would then get *half* of the total property left by the grandparents. When Mary died, assuming she also left no surviving spouse, she would probably leave her property to her three children. Collectively, they would get one-half of their grandparents' property. But individually, each grandchild would get one-third of their mother's one-half share, or *one-sixth* of the original property left by the grandparents. The net result would be that John's child gets three times as much property as each of his cousins.

This example illustrates what is called *per stirpes* distribution. Each child is treated as a separate family group and the children of that child share equally in the portion of what their own parent had. However, one grandchild ends up with half of the total estate of the grandparents and the other grandchildren each end up with one-sixth (or, collectively, three-sixths) of the estate. Does this treat grandchildren equally?

The alternative approach is what is known as a *per capita* distribution, where each grandchild would get one-fourth of her or his grandparents' property. If the per capita alternative were selected, in this case it would mean that Mary's children would inherit three-fourths of the total property left by the grandparents and John's child would inherit only one-fourth. Is this fair when, during their lifetimes, John would have been entitled to one-half of the estate while the other half would have gone to Mary?

The diagram in Figure 1 may help you to understand the difference between per stirpes and per capita.

Figure 1.

Fred and Dorothy, grandparents, have two children, John and Mary. They leave their property in trust for the lifetimes of their children, and on the death of their children the trust terminates and the property goes to their grandchildren. John has one child. Mary has three children.

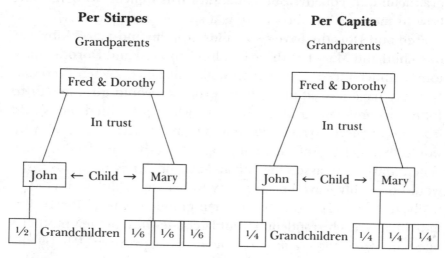

Per Stirpes: John's child inherits the share of his father and gets a full ½ of the trust. Mary's three children inherit the share of their mother and together receive a full ½ of the trust, or ⅙ each.

Per Capita: The total share of the grandparents is divided equally among the four grandchildren, each getting ¼.

There are no easy answers to the grandchildren conundrum. Most people generally choose the per stirpes alternative, treating each child as a single-family group and having the share of that child divided among the generation that follows. However, the majority is not always right.

Suppose Mary had four or five children instead of three? The disparity between what her children and her brother's child would each receive becomes even greater.

One of the most recent situations I have encountered in this area involved Homer and Helen, a couple of great wealth. They had three children. One was unmarried, one was married with one child, and one was married with four children. The heart of our discussion concerned the possibility of their taking advantage of a special provision in the law known as the *Gallo rule* because the tax benefit was lobbied by the Gallo family of wine-making fame in California. The tax background of the Gallo rule is that generally all large outright gifts (except for gifts to a spouse) and all gifts in trust are subject to gift tax, which can be as high as 55 percent. But if gifts are made to grandchildren or great-grandchildren, they are also subject to an additional very high tax known as the *generation-skipping tax*. The generation-skipping tax was an attempt by Congress to make up for lost revenue when grandparents transferred property directly to grandchildren, thereby avoiding the additional tax that would have been incurred if the property had passed to their children and had been included in their children's taxable estates. The special Gallo statute said that a taxpayer could give away up to $2 million to each grandchild and escape the onerous generation-skipping tax provisions of the Internal Revenue Code, provided that the gift was made before January 1, 1990. (The gift would still be subject to the regular gift tax.) Many extremely wealthy taxpayers considered taking advantage of the Gallo rule.

When Homer and Helen considered making Gallo gifts to their five grandchildren, questions of equality immediately arose. This was a strictly per capita rather than a per stirpes gift. What should be done about the child who was not married and had no children? What about the married child who, in turn, had only one child? Was it fair to give her child $2 million while her sister's children received $8 million?

I suggested that to meet this problem an adjustment could be made in the provisions of the donors' wills. Before dividing property equally among family groups, they could first make some outright gifts to their children that would take into consideration the fact that one family group received $8 million of gifts under the Gallo rule, another received only $2 million, and the third received none.

I suggested as a further adjustment that the couple might even add an after-tax interest factor, to run from the date of the gifts to the date of donor's death, which would take into consideration the fact that the grandchildren had earnings on the gifts that were given to them. In other words, the person who had no children would first get $8 million out of the estate, plus an interest factor such as 5 or 6 percent a year measured by the time span between the date of the gift and the date of the donor's death.

Even though from a tax-planning standpoint the Gallo gifts made sense, and even though there could be some general adjustment through the use of provisions in the wills of the donors, Homer and Helen finally decided that from an emotional and psychological standpoint they did not feel comfortable in creating such a wide disparity among their children as family groups. Despite the very favorable tax treatment afforded by the Gallo rule, they decided to pass and make no Gallo gifts.

I have developed a relatively simple per stirpes–per capita "combination share" compromise that I recommend clients consider as a possible solution in cases where the estate is not large enough to be subject to the generation-skipping tax. Let us go back to our example where John had one child and Mary had three children. The parents of John and Mary could have divided their property into three equal shares. The first share could be held in trust for John with the proviso that John receive the income during his lifetime and that the trustee have the power to invade the principal for his benefit, if needed. Anything left over on John's death would go to his child. The second share could be for Mary, with the proviso that Mary receive the income during her lifetime and that the trustee have the power to invade the principal for her benefit. On her death the property would be distributed to her three children. The third share could be a share for both John and Mary, with income to go to John and Mary in equal shares for their lifetimes. When one of them died, the survivor would continue to receive all of the income from that share. On the death of both John and Mary, the property could be distributed per capita, one fourth for each of the four grandchildren. This approach favors the child who survives, but most parents think this is an appropriate way to compromise.

Another practical alternative that I have often suggested for consideration is to go half and half—half per capita and half per stirpes.

Discussing these issues with an attorney who has substantial experience in estate planning can generally be very helpful. But ultimately the final decision is a personal one.

In looking at the conundrum of grandchildren equality, there is one other consideration, which, of course, is similar to questions that arise when one considers how to leave property to children. What will the grandchildren think? If one grandchild receives three times as much as his cousins because he or she happened to have no siblings, will this lead the cousins to feel that they were unfairly treated by their grandparents? Should this be of concern to the grandparents in their deliberations about how to leave the property?

Obviously, grandparents care about how their grandchildren might view these decisions. Some people have come to me and raised the possibility of discussing the per capita–per stirpes dilemma with their children and grandchildren and telling everyone how and why they have reached their decision. Perhaps in some families this would be helpful. However, my experience has been that in many families premature discussions about these decisions often create unpleasant situations for all concerned. In our hypothetical situation, Mary and her children might be upset with per stirpes and John and his child could be upset with per capita. Why open up this possibility?

If you are in doubt, I would recommend not discussing this emotionally charged issue with your family unless you think there is a compromise that would satisfy everybody. If any family disagreement arises, it will come at the time of ultimate distribution, when you will no longer be living. Accordingly, you will not be caught in any crossfire that might come about because of disagreements among grandchildren. If you feel it appropriate, you can leave a background memorandum explaining how you viewed the situation and why you elected to do what you did. But in my experience, you should not expect any amount of explanation to eliminate all possibilities of resentment. If bequests are equal, beneficiaries may complain that there were reasons that they should have been unequal. If bequests are not equal, beneficiaries are more likely to complain. The per stirpes–per capita dilemma will often—perhaps almost always—be a lightning rod for grandchildren's complaints, unless each child has an equal number of children.

These are questions for which there are no easy answers, and reasonable minds will surely differ. Per stirpes or per capita? What do you think?

For me, this is one of the most difficult decisions that arises in the estate planning field. Strong arguments can be made for both. If the differences in numbers of grandchildren are not too great, and you have no strong preferences of your own, I would recommend adopting the more common alternative of per stirpes. But if there is a situation where one child has only one offspring, and the other child has three or four or more offspring, then I would suggest a partial per capita approach, such as the combination-share compromise or the half-and-half alternative of leaving half per capita and half per stirpes.

As you struggle to resolve doubts in your mind, striving to be equitable and do your best, and hoping to avoid resentment in your children and grandchildren, remember another very important basic rule: Not all problems have solutions. And if you still are not quite sure what you should do, remember Basic Rule Number One, "There is more than one right way," and then turn to Basic Rule Number Two: "What advice would I give to my best friend if she or he had a similar problem?" In pondering this question, you will find a lot of wisdom within you that can help you determine what to do in your own family situation.

5

Blended Families
and Adopted Children

Most parents treat adopted children as if they were natural born, including parents who have both adopted and natural-born children.

However, in today's society, with higher percentages of divorce and remarriage, increasing numbers of people are living in what is known as *blended families*. There are literally hundreds of different blended-family situations that affect how individual family members plan their estates. The easier problems involve a remarriage where one partner adopts the children of the spouse.

Here is a typical example. Walter is divorced and has custody of his two young sons. He meets a young widow, Betty, who has one child, Gloria, from her first marriage. They decide to get married, and Betty asks Walter to adopt Gloria. Walter agrees, and the three children grow up together.

In later years Walter is deciding how he wants to leave his property after the death of Betty. Should he give Gloria a one-third share, even though she is not his natural daughter? After all, he cares for her and indeed adopted her as his child. What if he feels greater attachment to his natural-born children? No law requires equality of treatment of children. If a person dies without a will, the law in most states will generally treat natural-born and adopted children equally.

Suppose Walter never formally adopted Gloria but yet helped raise her? If Walter truly had a great deal of affection for Gloria and from Gloria's perspective was just like her own father, should Gloria not share in Walter's estate? To do this, Walter would have to include her specifically in his will. Without a will, Gloria would not be an heir and would receive nothing.

Estate-planning problems of blended families do not just involve parents and children. They also include grandparents. Here is a typical family situation. Joan was divorced, with a five-year old daughter, Mary, when she met David. Sometime later they were married and had two children together. Joan's first husband rarely saw Mary, and the only grandparents Mary knew were Joan's parents and David's parents. She called David's parents "Nana" and "Papa," as she did her mother's parents. Because Mary's father was still living and contributing a modest amount of child support (though far less than he should have) and because he would not give his consent for David to adopt Mary, she was not the legal grandchild of David's parents.

David's parents came to me to prepare their wills. They wanted to leave money to their grandchildren. But they were not sure whether to include Mary.

I asked them what they would have done if Mary had been adopted by their son. "By all means, we would have included her, too."

"But if you were going to include her in that situation, why not include her when, in substance, she is your granddaughter—she thinks of you as her grandparents—and the only problem is a technical one because she cannot be legally adopted?"

As we discussed the matter further, another concern was raised: "Suppose we leave money to Mary and something should happen to her, where would the property go?" The answer depends upon the laws of the state in which Mary lives. Generally speaking, if someone dies without a will and without lawful descendants, the property goes by operation of law to her parents—in this case, Mary's mother and natural father. Above all, the grandparents did not want the possibility of Mary's natural father ever getting any portion of their property.

We were able to resolve the problem quickly by putting the

portion set aside for Mary in a trust, administered by her mother and David, with the proviso that if something happened to Mary, the property would then go to the natural grandchildren of my clients.

What about David? Will he treat Mary the same in his will as he does his two natural-born children? Should he treat them all equally?

If they were all raised together starting as very young children, and if there is a strong bond of affection among them, the answer is probably yes. But if David had not married Joan until Mary was fifteen, perhaps the answer is no—in part depending upon the bond between the two. Yet, there is a third factor to consider, and that is how would unequal treatment affect the bond and relationship between David and Joan? These are not easy questions to answer, and it is one of the many examples of how decisions people make while they are living have many ramifications—far beyond the economics of dividing money.

In large part, the answers to all of these questions depend upon the personal relationships among the members of the family. My professional experience is that most parents treat adopted children the same as they treat natural children, and most grandparents treat adopted grandchildren the same way they treat natural grandchildren.

However, differences arise in blended-family situations where there is no formal adoption. In the majority of such situations that I have seen, a child from a first marriage who was not adopted by the partner in the second marriage would not receive any direct gifts from the grandparents. This can, of course, create problems in the relationships among the young people who grew up together.

There are other complicating factors that can arise. Let us return to Walter, who had two children from his prior marriage and who adopted Betty's daughter, Gloria. If Walter's parents had left substantial sums to Walter's two natural-born children but not to Gloria, this could have had a very destructive impact on the relationship between Gloria and Walter's two children, with whom she was raised and whom she thought of as siblings. But what if the parents of Gloria's deceased natural father left property to Gloria?

In essence, Gloria could inherit from three sets of grandparents. Should this affect how much Walter's parents should leave to Gloria?

The many variations in blended-family situations are compounded when there are differences in wealth between the husband and wife and also between their respective parents.

When counseling clients, I have three general suggestions that I make as a starting point for discussing how these problems can best be resolved:

1. Adopted children and adopted grandchildren should be treated the same as natural-born children and grandchildren.

2. In the case of blended families, where people are getting along well, do not exclude the person who may not have been formally adopted. This does not mean that one must give that person an equal share. What it does mean is that there should be sensitivity and consideration given to the ramifications of how the young people themselves will feel about how the money was left. To be sure, the people who have earned and accumulated the money have the ultimate decision. But sensitivity to relationships between younger people has to be one of the considerations in overall estate planning. Insensitivity can rupture relationships and cause enormous family rifts.

3. If there are special factors such as a potential large inheritance from a grandparent that blended-family siblings would not share, one should take these special factors into consideration in deciding whether strict equality is the best course to follow.

The rights of adopted children are generally covered by state statute. Subject to the terms of these statutes, a will can specifically state whether adopted children are treated the same as natural-born children. A will can also state the rights of illegitimate children. And, as a matter of fact, a will can specify that a child who has not been formally adopted shall nevertheless be treated as having been adopted, if this is the way the person who makes the will feels.

Where there is a blended family, it is even more important to consider the possibility of a trust. In our example of Walter and Betty, if Walter were to die before Betty and leave property outright to Betty, rather than in trust, there is every likelihood that Betty could in turn leave the property to her child and exclude Walter's two children from his prior marriage. The same situation could happen in reverse if Betty predeceased Walter and Walter had not adopted Gloria. In general, the best way to deal with the increasingly common circumstances of the blended family is to use the flexibility of a trust. Thus, instead of Walter leaving property outright to Betty, he could leave the property in trust for her benefit. The trust would provide that, during the remainder of Betty's life, she would get all of the income. The principal could also be used for her benefit and, if Walter so provided, for the benefit of all three blended-family children, if needed. On the death of Betty it would go in equal shares to Walter's two children and Betty's child, Gloria.

When I counsel clients in this area, I listen to their desires and concerns and then try to draft provisions to meet the particular circumstances in each family situation.

For instance, in our first example where Walter married Betty after the death of her husband, if Walter had not adopted Betty's child, Gloria, but still wanted to provide in some way for her, he could have placed the property in trust for Betty during her lifetime. On her death, the property could be divided into three shares—one for Betty's child, Gloria, and one each for Walter's two children from his prior marriage. These shares could continue to be held in trust. On the death of Gloria, her share could be either distributed to her children or redistributed to Walter's two children, if he so desired, or, if they were not living, to Walter's grandchildren. If Walter had no grandchildren, the property could then be redistributed to Gloria's children, if Walter so desired. (If there were no descendants, the property could go to Walter's brothers and sisters and their descendants, if Walter so directed.)

Similarly, if Walter's parents preferred to treat Gloria differently from Walter's children from his first marriage, but still wanted to do something for her, they could have used the vehicle of a trust in their will to provide income for a period of time for Gloria. Then, at some particular time specified in the trust instrument—

perhaps upon Gloria's reaching a particular age, or perhaps upon her death—the property could go to Walter's two children from his first marriage and their descendants.

My general recommendation is that where there are blended families there should be trusts. I also suggest that, if there is a close relationship between the stepparent or step-grandparent and stepchild or step-grandchild, then some provision should be made. It may or may not be an equal share, but if it is not an equal share, it should be some specific sum or partial share. If a stepchild or a step-grandchild is to be included, specific provision should be made about what happens to the property if that stepchild or step-grandchild dies without lawful descendants. If that contingency arises, most people want the property to revert to their own children and grandchildren.

Many estate-planning problems are fundamentally problems of human relationships defined through the ultimate medium of exchange—money. This observation is particularly applicable to blended-family situations. Because human emotions in these situations can create potential powder kegs, I would restate an additional suggestion that I made in the Introduction, namely that good communication between husband and wife and the sharing of natural feelings of concern are especially important when blended families plan their estates. It is essential that husbands and wives have tolerance for differences in each other's opinions, for most of these questions do not have black-and-white answers. If one partner has very strong feelings about a particular issue, and the other partner does not, then this should obviously have an impact on what final decision is reached.

The key is to understand that there are no absolute rules when it comes to blended-family situations. Leaving money wisely requires that there be sensitivity to the feelings of all parties involved and that, when final decisions are reached, the individuals who are planning their estates specify in writing exactly how they want to leave their property. Ultimately, it is the person who has the property to leave who is the final judge.

6

Second Wives
and Second Husbands

In today's society, increasing numbers of first marriages unfortunately often end in divorce. On the other hand, many people find great happiness in their second marriages, including those whose first marriages ended because of the death of a spouse. However, complications can arise when estate-planning issues are discussed.

One of the most sensitive areas of my work involves second-marriage situations where at least one of the partners has children from a prior marriage. There are natural conflicts people face when they deal with how they want their property divided between their spouse and their children. Questions of equity as well as issues of power and control are almost always present, particularly where there is disparity between the wealth of the two partners. Partners with the lesser amount of property want to feel that the contributions they bring to the marriage—their talents, capabilities, love and commitment, and, where the other partner has children, the willingness to share time and build a relationship with those children—are fully appreciated.

When second marriages work out well, the parties often want to leave more than the minimum amount the law requires that one leave to a spouse and more than the minimum amount that may have been established in a prenuptial agreement. The question

41

then becomes "How much should I leave my spouse?" and, if there are children from a prior marriage, "How should I best protect my children?"

Here is a typical family situation. Bud and Dolores were both previously married, and each had children from their first marriages. As they were contemplating marriage, Bud said that he wanted to protect Dolores if he died, but he did not want to be worried about having a divorce court take away any more of his property.

Many men approach this problem through a prenuptial agreement providing for life insurance, coupled with a provision that the spouse has no right to any other property. From the male point of view, if the marriage lasts and the husband dies first, the wife is well provided for through insurance. On the other hand, if the marriage doesn't last, the wife does not gain any of the husband's property (although she may be entitled to alimony). This may not be fair, but it is often what men with substantial means demand. When negotiations of this kind occur, they do not necessarily make the firmest foundations upon which to build a marriage.

Dolores unhappily consented to a prenuptial agreement that gave neither party any right to the other's property but that required Bud to pay the premiums on a $250,000 life insurance policy that named Dolores as the beneficiary. But the second marriage took hold—indeed, it was far better for both Dolores and Bud than their earlier marriages. Bud came to see me to discuss what more he could do for Dolores (although he wanted to keep the prenuptial agreement in force "just in case").

We talked about the amount of property that he had, and we talked about fractional shares. At first Bud said that he would like to set aside one-third of his property in a trust for Dolores. I responded, "I know that one-third to you seems fair, Bud, but how much income will this yield, together with the income from the insurance proceeds, and how much income would Dolores need to live comfortably?" It turned out that Bud wanted Dolores to have an income of $75,000 a year, and in order to do this he would need to set aside in a marital trust nearly half of his property for her. Of course, if he had been a much wealthier person, he might have left only a third of his property in trust, or possibly less, depending upon the couple's overall circumstances.*

This example illustrates one very important point: When you are considering how much you want to leave your spouse, do not just consider the fraction of the estate that you are leaving. Consider also the amount of income that will be produced.

There are many variations of these kinds of problems. Sometimes only one of the parties has been divorced and the other party has been widowed. On many occasions, only one of the parties has been previously married.

I believe that, if one is to err, it is better to err on the side of generosity because it has one major fringe benefit: It helps make the second marriage work. That can be far more important than arguing about one-fourth, one-third, or one-half of a person's property.

Above all, the parties should communicate openly and understand that reasonable minds can differ about what is fair. "There is more than one right way."

The problems can be compounded when there are children born in the second marriage. Then there might be three sets of children—the wife's children from the first marriage, the husband's children from the first marriage, and the children of the two together. Each partner wants to treat all of her or his children equally. But one child (assuming one child from the second marriage) will in a sense be ultimately receiving property from both parents in the second marriage. The children from the first marriage could inherit from additional sources, too—from the other natural parent or from grandparents. When children from neither marriage have a potential large inheritance from a source other than yourself, it is easier to determine a measure of equality between them. But when there are potential large inheritances that apply to only one set of children, it is more difficult to determine what is fair.

Occasionally, a parent is estranged from one or more children

---

*In some states, leaving more than the prenuptial agreement requires may open the door to claims that the agreement has been waived or canceled. This is an area that should be discussed with your attorney.

from an earlier marriage. In that situation the second spouse may ultimately receive most or all of the property. A number of years ago, a client who had lost contact with his children from a first marriage asked for my help. He said that his first marriage had broken up in part because his wife as a young child had been the victim of incest by her father, and she was afraid that her husband would do the same thing with their daughters, who were very attractive. The wife's feeling was affecting her physical relationship with her husband, and this contributed to his becoming involved with another woman, which in turn led to a divorce. After the divorce, his first wife "poisoned" the minds of his children, asserting that their father was an adulterer who had broken up the family home, and she took the children and moved to the East Coast. For years they had no further contact with their father.

"Why should I leave them anything? They never even call me on my birthday." I suggested the first item on his agenda was not to write a new will. Rather, he should try to do everything he could to establish contact with his children, who by now were adults. I recommended that he start with the child he felt might be the most receptive. If successful, he could in turn work through that child to rebuild the relationship with his other two children.

This story had a happy ending. He was able to rebuild a relationship with all of the children from his first marriage, and they are now beneficiaries in his will. (Of course, this meant that the second wife would ultimately receive less than what otherwise may have been left to her if the husband had not had any contact with his children.)

There are many variations on the central theme of what is the best way to leave property in the case of a second marriage. If there are no children from the first marriages, the problem is less difficult. But where there are children from earlier marriages, the problems become more complex. Most attorneys advise that the property set aside for the surviving spouse should be left in trust with income to the spouse for life, with power given to an independent trustee to invade principal, if necessary, to provide for proper care, support, and maintenance. The trust provisions would specify that, on the death of the second spouse, any remaining property would go the children of the first spouse, either outright or in trust.

The amount of the share to be set aside for the spouse depends in part upon the total assets of each party, their respective earning power, the duration of the marriage, how close the parties are to one another, and also their relative ages. A husband married to a much younger wife might not want to have everything withheld from his children during her lifetime because they may not get any property until they are seventy years old, or even older. Obviously, the particular circumstances in each family situation will have an impact on how the trust is structured.

How much should be included in the trust? Look at this from the perspective of both the fractional share set aside and the income it will produce. Also take into consideration the independent financial means and earning power of each party. In larger estates where there are tax consequences, there are opportunities, as we will see in Chapter 18, to take advantage of the marital deduction provisions of the Internal Revenue Code.

Assuming that the second marriage is a happy one, there is no objective reason to leave the second spouse with less income than in the case of a first marriage. Moreover, when a second marriage turns out well, it is also important to consider giving your partner a right to control the disposition of a portion of the principal, even though it may disadvantage your own children. After all, one of the things that she or he brought into the marriage was the capability of giving not just to you but to your family, and over the years this can involve a major commitment of time and energy. Is it not fair—is it not appropriate—in the case of a happy second marriage to give the surviving spouse a full participation in not just a portion of the income but also a portion of the principal and the right to control its ultimate disposition? Not only is this equitable, but it can contribute in a very important way toward cementing the relationship between the parties. One of my favorite sayings is that "money is the cheapest commodity." Where your second marriage is a happy one, generosity can bring the couple even closer.

One additional piece of advice: One of the best ways to reach the heart of a partner is to reach out to the hearts of your partner's children. At times it may not be easy, because they may look upon you with some degree of jealousy or suspicion. The effort required in these circumstances may be extraordinary—70 or 80 percent of the way—but the potential rewards and the psychological satisfaction that can come from building a relationship of this kind are great. Even if you do not succeed as well as you might like, the effort that you undertake will have a major positive impact on your marriage. This in turn will help make it easier to resolve potential disagreements about how each of you will leave your property.

Estate-planning problems involving second wives and second husbands can be complex, particularly where there are children from prior marriages. The competing psychological pulls between love of spouse and love of children are often hard to resolve. But with flexibility and understanding on the part of both parties, and creative help from expert counsel, happy solutions can be reached. There is more than one right way.

7

Prenuptial Agreements and Estate Planning

We are living in the age of remarriage and the prenuptial agreement. "I got burned the first time and I'm not going to get burned again" is a common complaint of men with financial means. Women who have substantial property also often want a prenuptial agreement the second time around so that if the new marriage falls apart, each partner will keep her or his own property. Prenuptial agreements are even becoming common in first marriages, particularly where one or both of the partners are over thirty-five.

The recent nationwide press coverage of the Donald and Ivana Trump soap opera has brought to the forefront the central role that money often plays in marriage relationships. I do not propose in this book to cover all of the terms and conditions that should be considered in a prenuptial agreement. Rather, I want to highlight several estate-planning areas of common concern and underscore the importance of understanding differing perspectives.

The starting point is to understand that the state of one's residence governs what happens in the event of one's death. In most, if not all, states, unless there is a prenuptial agreement, a surviving spouse is entitled to a minimum fractional share of the estate of the deceased spouse, no matter what the will may provide. In many states, that share is one-third, if the deceased partner left surviving children. Even though one might be satisfied with the laws of a

47

particular state, and therefore not seek to include estate disposition provisions in a prenuptial agreement, it is important to recognize that those laws can be changed. Moreover, we live in a mobile society, and if a couple moves from one state to another, the controlling jurisdiction generally will be the state of residency at the time of death—not the state in which the parties were married.

In a second marriage where one or both of the parties have children from previous marriages, many people do not want the children of a surviving spouse ultimately to inherit a substantial portion of their estates. This is particularly true if the parties had only been married for a year or two when the death occurred. On the other hand, the surviving spouse might very well take the position that he or she entered the marriage on the assumption that it would continue for the lifetime of the parties and might therefore ask, "Why should I receive less when I committed myself for life and it was a premature death?"

My general recommendation is that this is the area of prenuptial agreement negotiations where people can afford to be the most generous. After all, the condition of death is not likely to arise very soon in most marriages. Therefore, why not be inclined to accede to your partner's wishes when, by hypothesis, the property at stake will not be divided for ten, twenty, or thirty years, or more, and in the interim you will hopefully have lived together very happily—perhaps more happily than either party did in any prior marriage.

If it turns out that the second marriage goes sour, and there is a divorce, any generous estate-planning provisions in your prenuptial agreement will be irrelevant.

There is another aspect of this area that is important to take into consideration: the concept of present value. The right to a dollar ten years from now is worth much less than a dollar today, since you can invest the dollar today immediately and have it produce income. The right to a dollar twenty, thirty, and forty years from now is worth much, much less. The exact difference can be mathematically determined by printed tables or by calculation. The key factors are the numbers of years involved and the interest rate that is assumed.*

*The concept of present value is discussed in greater detail in Chapter 30, when we look at what is known as charitable lead and charitable remainder trusts.

The important principle to understand when negotiating estate-planning provisions in a prenuptial agreement is that the dollars you are talking about will not be paid for many years. Therefore, the present value of those dollars is not nearly as great as one might initially assume, and they are not as important as provisions pertaining to what happens in the event of divorce.

Moreover, many estate-planning issues and prenuptial agreements concern not just how much the surviving spouse is to receive, but what happens to that property on the death of the surviving spouse. That event could be thirty or forty years away. The "present value" of those dollars might be as little as twenty-five cents, or less, depending on what interest rate assumptions are used.

In other words, if you have an estate of $600,000 and are negotiating whether or not to give your surviving spouse one-third of that amount (which is $200,000) or one-half of that amount (which is $300,000), the real difference you are talking about in terms of present value is not $100,000, because those dollars will not be going to your spouse for another twenty or thirty years, depending upon your life expectancy. In "present value" terms, you may be talking about only $25,000.

Similarly, if you are arguing about what might happen to the property on the death of your surviving spouse, you should understand that, in the first place, your surviving spouse may not survive you, so the argument may become irrelevant. And if he or she does survive you, and the argument is whether the property should be left outright or in trust with income for life and the balance to your children on the death of your spouse, you may be talking about an event that will not take place for thirty or forty or fifty years, and the argument, instead of being about a present value of $25,000, could be about a present value of $15,000, or even less. Therefore, I suggest that people with means can afford to be generous in that portion of the prenuptial agreement involving what happens to their property on their death.

Unfortunately, people do not always agree about what constitutes relative generosity. For instance, several years ago, Daniel, a widowed man with four children, consulted with me about a prenuptial agreement and estate plan. His intended spouse, Eileen, had been married previously but had no children. She had some property in her own name and had the expectancy of a substantial inheritance from her own family, although they were not nearly as wealthy as Daniel. Daniel had first sought advice from some of his business friends. They recommended a prenuptial agreement with a $1 million life insurance policy so that, in the event of his death, Eileen would have ample income for the rest of her life.

When Daniel proposed this to Eileen, she was extremely upset and felt that it was not fair. An argument ensued. Daniel came to me for my advice.

As I am often prone to do, I turned the tables and asked Daniel, "What would you advise your best friend to do under these circumstances?"

"Well, I would probably tell him to leave maybe a fourth or even a third of his estate in a marital trust, giving her the income for life, and then having it go to his kids."

"Daniel, you have lots of money. Why don't you give Eileen a full third—make her feel really good—get everything off on the right foot. After all, it's only money."

Less than two weeks later, he was back in my office. Since his own children were well provided for, he determined that he would set aside the full third of his estate in a marital trust. This would give Eileen an annual income of more than $150,000. Then, on her death, the property could go to his children.

"What was Eileen's reaction?" I asked.

"She was very angry," Daniel responded. "She said that one-third of my estate was fine, but she wanted to have the right to decide where it would go on her death. She said that she recognized I brought into the marriage a large amount of property, together with all of my other qualities, but she said that she brought into the marriage, in addition to all of her qualities, a commitment to build a relationship with and spend time with my children. She claimed that for me to remove from her the right to determine where any portion of the property would go on her death smacked of me trying to control the property from the grave."

The point of the story is not whether one party was right or one party was wrong. The point of the story is that reasonable minds can differ greatly over what is right and what is wrong. What seems generous to a husband may not seem generous to a wife, and what is viewed as not generous in the eyes of one woman or man may be exceedingly generous in the eyes of another. If you are discussing with your second wife or husband what you plan to do, or if you are discussing this with your fiancé and either one of you has previously been married, be aware of the fact that these are sensitive and often volatile issues. People differ in their views and perceptions of fairness. Be prepared for the unexpected response.

In the case of Daniel and Eileen, I tried to help bridge the gap by suggesting to Daniel that he "split the difference" and give Eileen the right to decide where half of the trust property would go on her death and leave the remaining half to his children. Daniel said he was willing to do this, although he remained "disappointed" because he felt he had been more generous than most others in his circumstances and Eileen had not recognized his generosity. "She denies me the pleasure of having her appreciate I am giving more than almost anyone else I know." Eileen was unhappy because of the timing of the discussions and her feeling that Daniel was too concerned about money matters.

Unfortunately, the story of Daniel and Eileen did not have a happy ending. They broke off their relationship, in part because each thought the other was too unyielding and lacked understanding of the other person's perspective of what would be a fair division of Daniel's property upon his death.

This example vividly illustrates why it is difficult to arrive at general recommendations about what specific estate-planning provisions should be included in prenuptial agreements. However, the estate-planning provisions of most prenuptial agreements drawn by attorneys generally provide that, where there are children from prior marriages, property that is left to a surviving spouse is almost always left in trust, with income for life. Usually, there are provisions to invade principal, if necessary to provide for proper care, support, and maintenance. On the death of the surviving spouse, the principal usually goes to the children of the partner who died first.

If both partners have substantial independent means, they may sometimes agree in advance that neither party will make any claim to the other partner's property on death. The relative ages of the

parties and the duration of the marriage, as well as their independent resources and respective earning power, are important factors that are taken into consideration. In some cases, particularly
those involving older people, the prenuptial agreement will contain a specific provision that reduces the amount of property a
surviving spouse would ordinarily get if death occurs within the
first few years of the marriage.

In the case of first marriages, most wills generally give a surviving spouse more than the minimum to which he or she is entitled
under state law. This is one of the reasons I generally recommend
to clients who are getting married for the first time that, if they do
desire a prenuptial agreement, they exclude from that any limitations on what might happen in the event of death.

(I generally go one step further and recommend that there be
no prenuptial agreement at all, except possibly in situations involving families of substantial wealth. I recognize that there is a risk
that, if the marriage ends in divorce, a partner may be disadvantaged because there was no prenuptial agreement. On the other
hand, the foundation for a good marriage can be much firmer if
at the very beginning there are no extended contract negotiations
about the terms of a prenuptial contract—negotiations that can
sometimes get out of hand because of the advocacy of the respective attorneys for the parties. The potential gain from avoiding this
legal confrontation may be worth the gamble of potential disadvantage in the event the partners decide to split.)

One can argue that, if my general advice in first marriages is to
exclude estate-planning provisions from prenuptial contracts, why
should it not also apply in second marriages, because in many
cases second marriages turn out at least as well and sometimes
better than first marriages? There is a lot of merit in this perspective, and certainly it is an important factor to consider. However,
in second marriages there is often a potential conflict of interest
between the surviving spouse and the children of the first marriage. Also, people are generally more understanding of the need
for a prenuptial agreement when one or both of the parties have
gone through the trauma of divorce settlement negotiations in
prior marriages.

There is another aspect of risk taking to take into consideration, and that concerns the fact that in many situations, when marriages work out very well, wills are changed to provide for more than the minimum that is required in a prenuptial contract. It has been a wonderful experience for me to visit with clients who have been happily married for a number of years and who are executing new wills, smiling and outwardly showing great affection as one spouse signs a new will leaving far more to the other partner than the minimum required by the prenuptial agreement. Of course, "a contract is a contract," and some people choose to stick by the terms of a premarital contract. Therefore, one should not necessarily agree to the terms of a prenuptial agreement on the assumption that, if things work out well, the terms will be liberalized.

If you are involved in discussions about a prenuptial agreement, you will probably need a lawyer with expertise in the area to counsel you. However, lawyers can sometimes end up in legal confrontations with one another and, if the negotiations take a turn for the worse, consider bringing in a family counselor as well as a lawyer. The psychological and emotional aspects of these discussions go far beyond the traditional aspects of a lawyer's training. It can be very constructive to turn to a person such as a psychiatrist, psychologist, or other family counselor who has professional training to help facilitate a happy resolution of any disagreements that may arise.

If you are the person with the greater amount of wealth, be sensitive to the fact that your intended spouse does not want to feel like you are the potentate distributing your largess. Marriage is a mutual undertaking—an opportunity for both people to give everything they have to help make the marriage a success—and the nonmonetary aspects of what people can contribute are more important than the dollars involved.

On the other hand, if you are the partner with less financial resources and your intended spouse is willing to share his or her estate with you in amounts greater than what most others do, it is important to have an understanding of his or her perspective and to voice recognition and appreciation of that generosity.

If you feel that you must have a prenuptial agreement, the place that you should be ready to give the most is in the area of what happens to your property if you are no longer living. And if you really want to enhance the happiness of your marriage, consider at an early date amending your will or living trust to provide substantially more than the minimum you are required by contract to do.

As I said in the previous chapter, though these problems may be difficult in their resolution, happy solutions can be reached with creative help from expert counsel and with flexibility and understanding on the part of both parties.

8

Leaving Money to an In-Law

"I really love Max, my son-in-law. But I'm just not sure that ten years from now Max and Betty will still be married. With the divorce rate being what it is, how do I know?"

You never really do know. People divorce after twenty-five, thirty, thirty-five and even after forty years of marriage. One of the worst aspects of these divorces is the insecurity fallout that affects the children—even adult children. "I thought Mom and Dad had a good marriage—not great, but good. But now I wonder about my own situation. How do I know my husband won't leave me for another woman thirty years from now the way Dad left Mom?" Or "How do I know my wife won't leave me if my business career starts faltering?"

When counseling clients, I have talked about all of the things one can do to make a marriage great. Good communication stands on the top of my list, along with mutual understanding, tolerance of differences, and all the other qualities that are so important.

I mention one of my favorite sayings regarding relationships and marriage—"It takes two to make it"—and if clients ask for the best advice I can give about marriage, I relate to them what my father said to me shortly before my wedding day—the greatest marital advice I ever heard.

"David, everyone says if you want to have a good marriage, you and your wife each have to be willing to go fifty percent of the way. But I say that fifty-fifty is not good enough. If you want to have a great marriage, it should be sixty-sixty, because if you try to go only fifty percent of the way, you may not really get there, even though you think you have. The same thing goes for your wife. All too often, you'll start thinking that your partner really didn't go fifty percent of the way, and you'll start to get angry. But if you and Connie each try to go sixty percent of the way, even if you don't quite make it, you'll probably generally go at least fifty percent— and that will help lay a terrific foundation for building a happy marriage."

Unfortunately, even marriages that flourish in the beginning do not always remain happy. And when a marriage starts to fall apart, people who have made substantial gifts to in-laws have a lot of second thoughts.

Here is a practical example of what can happen in a family where, from all outward appearances, there are no problems. A wealthy client from a community-property state bought his daughter and son-in-law a house as a tenth-anniversary present. Five years later, the husband became involved with another woman, the marriage disintegrated, and eventually there was a divorce. Because the deed had been drawn in the names of both parties, the husband ended up with half of the house. As a part of the divorce settlement the house was sold, and the proceeds were divided. The wife then moved into a smaller house.

"But what were we to do? We loved our son-in-law. We thought about giving the house just to our daughter, but we wanted our son-in-law to know that we looked upon him as a son, and we didn't want him to feel uneasy about his relationship with us." I assured my clients that under all of the circumstances they had acted reasonably. But the good intentions they had by placing half of the house in their son-in-law's name were to no avail.

On the other hand, there are many happy marriages where a divorce never occurs, and the bonds of family between parents and son- or daughter-in-law become ever strengthened. What can you do to cover both alternatives and most of the possibilities in between?

My general recommendation to clients is that, if they want to leave money in their wills to their in-laws, if the amounts are relatively small, then outright distribution should create no problems. But if the amounts are large, they should probably put the property in a trust for both their children and their in-laws and give their children (but not their in-laws) the right to make any decisions of outright distribution.

Here is an example involving Max and Betty, a married couple with no children. Betty's parents decided to leave Betty's share in trust, with mandatory distribution of all of the income to her and with the trustee given the right to invade principal to provide for her proper care, support, and maintenance. On Betty's death, if she still had no lawful descendants, the property was directed to go to Betty's brother, if he was living, and if he was not living, it was directed to go to the children of her brother. In other words, the testators wanted the property ultimately to go to their grandchildren. However, they gave Betty the right to direct that half of the property that had been set aside in trust for her could continue to be held in trust for Max during his lifetime, with Max to get all of the income. On Max's death, it would then revert to Betty's brother and his children.

Betty's parents did not want the property to go outright to Max, because on Max's death, if Betty was not living, Max might direct it to go to his brothers and sisters. But they felt close enough to Max to allow him to be a permitted beneficiary, if Betty so desired in her will. The designation of Betty as the decision maker regarding her trust is what lawyers call a *power of appointment.* *

There is another common way to include in-laws as beneficiaries without the in-laws getting the property outright. This is through the use of what is known as a *sprinkling* or *spray trust,* which distributes income and principal among a named group of beneficiaries. The purpose of the sprinkling trust is to give an independent trustee the discretion to distribute income among the members of a family group in accordance with their needs. Usually, the trust instrument specifies a standard along the following lincs:

My trustee shall distribute so much of the income and principal of the trust among the members of my family group consisting

*Powers of appointment are discussed in greater detail in Chapter 17.

of my child and her children to provide for their proper care, support, maintenance, and education in such sums as my trustee in my trustee's sole discretion deems necessary or advisable.

The trustee will usually distribute the income to the child directly, unless for tax or other reasons it is desired to have property distributed to grandchildren. If substantial wealth is involved so the generation-skipping tax is applicable, there are certain limitations that have to be taken into consideration.

The testator, if she or he so desires, can include a son-in-law or daughter-in-law as a part of the permitted class of beneficiaries. In other words, instead of just leaving the property in trust for "my daughter, Susan, and her lawful descendants," the trust provisions would say, "my daughter, Susan, and her husband, Harry, so long as they have not separated or divorced, and Susan's lawful descendants." If Susan and Harry remain married, and Susan later dies and Harry lives to be an old person and has financial need, the trust instrument gives the trustee the discretion to help Harry financially.

It makes sense to differentiate in-laws from children and grandchildren, for as the old saying goes, "Blood is thicker than water." In an age where there is a high incidence of divorce, occurring with ever-increasing frequency among people who have been married twenty years and longer, it is wise to consider leaving money to an in-law through the vehicle of a trust.

The same types of trust provisions can be used to take care of a mother-in-law or father-in-law in cases where the younger generation has substantial means and wants to cover the contingency that an older person might outlive them. This also obviously applies to brothers- and sisters-in-law.

My general recommendation to clients is that if they have any concerns about leaving money outright to their in-laws, they can resolve most of their doubts by putting the money in trust. Where appropriate, sprinkling provisions can be used, and there can be a condition that any interest ceases in the event of separation or divorce. If there is a strong bond of affection with the in-law, the trust can also give the testator's own child a power of appointment to direct where the property will go on that child's death. The

power of appointment may include the in-law as a potential beneficiary. It may limit the in-law's right to distribution of income, but
it can also include distribution of a portion of the principal, or even
all of the principal, if their own child so directs. However, if there
is tension in the marriage, the reluctance of the child to exercise
that power in a will can exacerbate marital problems.

The use of a power of appointment clause in a trust protects the
family from the fallout of a divorce. Obviously, if a divorce should
occur, the in-law would receive nothing under the power of appointment.

These are tough issues to confront. But a high incidence of
divorce is a reality in today's world, and it is therefore important
to be aware of alternative means for leaving money to an in-law.

9

People Without Children: Leaving Money to Collateral Relatives

"I feel a lot closer to my brother's children than I do to my sister's. Maybe it's because my brother's kids grew up nearby in Chicago, and I spent a lot more time with them than I did with my sister's children, who grew up in California. Still, I have some guilt about not treating my nieces and nephews equally."

How would you advise someone who came to you with this problem? Does it make any difference if the relatives are first cousins instead of nieces and nephews?

There are no easy answers. There are no rights and wrongs. The key is what a person really wants to do and how much that personal desire should be limited by feelings of guilt or concerns that differences in treatment may breed ill feelings among brothers and sisters, nieces and nephews, and cousins—the group generally called *collateral relatives.*

The majority of persons who raise issues concerning collateral relatives are unmarried with no children or grandchildren, and the family situation that seems to create the greatest difficulty involves differences in treatment between siblings. There are two general areas of concern:

1. Will a brother who got less be angry because his sister was left more than he was?

2. Will he be angry with his sister because she got more? Will it have an adverse impact on their relationship with each other?

A somewhat similar concern occurs when the question involves the children of sisters and brothers. It is not just a question of the nieces and nephews becoming jealous of one another—it is also a question of how their parents might feel toward one another and toward the person who made distinctions in a will.

Of course, the gifts do not occur until after the death of the testator. Even so, people have a real concern about how their family will remember them after they have passed away.

Sometimes a person establishes differences in a will because of differing emotional ties. Sometimes these arise because of differing economic circumstances. Sometimes differences are established because of life-styles or philosophy, such as religious affiliation.

I generally advise clients that one should not automatically be restricted by the doctrine of absolute equality in treatment of collateral relatives. There are natural reasons for differences, and the decision of how much should be given to any particular brother, sister, niece, nephew, or cousin should be based on knowledge, sensitivity, personal feelings, and judgment, and not on arbitrary rules.

In the face of the complicated issues involved in making choices, the single person sometimes thinks about avoiding the problem and simply not executing a will. The property then is generally distributed in accordance with the statutory law of the state where the deceased person resided. In most states this would mean that the property would go to the parents, and if neither parent were living, to the brothers and sisters, and if there were none, to the children of brothers and sisters (per stirpes). If a single person without children does not want this chain of events to take place, it is necessary to have a will.

Often the question is raised, particularly by single people: "What happens if the person to whom I leave property does not survive me?" The laws of the state of residence generally apply, and in most cases, if that person had children, those children would receive the share that otherwise would have gone to their parent. Sometimes a testator does not want this to happen, and the easiest way to avoid this eventuality is to use language in a will that clearly specifies that the person is to get the money only if she or he survives. In most situations I recommend a clause that contains a minimum survivorship period: "I will $10,000 to my niece, Barbara, if she survives me by a period of six months, and if she does not survive me by a period of six months, this $10,000 gift shall lapse." Or, in the alternative: ". . . and if she does not survive me by a period of six months, this $10,000 gift shall go to her children in equal shares."

One other very important consideration in leaving money to collateral relatives should be mentioned here. If the beneficiaries are under twenty-one, complications can arise in transferring property to them because they are not of legal age. Accordingly, most well-drawn wills will contain provisions to cover this situation. Either the property will be kept in trust for the beneficiary until the beneficiary reaches at least the age of twenty-one or, under statutes that have been adopted in most states, property will be given to someone to hold as custodian for the beneficiary until that person reaches legal age. What happens if the child dies before attaining legal age but leaves children of her own or his own? That, too, can be covered in well-drafted wills, so there will be no need for guardianship or conservatorship proceedings.

The problem of how to treat collateral relatives is not limited to single persons. Many people in planning their estates want to leave something to brothers and sisters or to the children of brothers and sisters. The same concerns about equality of treatment arise in these situations, similar to concerns about equality of treatment of one's own children or grandchildren. However, they are compounded by one additional factor. If a single person without children favors one brother or sister over another or one or more nieces or nephews over others, when the single person dies, there will be no descendants to face the problems that ill feelings and jealousies can cause. On the other hand, when someone with children decides to favor one collateral relative over another, she or he should take into consideration the fact that any ill feelings or jealousies among the relatives could be directed toward the testator's children. Although this consideration may not affect your final decision, it should not be overlooked.

Related to questions of leaving money to collateral relatives are questions that arise in what is known as an *absence of takers* situation. Where does the property go when all the named beneficiaries have died?

The typical will says that the property will go "to my heirs at law." Most people don't give this possibility much consideration because they assume at least some of the named beneficiaries will survive.

Yet I have seen situations where the named beneficiaries did not survive, and property was distributed to "heirs at law" who may have been remote cousins for whom the testator had no personal attachment.

Therefore, it is important to consider when planning one's estate where the property should go in case no named beneficiary is alive. One possibility, of course, is to leave the property to lawful descendants of named beneficiaries or to more remote collateral relatives—first or second cousins and their lawful descendants. Another possibility is to leave all or a portion of the property to a particular charity or charities. Close friends are often another option to consider. Obviously, there are many possible alternatives, including having various portions of property go to collateral relatives, close friends, and charities if an absence of takers situation should arise. The possibility may be remote that an absence of takers problem might occur in your family situation, but any well-drawn will should include this contingency.

Often a husband and wife will have similar absence of takers paragraphs in their wills so that the property will go half to the husband's nearest collateral relatives and half to the wife's nearest collateral relatives. One problem with this approach is that the surviving partner has the final word and may change the absence of takers clause in her or his own will, favoring the collateral relatives on the survivor's side of the family. There is a doctrine known as a *joint and mutual will,* which can lock in specified provisions upon the death of the first of the two parties. However, questions can arise in estates where there is a federal estate tax problem, and there is a risk of litigation where the survivor tries

to change the will. These are complex issues, and people s
discuss them with their own attorneys.

My own recommendation for making gifts to collateral relatives
would be for a husband and wife to divide their property approximately equally between one another. They would then each
execute wills or living trusts that would provide income to the
surviving spouse for life, with the independent trustee empowered
to invade the principal, if needed, to provide for the proper care,
support, and maintenance of the survivor. On death, each will
would provide that the property would go directly to the respective
collateral relatives of the decedent or to whatever other beneficiaries the decedent prefers, such as close friends or charities. This,
of course, assumes that the principal of the trust of the person who
died first was not used to meet the needs of the surviving spouse
so there is nothing left to go to the ultimate beneficiaries of the
person who died first.

If you really want to favor one or more collateral relatives but
have some concerns about how the unfavored group will think of
you, I would offer this observation. It is important to have sensitivity to the consequences of differences in treatment. People should
be aware of these consequences when they plan their estates. But
to let absolute equality override everything else is unwise. Therefore, my ultimate advice is to understand the alternatives that you
have and, after careful consideration, give your own personal preferences the greatest weight. It is your property to enjoy during life,
and it is your property to leave as you wish. You should be your
own judge. Upon your death, the decision of the judge will be final.

PART II

*Special Problems
to Consider*

10

Avoiding Probate: The Living Trust

There are all kinds of disparaging jokes about lawyers.

Q: When a lawyer falls overboard in shark-invested waters, why do the sharks leave him alone?
A: Professional courtesy.
Q: What's black and rust and looks good on the throat of a lawyer?
A: A Doberman pinscher.

Legal fees are a constant subject of comment in both business meetings and social gatherings. As an attorney, I am obviously aware of probate costs, and I have planned my estate in a way to minimize these costs, just as I recommend to clients. I have executed a living trust and have transferred all of my assets to that living trust.

My house and my car are not registered in my name. Rather, legal ownership is in the name of the David W. Belin Living Trust.

My checking account is not in my own name. When I sign checks, I merely sign my name, but below the signature line is the word "Trustee," and the actual bank account is in the name of the David W. Belin Living Trust.

Everything I own is in the name of the David W. Belin Living

Trust—stocks, bonds, real estate, and even household furniture and furnishings, which I transferred to the David W. Belin Living Trust by signing a printed "bill of sale" form prepared by the Iowa State Bar Association.

When I die, since all of my property has been transferred to my living trust, there will be no estate to probate and no need to have ancillary probate proceedings in any state outside of Iowa where I might have a real estate investment. As a result, there will be no executor's fees to pay, and although there will be legal fees to take care of such matters as filing any estate and inheritance tax returns, these fees will be minimized. My family privacy will also be protected, because no inventory of property will be filed in a probate court, which would let the whole world know the amount of property I own. No one, other than the beneficiaries of my living trust, will know how much money I left to individuals, how much money I left to charities, and how I disposed of the remaining part of my estate. There will be no probate of my estate, except for what is called a *pour-over will,* which will cover the contingency that all of my assets may not have been transferred to my living trust and which will merely say that whatever assets I may own (that I have not previously transferred) will be distributed to the trustees of the living trust.

Since at the time of my death all of my assets, hopefully, will already have been transferred to a living trust, these assets can be sold, new assets can be bought, distributions can be made to my heirs without any delays, and all of the red tape of probate will have been avoided.

I accomplished all of this, and more, by a very simple device known as a *living trust* and more technically known as a *revocable trust.* The other major type of trust is called *irrevocable* and cannot be changed, once it has been executed.

A revocable living trust requires no separate tax returns, if the settlor is also a trustee. Rather, all of the income is reported on one's own individual tax return. Stocks and bonds owned by the living trust do not have a separate tax identification number. If you are a trustee, your own social security number is used.

I recommend that all of my clients with substantial estates consider using living trusts. I recommend that all of my older clients, regardless of the size of their estates, consider using living trusts, and I recommend that families of great wealth consider discussing living trusts with their children as soon as the children reach legal age.

How does a living trust work? Very simply. First, you decide on the provisions you would desire in your will. Once those decisions have been reached, you prepare a document which in essence says: "I hereby transfer all of my property to the _____ Living Trust . . ." (fill in your name), and designate as trustees yourself and one other person, who can be a spouse, a child, a trusted friend, a close collateral relative, or a bank or trust company. The trust instrument will say that, during your lifetime, the trustees (the dominant trustee being you as long as you are living and in good mental health) will use whatever amount of income and principal is necessary for your proper care, support, and maintenance. The trust instrument will also provide that at any time you can change any term of the trust instrument. You can amend it, or you can revoke it completely. On your death, the living trust becomes irrevocable. It governs the disposition of your property, just as a will would do, except that there is no need to probate an estate because your assets are already in the trust.

Not only does the living trust avoid the necessity of probating an estate, but it has one other basic advantage. In the event of your temporary or permanent incapacity—through physical or mental illness—the trust instrument continues to own your property, and the other named trustee can manage your affairs without going into court and undertaking any formal legal proceedings in the form of a conservatorship or guardianship. This can be a tremendous advantage in the case of mental or physical incapacity. It not only avoids the expense of a conservatorship or guardianship, but also allows far more flexibility in handling property.

When you execute a living trust, you should also execute a pour-over will, a very short document that, in substance, states that all of your debts should be paid and everything else turned over to the trustee of your living trust. It will also protect you in the event you own property that has not been transferred to the trust.

What are the disadvantages of a living trust? Very few. Time and expense are involved in working with a lawyer to prepare the trust instrument. However, this is really not very different from the time and expense involved in preparing a will. Transferring property from your own name to the name of the living trust also requires some time and effort. It can involve a deed for real estate, or a transfer of title for an automobile, or working with a broker to have all of your stocks and bonds transferred from your name to the name of the living trust. I can guarantee that the time and effort required to effect these changes while you are living, however, is far less than what would be required if your property had to be transferred through probate.

If you name a corporate trustee or co-trustee, there will be additional costs, but if you are living and in good health, these costs should be relatively small, assuming you, yourself, as a trustee will be handling most of the trust affairs and the management of trust assets.

What about life insurance? If the estate has been named as a beneficiary, have the beneficiary provisions changed to the name of the living trust. And if you are the owner of the policy on your life, transfer the ownership to your living trust. There are other questions about ownership of insurance policies that have estate tax implications. These should be discussed with one's tax adviser.

If you open an account with a brokerage house, you will want it to be in the name of the living trust. The brokerage house will then want to have a copy of the trust instrument, but you can delete those terms of the trust which designate how the property is to be distributed. The brokerage house does not need to know how you want to leave your property. All it needs to know is that the trustees have the power to buy and sell stocks. Although there is a little bit of red tape involved in giving copies of part of the trust instrument to other people, it is far less time consuming and also less expensive than the one- or two-year process of probating an estate.

What does a living trust not do? It does not save federal estate or state inheritance taxes; tax returns still must be filed. It does not save income taxes. It does not avoid valuation problems and tax problems that arise upon one's death and the professional fees necessary to deal with these problems. And, if you are not thorough in transferring all of your property to the trust and leave part of your property outside of the trust, which may necessitate extensive probate proceedings, there may be no material savings of lawyers' fee and other probate costs.

In order that you can see what a living trust looks like, I have included in this book as Appendix C an example of a living trust with a lot of optional provisions to be included, such as powers of appointment. The key provisions to understand are that you can be one of the trustees, you can have all of the income and all of the right to principal during your lifetime, and you can have the right to amend or revoke the trust at any time you desire.

Do you need two trustees? In most states (if not all), you do not need a co-trustee. However, I generally recommend a co-trustee, for two reasons. First, if you are physically or mentally unable to manage your affairs for a period of time, or if you are out of town and must have something taken care of in your absence, there is a second person already named in the instrument who has the power to take care of any emergencies or needs that arise.

Second, in the event of your death, there will be another person immediately ready to step in to take care of all of your affairs without any interruption in the management of your assets.

If you change your mind about a trustee that you have initially named, you always have the right to designate another trustee. Also, just as a good will should include the names of successor trustees or a means for selecting successor trustees (where trusts are established), the same sort of provision should be included in a living trust.

Every single provision that you might want to include in a will can be included in a living trust, for upon your death your living trust in essence becomes your will. The major difference is that it will distribute your property automatically, without going through the cumbersome and expensive provisions of probate.

"Well," you might say, "if living trusts are so great, why aren't more living trusts used?" There are a number of reasons. I think that individual apathy is probably the primary reason that more people don't use living trusts, for some initial work is involved in transferring all of the assets from an individual's name to the name of the living trust. However, that time is a small fraction of the time that would be involved in the probate of an estate.

Another reason is that often people do not want to think about death, and they therefore avoid spending time and effort planning ahead.

Some people are afraid of living trusts because they do not understand the concept of a trust and are afraid of becoming involved in what they erroneously perceive to be a very complicated situation. They therefore shy away from considering a living trust for themselves. On the other hand, there are some people who learn about the concept, understand its relative simplicity, and assume, erroneously, that because the concept is so simple there must be something wrong.

Lawyers are occasionally accused of discouraging living trusts because the fee for the preparation of a trust instrument is substantially less than probate fees. My experience is that most lawyers with expertise in this area do not discourage living trusts because they may be fearful of losing probate fees.

There are some legitimate reasons for not using a living trust. If there are potential claims against the decedent, a probate proceeding forces claimants to file within a relatively short period of time. If claims are not filed, they will be cut off. Therefore, as a precautionary measure, many attorneys file a pour-over short-form will, which leaves everything to the living trust, and a simple probate proceeding is commenced, primarily to cut off claims. The fees for this should not be great.

In larger estates, there can be some minor loss of flexibility in allocating income and expenses between the decedent's estate and the eventual trusts that are established. However, my personal experience is that whatever minor loss of flexibility occurs is far less troublesome than the time, expense, and other disadvantages involved in probating an estate.

If your estate is relatively small, you may want to avoid having a financial institution be a trustee because, for a smaller trust, the fee of a corporate trustee can be disproportionately large when compared with the trust income, since there are certain minimum costs to handle any trust. If you have any questions, obviously you should approach several financial institutions to determine which might best meet your needs for the maximum benefit and the minimum cost.

Once you decide to have a living trust, you cannot just leave it alone. Just as a will has to be updated from time to time, to take into consideration changes in your own desires as well as possible changes in the tax laws, you should review your living trust from time to time. But the cost of amending a living trust instrument is no greater than amending a will. And if at any time you desire to revoke your living trust, you always have the right to do so.

Should a living trust be used by everyone? Not necessarily. However, in my entire practice, I have never seen a situation where a person revoked a living trust and went back to having all of his or her assets subject to probate. Changes in the trust instrument? Yes—often. Revoking of the trust instrument, without a substitute? If not never, almost never.

If you want to leave money wisely, I urge that you consider adopting a living trust. It avoids publicity. It avoids tying up property in probate courts. It avoids executor fees. It substantially reduces legal fees. Perhaps most important of all, a living trust in essence is a posthumous gift to your family, for it can save them a lot of time and effort and avoid the frustration that often comes when one has to deal with the complexity of probate courts.

11

How Best to Divide
Tangible Personal Property

The last thing a parent wants is to have children argue about who gets particular items of furniture, jewelry, or other family heirlooms—items that are known as *tangible personal property* and that are often simply called *personal property,* as contrasted with real estate. (Stocks and bonds are sometimes referred to as *intangible property.*)

Generally, in a first marriage where there are no particular family complications, the husband and wife leave their personal property to each other. If there are children, the survivor will leave all personal property equally to children, with adjustments sometimes made where there are specific items of property that parents might wish to go to particular children. A mother might naturally want her jewelry to go to her daughters, rather than to her sons. A father might want a watch to go to a son rather than to a daughter. Sometimes there are specific items of furniture or other tangible personal property that a parent might want to leave to a particular child, such as a piano or violin, when that child plays the instrument.

Many states permit individuals to leave a separate memorandum on how they want personal property to be distributed. This allows individuals to change their designation from time to time without going through the formalities of changing a will.

If one child gets more personal property than another, a fair adjustment can be made to help equalize matters by having a lump sum of cash also distributed in the will to those children who did not receive particular items of property. This is an option that is sometimes adopted where parents are particularly concerned about trying to make things as equal as possible.

But if there is a substantial amount of personal property that is left to be divided equally among children, what can be done to avoid family arguments about who gets which items? My favorite technique is the rotation method. The executor is directed to place approximate valuations on various items of personal property. Then each child will have a chance to make a choice in rotation. For instance, assume there are items of personal property having an aggregate value of $20,000 and there are four children: Ann, Bill, Connie, and Dan. Each person would be entitled to $5,000 worth of the property. Each child in rotating order will select a particular item, with the first being by Ann, the next Bill, the next Connie, the next Dan, the next Ann, etc., until that particular child has selected items totaling $5,000. When that level is reached for him or her, the remaining children who have not yet selected items totaling $5,000 will continue selecting on a rotating basis until the full $20,000 is allocated.

The next question becomes, Who decides who will go first? Most often it is done in chronological order, with the oldest child getting the first choice. However, this is not necessarily the fairest method, so sometimes it is done with changes in the order of rotation. For instance, in the first round the names might be in the order of birth, but in the second round the second oldest would choose first, with the oldest choosing last; and in the third round the third oldest would choose first, with the second oldest choosing last, etc.

Sometimes the initial order of selection is decided by lot, and the this order is continued in each round. Sometimes there is a change in each round, with the person who chose second in the first round choosing first in the second round, etc.

A single person with no children who leaves personal property to collateral relatives or friends can also find the rotation method very helpful.

A little extra language in the will or living trust is required to cover these contingencies, but in the long run this attention to detail is well worth the trouble because it avoids a lot of the disagreements that might arise in the trauma of dividing the personal property of a loved one.

In families where the husband or wife has been previously married, the division of personal property becomes more complicated, particularly where there are children from the previous marriages. Generally speaking, the personal property of each partner is not automatically given outright to the other, although the duration of the second marriage affects this decision. The longer and happier the second marriage, the more likely it is that personal property will be left outright to the surviving partner, except for particular family jewelry or other heirlooms that a parent might want to leave directly to her or his own children. Most couples are very understanding of these situations, and I have seldom seen many problems arise where there are good relationships within the family and where the values of items are not great.

On the other hand, I have seen major conflicts between the second spouse and the children of the first marriage where there were a number of valuable antiques among the personal effects of the decedent. Sometimes the controversy starts before the actual death occurs. Not so long ago I was retained by the children of a wealthy New York executive, who was hospitalized with a terminal illness. His children, who were from his first marriage, believed that his second wife, to whom he had been married for only eighteen months, was avaricious. They feared that while their father was still living she might take matters into her own hands by spiriting some of the most valuable antiques out of their Upper East Side New York City townhouse.

My first recommendation was for the children to take a camera and photograph every portion of each room of the townhouse to include all of the household furnishings. I suggested that this be done when their stepmother was not at home and that they not let her know that the pictures had been taken. Subsequently, when the estate was probated, the stepmother provided an inventory that supposedly included all of the household furnishings. Unfortunately, her itemization was incomplete. She left out some of the most valuable pieces, which she had removed from the house. With the photographic evidence, the children were able to protect their rights. And with the proof she had lied about the list, they were able to gain a psychological upper hand in all subsequent disputes involving the estate.

Relationships can be complex, particularly in "blended family" situations. The best way to avoid controversy is to anticipate the problems in light of the particular personalities and relationships within the family.

Even where there are no second marriages and blended families, great controversy can arise about how tangible personal property should be divided. Sometimes the will may provide that the executor has the power to resolve any differences. However, from my experience, the rotation method is a practical way to minimize problems where there are two or more children involved.

12

Contractual Rights: Joint Property, Retirement Plans, and Life Insurance

When Clara and Bruce fell in love, everything seemed perfect. They had both been widowed, they both had a modest amount of property and some degree of financial independence, and for people in their seventies they both were in relatively good health. Before they were married, they signed a prenuptial agreement to make sure that, upon the death of either one of them, property would be left in trust. Half of the income would go to the survivor (with the other half going to children). On the death of the survivor, the trust would end and all assets would be distributed to their respective children.

Soon after they were married, they bought a new house. The real estate agent did not know that this was the second marriage for both. At the time of the closing, deeds were drawn in the customary manner where couples are involved, which resulted in the property being conveyed to Bruce and Clara, "husband and wife, as joint tenants, with right of survivorship." What Bruce and Clara did not realize was that joint tenancy is a contractual arrangement. Under the laws of most states, this means that, when one of the joint tenants dies, the surviving joint tenant becomes entitled to all of the property.

Clara erroneously assumed that she had a one-half interest in the property and Bruce had a one-half interest in the property and that, on her death, the prenuptial agreement would control the situation. If she predeceased Bruce, her half would be held in a trust during Bruce's lifetime and on Bruce's death would pass to her children. Clara was wrong. In fact, wills do not control the disposition of property held by two people in joint tenancy. Rather, the disposition of property is governed by the contractual nature of the joint tenancy, which means that the property will pass directly to the surviving joint tenant, without going through the processes of probate.

In the case of Bruce and Clara, the arrangement proved satisfactory for Clara's children because, after Clara's death, Bruce knew that the mistake had been made. He recognized his moral obligation to Clara and her children and in his will left Clara's children one-half of the proceeds from the disposition of the real estate that had been held in joint tenancy. However, an additional state inheritance tax was levied on Clara's children because they were not Bruce's children and thus were not eligible for the exemption that many state statutes give to property that passes by inheritance to a surviving spouse or children.

Joint tenancy is an alternative to consider when the combined estates of the couple are below the threshold level of federal estate taxes and when the parties want to leave everything to each other without going through the formalities of a will, and without worrying about children. However, when the surviving joint tenant dies, then the property will pass by the terms of a will.

Another possibility to consider is what is known as *simultaneous disaster*. Where does the property go if both joint tenants are killed at substantially the same time in an airplane or auto accident? If one of the parties lives a few hours longer, the entire joint tenancy will pass through the will of the survivor.

Joint tenancy raises another problem if the parties are living together but are not married to each other. Gift tax implications arise where unmarried parties who purchase property in joint tenancy do not equally contribute to the cost. If you have any problems in this area, you should seek expert advice.

If the parties are married, there is no gift tax to worry about. However, there are estate tax implications. Prior to 1982 the federal estate tax law provided that upon the death of a joint tenant all of the joint tenancy property for which she or he had paid would be included in her or his estate for federal estate tax purposes. The law has since been changed to provide that, regardless of who provided the purchase price, only one-half of the joint tenancy property will be included in the estate for federal estate tax purposes. Generally, estate-planning experts support this change, but one adverse aspect concerns what is termed the *tax basis* of the property for determining capital gains on a federal income tax return.*

Here is a typical example. Sam and Mollie bought a house in New York in 1960 for $50,000. In 1988, when Sam died, the home was worth $500,000. The house was purchased in joint tenancy, and one-half of the value of the house, or $250,000, was included in Sam's estate for federal estate tax purposes. He did not have many other assets, and there was no federal estate tax.

In early 1990 Mollie sold the house for $500,000. For federal income tax purposes, the tax basis was $275,000—$250,000 representing the federal estate tax valuation in 1988 (when the property was also worth $500,000) for the one-half interest owned by Sam, and $25,000 representing the tax basis for Mollie's one-half interest in the property. This tax basis was allocable to her, even though Sam paid the entire price. Therefore, there was capital gain income of $225,000 ($500,000 less $275,000). Fortunately, from Mollie's perspective, federal tax laws provide a special exclusion of up to $125,000 of capital gain if it arises from the sale of the principal residence and if the seller has attained the age of fifty-five. (There would be a deferral of the entire capital gain if the proceeds were reinvested in other residential property. There are also special factors to consider in a community-property state.)

I generally recommend that couples not use joint tenancy as a

---

*Capital gain is ordinarily determined by the excess of the net sales price over the tax basis, which is usually the original cost of the property, plus any capital additions, less any tax-deductible depreciation or amortization. If the owner dies, there is ordinarily a new tax basis for the property which is its valuation at the time of death. Since this is usually higher, it is called a *stepped-up basis*. This is discussed in greater detail in Chapter 22.

substitute for a will or a living trust. If there is a second marriage, I also point out the complicating factors that can arise.

Complications in the area of retirement benefits often arise in second marriages. The terms of a will do not govern who receives the funds under a retirement plan. That is a matter of contractual right and is governed by the terms of the retirement plan. The current rules are very technical. If your retirement plan benefits are large, you should obtain expert advice about how to withdraw them. As a matter of fact, excess retirement accumulations can lead to an extra 15 percent tax on excess distributions. Complex income tax rules are also affected by the amount of the distributions and whether they are paid in a lump sum or are distributed over a period of years. Penalty taxes can be incurred on premature distributions, on failures to make minimum distributions, and on excess distribution and accumulations. There are certain extra tax savings possible where benefits are payable to a surviving spouse.

In addition to these tax complications that have been imposed by new amendments to the Internal Revenue Code, recent congressional legislation has created another major problem. At one time no federal restriction dictated how a person left the proceeds of his retirement plan. He or she could leave it to a spouse, children, friend, or anyone else. Unfortunately, there are many unhappy marriages in this country, and increasing numbers of individuals with retirement plans designated people other than their spouses as beneficiaries. Most often it was their children, but sometimes it was another party.

Women's action groups saw this as a problem and lobbied to have Congress pass a law requiring that a surviving spouse be entitled to 100 percent of the retirement benefits under a qualified retirement plan unless she or he gives written consent to part of the proceeds going to another person. Consent is required, even if the other person is a child.

Initially, many people felt that this was constructive legislation. However, new legislation often has unintended consequences, and recently clients have come to me with problems involving death and remarriage. Here is an example. Ted's first wife, Shirley, passed away in 1980. They had three children. In 1985 Ted married Nancy, who had some independent means of her own and children from her first marriage, which ended in divorce. Ted and Nancy did not sign a prenuptial agreement. They each planned to leave the other at least what the law requires, which in Iowa is one-third of an estate. In other words, in Iowa, as in many states, you cannot disinherit a spouse. If you prepare a will and leave nothing to the spouse, the spouse can "elect" against the will and take what the law allows, which if there are children is one-third of the estate.

Ted recently prepared a new estate plan, which included a living trust. He went to his employer to have the beneficiary of his retirement plan changed to provide that his living trust would be the beneficiary. His employer informed him that new federal legislation required that he get the written consent of his wife to do this. When Ted went to Nancy, she told him that she felt she ought to have the right to the entire income from that plan, as long as she was living. A major family argument ensued.

Eventually, a compromise was reached whereby Nancy, if she survives Ted, will receive the income from half of the retirement plan and Ted's children will get the other half. But Ted believes this is very unfair because Nancy already has an independent estate of her own and his children could really use the money. From Nancy's perspective, she felt she was being more than fair because she could have demanded that she receive not just the entire income from the plan but all of the principal from the plan as well. This is a typical example of there being no black and white answers. Whichever position one supports, one must recognize that an opposite position may also have merit.

All kinds of variations occur on this story. Ted's first wife, Shirley, would have wanted their children to have a substantial interest in the retirement plan. If the major portion of the benefits were earned while the first wife was living, should the second wife be entitled nevertheless to all of the benefits? Suppose the second marriage is only two years old when the employee dies. Should Congress automatically require that the surviving spouse get all of the benefits? I leave it to you to answer that question.

If you are planning to get married, and if you have significant benefits in a retirement plan, this should be a subject of discussion if you do not think it fair that your intended spouse receive all of the benefits under your retirement plan. In any event, as you review your estate plan you should be aware of the fact that, regardless of what you say in your will or your living trust, the beneficiaries of your retirement plan are determined by the retirement plan contract itself.

Insurance policy proceeds are also not governed by the terms of a will unless the policy itself is payable to the estate. Many people who are aware of this simply leave the policy proceeds directly to their estate. However, under the laws of some states, this would make the insurance policy proceeds subject to state inheritance taxes. In contrast, if they were payable to a named beneficiary or beneficiaries or to a living trust, there might be no state inheritance tax.

If your estate is large enough to have a state inheritance tax problem, you probably will have trusts established in your will. You can discuss with your attorney whether, under the laws of your particular state, the designation of testamentary trusts in a will as a beneficiary will allow the insurance policy proceeds to escape state inheritance tax.

If you use a living trust, you can name the trust as the beneficiary of the insurance policy proceeds. Of course, if there is more than one trust established under a will or a living trust instrument, you should specify which particular trust is to receive the proceeds of life insurance.

One final word about life insurance. Many people are undecided whether the proceeds of life insurance should be paid out in the form of an annuity over the lifetime of the beneficiary or in a lump sum payment with the proceeds to be invested. I generally recommend that if the proceeds are $100,000 or more, and if the proceeds are going into a trust that will be managed well, the lump sum is preferable because it will allow the investment of funds in a manner to keep up with inflation. The real purchasing power value of an annuity payment will diminish each year to the extent of inflation.*

In all of these contractual right situations involving distributions

---

*I will discuss this further in Chapter 21 when I talk about inflation insurance and the need to preserve purchasing power.

from retirement plans and life insurance, the beneficiary provisions of the contract itself determine who will get the property. Integrate this with your will or living trust. And above all, if you want your will or living trust to control the distribution of all of your property, do not use joint tenancy.

13

Special Problems
of the Aged, the Disabled,
and Medicaid Recipients

Millions of Americans are now over eighty-five. These numbers will grow substantially over the next few decades. Life expectancies are also increasing. The life expectancy of an eighty-five-year-old person today is approximately five years.

As people age, greater problems of physical and mental disability occur.

What can be done to protect the individual and his assets when mental and physical faculties start to decline? The best way, by far, is to use a living trust, provided that there is a capable trustee or co-trustee to assure proper management of the trust. The co-trustee can be a family member, trusted friend, or a bank or trust company. If a corporate trustee is designated, you should make sure that you know ahead of time what the costs of trust management will be. Trust fees vary from company to company, and sometimes they may be negotiable, particularly in the case of a living trust where the person who created the trust is generally managing the trust affairs.

As long as there is no incompetency or senility, the settlor, who created the trust, can continue to act as his own trustee. Some people, when they begin to slip mentally, will voluntarily relinquish being a trustee. But sometimes increasing age has many collateral effects, one of which is deep insecurity and fear that loved ones will try to take property away and there will not be any property left.

Here is a typical example. Jean, a widow who is eighty-seven, has an only child, Cara, who for many years has looked after her mother and helped take care of her mother's affairs. I urged Cara to talk to her mother about setting up a living trust to avoid problems of probate and problems of management of her mother's property, if she should become disabled. The family put it off. Early last year Cara came to me and said that her mother was becoming more and more "paranoid" about her daughter trying to steal her property. She told me she was afraid that the situation would get gradually worse and that her mother would start making some unwise investment decisions.

I again asked her to talk to her mother about creating a living trust. Cara finally did, but it was too late. Had the conversation taken place a year or two earlier, the living trust plan probably would have been adopted.

One special area of sensitivity in drafting a revocable trust instrument concerns how to provide for the time when the settlor who creates the trust is no longer capable of serving as a trustee. Obviously, the settlor-trustee can always resign in favor of another trustee. But what happens if the trustee refuses to resign and then becomes senile? Some trust instruments provide for what are known as *voluntary relinquishment* clauses and *automatic relinquishment* clauses.

The voluntary relinquishment clause merely states that the settlor who is also a trustee has the right to resign at any time. A successor trustee or trustees are named.

The automatic relinquishment clause has many possible variations. For instance, the trust may specify that the automatic relinquishment clause must be triggered by a written instrument signed by two physicians, each of whom is a member of a recognized medical specialty board. Both doctors will have to state that they have examined the settlor-trustee and have determined that because of physical or mental illness, progressive or intermittent physical or mental deterioration, accident, or other similar cause, the settlor-trustee has become incapable of exercising prudent judgment in managing the assets of the trust. The receipt of such a written document shall constitute an automatic resignation by the settlor-trustee, and the remaining trustee shall continue to manage the affairs of the trust in accordance with its terms. These terms may or may not provide for the succession of a second co-trustee.

The trust can provide for recourse if there should be a subsequent return by the settlor to sound mental capabilities.

Another alternative to consider where declining mental capability is a potential problem is known as a *power of attorney*. This does not involve the kind of an attorney licensed to practice law. This is the power given by one person to another, who is known as the *attorney-in-fact*, to manage all of the affairs of the person granting the power—including such power as signing the person's name on checks or other written instruments, paying debts, buying and selling assets, and everything else a person could do to manage his or her own property. Of course, one has to be certain that the person to whom the power of attorney is given will act responsibly and in the best interests of the donor of the power. Sometimes powers of attorney are specifically drawn to provide that they continue in effect even after the donor has become mentally incompetent to handle his or her affairs. This is sometimes known as a *durable power of attorney*. Its validity depends upon the laws of your state, and you should discuss this with your own lawyer.

Another vehicle sometimes used is putting property in joint ownership. Potential gift-tax problems can arise where the new co-owner is not a spouse. Moreover, once property is placed in joint tenancy, as we have seen, its disposition falls outside of a will or living trust. Rather, its disposition generally goes automatically to the surviving joint tenant.

Occasionally older people are confronted with an entirely different set of problems, such as an avaricious child who seeks to gain access to the parent's property. Here is a recent example. Gino, a retired businessman in his early eighties, is worried that a son, an ambitious entrepreneur, wants to get hold of his father's money in order to invest it in a venture that Gino thinks is too risky. Gino recognizes that he is not as alert as he once was. He worries that his son might employ a lawyer to bring a court conservatorship proceeding in which Gino's son would be appointed as a conservator of his father's property. If that were to happen, Gino could lose control of his property. Sometimes conservatorship proceedings of this kind are warranted, but in many cases they are not. If a parent feels threatened that a child may try to gain control over the parent's property, one of the best ways to prevent this from happening is through the use of a living trust with an independent corporate trustee.

How often do situations of this kind arise? More often than one likes to think.

The more common situation, of course, occurs when children want to provide in their wills sufficient funds to take care of elderly parents. Generally, a trust is the most practical way to accomplish this, but there are potential problems that should be considered. For instance, if the trust provides for mandatory distribution of income and specific rights to principal, you should give attention to how this may affect the parent's eligibility for rights she or he would otherwise have to governmental assistance such as Supplemental Security Income, Medicaid, and even food stamp programs.

Of course, if the trust is large enough, you don't have to worry about government assistance. But for many people of modest or middle-income means, a trust with mandatory distribution provisions can create problems with government agencies trying to make claims on property that was originally intended to provide for extra funding to create a more comfortable standard of living for a loved parent.

Sometimes parental support is provided through the use of a sprinkling trust. The trust gives to the trustee the discretion to provide whatever amount from the income and principal is necessary to provide for the proper care, support, and maintenance of the parent. This is used under the assumption that the court cannot force the trustee to provide income in lieu of Medicaid benefits. However, there have been cases where courts have held that the public interest prevails over private concerns; therefore, nursing home benefits that otherwise would have been paid by the state are terminated under the theory that there are discretionary funds that would be available through a trust.

The laws differ from state to state. If these are potential problem areas for your family, you should discuss them with an attorney who has appropriate expertise.

Another way to handle the situation is through an informal understanding among the children involved and, in turn, their children, so that direct payments are made from time to time to take care of the extra needs of the aged or infirm parent. If one of the children dies prematurely, other members of the family can assume an appropriate share of the burden.

Related to this area are problems involving retarded or otherwise disabled children. Once again, gifts in trust can affect entitlements to public aid. In some states a discretionary trust is an effective means to provide for disabled persons. The National Association for Retarded Citizens, for example, provides help and assistance in this area, and you may want to contact that and other associations before you meet with your attorney.

Dealing with problems of aged, disabled, and Medicaid recipients has often led me to give this advice to older clients: If you really want to give your husband (or your wife) a present, execute a living trust so your spouse won't have to go through the red tape of dealing with the courts in the event of your death. And if you have real estate in more than one state, a living trust will avoid the necessity of opening a second probate proceeding in that state (known as an *ancillary administration*). If there is no living trust, an ancillary administration may be required in order to have the property transferred from the name of the deceased person to the designated beneficiary.

Moreover, there is a second benefit that inures directly to you. If you have the misfortune of becoming physically or mentally disabled (and this can happen to any one of us), a living trust will assure your affairs being managed in a sound manner to give you the kind of support you need.

So, to protect yourself, consider giving yourself the gift of a living trust. And to help the members of your family, consider giving them a living trust so they can avoid the extra time and expense and the many problems that can arise because of probate.

14

Choosing an Attorney: Some Dos and Don'ts

One of my favorite lawyer stories involves the argument between a doctor, an engineer, and a lawyer about whose profession was the oldest. The doctor asserted with great authority that the medical profession was obviously the oldest because, when God created Eve out of Adam's rib, that was a medical act. "But," said the engineer, "before God created man and woman, He created heaven and earth out of chaos, and this was obviously the greatest engineering act of all time."

"But," said the lawyer, "who created chaos?"

In the minds of many people, the word "lawyer" connotes frustration, dissatisfaction, and high fees. Yet, although some lawyers may deserve that antipathy, my observation is that the great majority of attorneys seek to serve their clients well.

One complaint about lawyers is the amount of fees they charge. Here lawyers are at a disadvantage when compared with doctors because the time that most doctors spend with particular patients is measured in minutes, whereas the time of a lawyer is measured in hours. If the lawyer spends a full day working on the estate plan of one client and has a billing rate of $150 an hour, the total gross income for that lawyer for an eight-hour day will be $1,200. If a doctor sees four patients an hour and charges $75 per consultation, the doctor in an eight-hour day can gross $2,400. Most patients will not complain about a $75 fee. But many clients will complain about a $1,200 fee.

Moreover, from a public relations perspective, lawyers make a mistake when they quote hourly rates without reference to office overhead. When a lawyer tells a client, "My rate is $150 an hour," many clients think that the entire $150 is going to go to that lawyer, and they multiply that $150 by 40 hours a week and quickly arrive at $6,000 a week, and they multiply that by 52 weeks and quickly arrive at more than $300,000 a year. They do not consider vacations; they do not consider sickness or holidays. And most important of all, they do not account for the fact that out of the gross income the lawyer has to pay for rent, secretarial help, telephone, and all the other items of overhead.

If lawyers were as smart as most of them think they are, instead of saying, "My hourly rate is $150," they would say, "My hourly rate is $90, and there is a factor of 67 percent to take care of items of expenses such as secretarial help, rent, and other items of firm overhead."

Ultimately, the bill will be the same, but the clients will be better able to understand that the entire $1,200 did not go to the lawyer.

However, understanding the composition of a bill is not nearly as important as trying to reduce the bill. Here are a few things that you can do:

1. Before you confer with your lawyer about preparing a will or a living trust, think about how you would like to leave your property. If there are any specific bequests to members of your family, collateral relatives, friends, or charities, jot this down. If you have any preliminary thoughts about whether to leave property outright, or in trust, write these thoughts in a memorandum. Then, prepare a letter to your lawyer outlining your thoughts.

2. The discipline of writing this letter will help focus your perspective and help make more efficient use of your lawyer's time. Understandably, your letter will be only a starting point for discussion, and you may make many changes as a result of the conferences you have with your attorney. But a letter

of this kind can save many hours of drafting and redrafting, and an hour saved means dollars and cents for you.

3. When you receive a preliminary draft of documents from your lawyer, review it to see if it reflects your desires. If you want changes made, give some careful thought, so the first set of changes will be the last or, if not, so any final changes will be minimal. If there are areas where you are vacillating, mark these for special discussion with your lawyer to make sure you receive good counsel.

Now for some "don'ts":

1. Don't be afraid to ask about fees. The lawyer may not be able to give you a definitive number because she or he may not know how much time will be involved in overall redrafting, but if you have a general letter outlining what you want, the lawyer should be able to give you a ballpark figure about what fees to expect.

2. Don't fall into the trap of thinking that, because one lawyer charges a higher hourly rate than another lawyer, that automatically makes her or him better. High hourly rates do not necessarily mean better capabilities.

   I learned this lesson when I had been in law practice for just a few years and was devoting the majority of my time to litigation. No-fault divorce had not yet come into vogue, and a client of the firm was involved in a bitter divorce lawsuit. His wife's lawyer was reputed to be one of the best divorce lawyers in town because he commanded by far the highest fees. He generally represented women and had wonderful personal rapport with his clients. In turn, he received great "word of mouth" recommendations.

   Large amounts of property were involved, and I quickly learned from my senior partner that the best way to deal with the situation was to contest every financial demand made by the opposing attorney. When it came to the time of trial, the opposing counsel would probably try to settle on the courthouse steps. The big concession we would make would be on the amount of attorney fees he would demand our client pay.

If opposing counsel demanded $10,000 but was really only entitled to $5,000, let him have the $10,000. But make sure that the concession we obtained was at least an extra $100,000 of property division.

As a matter of fact, in this particular case the lawyer got a $20,000 fee—far more than he would have received from the award of a court. But from our client's point of view, the final property settlement we negotiated for him was hundreds of thousands of dollars better than it probably would have been had the matter gone to trial.

The moral of the story: Top fees do not necessarily mean top representation. By the same token, lower hourly rates do not necessarily mean the best representation, either.

3. Hourly rates are only one component of a bill. The other major component is the number of hours spent on a project, and that in part is influenced by the expertise and efficiency of the attorney. If a lawyer with an hourly rate of $125 spends ten hours on a project and another lawyer who bills at a $150 rate can do the same work with at least as good quality in six hours, the lawyer with the higher rate will have a lower bill. Of course, the most important criterion is not who will present the lowest bill, but who will do the best job for you.

This poses another problem. How does one know that a particular lawyer has sufficient expertise in estate planning? Sometimes the credentials of a lawyer can tell you a lot about his area of expertise. If he or she is a member of the American College of Probate Counsel or a member of the section of probate or the section of taxation of the American Bar Association, this is evidence (not necessarily conclusive) that the lawyer does have expertise in the estate-planning area. Many lawyers who do not have these credentials nevertheless are very capable estate planners.

There are also general questions you can ask in your initial conference to help you reach a final decision. Here are three questions I would suggest:

1. Can you tell me about your experience in preparing both wills and living trusts?

2. Can you tell me about your experience in the use of sprinkling trusts and powers of appointment?

3. What experience have you had with generation-skipping trusts?

Most lawyers will answer these questions honestly. If they do not have sufficient experience in these areas, you may want to consider choosing other counsel, depending upon the complexity of your estate.*

Sometimes people work for years with one lawyer and think about changing but are reluctant to tell the first lawyer that they want to go somewhere else. The client may think the problem is compounded if the original copy of the will currently in effect is in the lawyer's safe. Actually, there is no need to communicate to the first lawyer that you are executing a new will. There is not even any need to destroy the first will (although everything else being equal, it is better not to leave old wills lying around). The opening paragraph of almost every well-drawn will includes the clause "I hereby revoke all former wills and codicils made by me." Even if the previous will has not been destroyed, it is void if a new will has been prepared and properly executed by a person of "sound mind and disposing memory."

Most lawyers expect that, if they have prepared the will, they will be selected to probate the estate. Lawyers often reduce the legal fees for drawing wills, with the expectation that they will make it up out of fees when the estate is probated. Corporate trust departments and lawyers often have an unwritten agreement that, if the bank is named executor in a will that is drawn by the lawyer, the bank will almost always require that the lawyer be retained as the attorney for the estate. This encourages lawyers to name banks as executors, which in the case of larger estates provides the bank with handsome executor fees. It also makes the job of the lawyer much easier, because the bank is well equipped to do the detail work. Yet the lawyer may still charge the same probate fee, which is often a percentage of the estate, such as 2 or 3 percent. Most

*See Chapter 35, which includes a discussion of information sources to find a competent lawyer.

people do not know that these fees are generally negotiable. The lack of knowledge is exacerbated by the fact that, at the time a lawyer is retained to probate an estate, the family is suffering emotional distress over the death of the testator. In times of trauma, people are ill equipped to negotiate with lawyers.

Ordinarily, there is no requirement that you have to rush to open a probate proceeding immediately. When you do contact a lawyer about probating an estate, you should determine whether the lawyer or someone in her or his firm has probate experience. Most firms with expertise in estate planning also have probate expertise. Ask what the probate fees will be and whether they include the work involved in filing a federal estate tax return and a state inheritance tax return.

Obviously, if substantial tax problems arise during the probate, the client should expect to pay greater fees. In the case of a living trust, where there is no estate to probate, most of the work will be in preparing and filing the federal estate tax and the state inheritance tax returns and related problems. In the case of large estates, a full and frank discussion at the beginning about attorney fees and executor fees can save thousands and sometimes tens of thousands (and with very large estates hundreds of thousands) of dollars.

If you are not satisfied with the fee discussions, you should contact other lawyers to see what alternatives are available.

The probate of an estate without tax and valuation complications or family controversy is ordinarily not very complicated, assuming there was a well-drawn will by a legally competent decedent. The will is filed in a probate court; the executor is named; notice of probate is given; the inventory of the estate is filed; debts, fees, expenses of the last illness and funeral are paid; and the federal estate and any state inheritance tax returns are prepared and filed, together with the tax payments. In many states there are provisions for paying a surviving spouse a sum called a *widow's allowance* during the course of probate. While the estate remains open pending the settlement of all taxes, partial payments can be made to beneficiaries. Once all debts, fees, and taxes have been paid and a final accounting has been accepted by the court, the estate can be closed.

The process is often painstakingly slow, but it is not difficult. If

I were to analogize with the medical profession and compare difficulties in surgery ranging from an appendectomy at the lower end and brain surgery at the higher end, the probating of an estate would fall in the appendectomy category (assuming a well-drawn will, validly executed, without any family fight and without any complicated tax or allocation problems). Obviously, the better the input in the preparation of a will, the less complicated the probate. And if probate fees have been negotiated, fewer complications should mean lower costs.

In addition to your will, you should prepare an informal memorandum itemizing your property and the location of specific assets. You can have the best lawyer in the world probating an estate, but if the lawyer has no knowledge of the location of specific property, that property may be overlooked and title not transferred to the proper beneficiaries on your death. Moreover, the estate may have to be reopened and all of the tax returns amended.

In my case, I have a *memo to file concerning assets* that is in the file with my living trust. It lists my assets, including any stock in closely held corporations that may not pay any dividends and that would therefore not be shown on an income tax schedule. It also includes a list of life insurance policies and the names of the insurance agents who sold the policies and who will provide service in collecting the insurance after my death. Also included is a list of any real estate holdings, interests in partnerships, references to contractual rights, and anything else that would be of value to my heirs.

A memorandum of this kind will save countless hours of work for your attorney. It is all part of planning ahead.

One additional factor in choosing a lawyer is at least as important as rates and competence. This involves the counseling aspect of estate planning and probate—the overall judgment and perspective of the attorney. Traditionally, a lawyer has often been known as a *counselor.* In this age of ever-increasing specialization, the broad perspective of a wise counselor is becoming relatively rare.

One can always find attorneys who have the technical competence and tax background and expertise to prepare well-drawn wills and living trusts. But many issues involve far more than technical legal capabilities. They involve matters of judgment that cross over into the areas of the psychologist and family counselor. After all, when one thinks about leaving money to husbands and wives, daughters and sons, nieces and nephews, and close friends, she or he is talking not just about dollars and cents but about relationships with people. These are areas of great sensitivity, where there is more than one right way to handle a particular situation. Here a lawyer has the opportunity to rise to the pinnacle of his profession—to serve not just as a sage legal counselor but almost like an impartial friend of the family. The wise lawyer will not try to impose his values upon his client. Rather, the truly wise lawyer will seek to bring out the client's own desires, season this with legal counsel and experience, and help the client achieve the ultimate goal of leaving money wisely.

A final word on choosing an attorney. Lawyers do not have crystal balls, nor do they have any monopoly on wisdom or on how to solve problems. Lawyers may gain wisdom through experience, but just because it is a lawyer's idea does not make it necessarily best.

I have seen the limitations of lawyers and their advice in many situations, ranging from the business world to family estate planning and other personal matters. Lawyers may know the law, but when it comes to family members they do not know your own needs and desires, nor do they know as well as you the potential beneficiaries of your estate and their attributes, needs, and desires.

Lawyers can be of tremendous assistance in helping you choose your financial destiny. They can keep you abreast of changes in the tax laws—a particularly important element today because the estate tax rates are so much higher than income tax rates, and estate tax savings therefore deserve even more thought. Lawyers can draft legal instruments to implement the plan that you choose. But the ultimate decisions are not legal decisions but are rather personal decisions that you yourself must make.

Many of these decisions concern psychological issues—questions of power and control—and at times these issues involve the spreading branches of a family tree. A family tree is not a pyramid with a solid base—it has a narrow base, with a broad top, and can become inherently unstable and find it hard to stand against the winds of change.

It is you who knows the family tree best. It is you who can make the best decisions. Your lawyer can be of great help—but look upon him or her as a resource person for you, rather than as a decision maker. Working together with your lawyer from this perspective is the best path to help you reach your goal of choosing your financial destiny and leaving money wisely.

PART III

*Important Issues for
People of Wealth
or Potential Wealth*

(At Least $200,000, Including Home,
Insurance, and Retirement Plans)

15

Minimizing the Federal
Estate Tax

An old Iowa politician once told me that, when it comes to getting elected, the three most important issues are taxes, taxes, and taxes. If you walk into the office of a typical estate-planning expert, she or he will often concentrate the discussion on taxes and tax savings. If you know the structure ahead of time, you can cut through a lot of the tax thicket and concentrate more time on the personal and philosophical issues, which are ultimately more important.

The primary tax consideration in estate planning centers on the federal estate tax, which currently has a top bracket of 55 percent (with an extra 5 percent for taxable estates between $10 million and $21.04 million to put the entire estate at the 55 percent level to the extent that the tax rates below $10 million average less than 55 percent). Although most people believe that the federal estate tax is complex, the basic rules are easy to understand. The starting point is to know what property is subject to the tax.

For federal estate tax purposes, an *estate* includes all property owned of every kind and nature—the house, household furniture and furnishings, jewelry and other personal effects, life insurance, retirement plan benefits, stocks, bonds, bank accounts, real estate investments, partnership interests, joint venture interests, all contract interests, and any other asset of value. Also included for tax purposes are joint tenancy interests, general powers of appointment, and trusts or other property where there has been a reservation of rights to income until death. Of course, debts are generally deducted in determining the value of an estate for federal estate tax purposes. So are charitable bequests.

Federal estate tax rates are steep. The tax bite is at the 37 percent level when there is over $600,000 of property. The tax rate rises to 39 percent at the $750,000 level, 41 percent at the $1 million level, and continues up to 55 percent for estates with a valuation of over $3 million. (Under current law, beginning in 1993, the 55 percent level will supposedly be reduced to 50 percent for any taxable estate over $2.5 million.) Here is the actual schedule:

If the Amount with Respect to Which the Tentative Tax to Be Computed Is:	The Tentative Tax Is:
Not over $10,000	18 percent of such amount
Over $10,000 but not over $20,000	$1,800, plus 20 percent of the excess of such amount over $10,000
Over $20,000 but not over $40,000	$3,800, plus 22 percent of the excess of such amount over $20,000
Over $40,000 but not over $60,000	$8,200, plus 24 percent of the excess of such amount over $40,000
Over $60,000 but not over $80,000	$13,000, plus 26 percent of the excess of such amount over $60,000
Over $80,000 but not over $100,000	$18,200, plus 28 percent of the excess of such amount over $80,000
Over $100,000 but not over $150,000	$23,800, plus 30 percent of the excess of such amount over $100,000
Over $150,000 but not over $250,000	$38,800, plus 32 percent of the excess of such amount over $150,000

If the Amount with Respect to Which the Tentative Tax to Be Computed Is:	The Tentative Tax Is:
Over $250,000 but not over $500,000	$70,800, plus 34 percent of the excess of such amount over $250,000
Over $500,000 but not over $750,000	$155,800, plus 37 percent of the excess of such amount over $500,000
Over $750,000 but not over $1,000,000	$248,300, plus 39 percent of the excess of such amount over $750,000
Over $1,000,000 but not over $1,250,000	$345,800, plus 41 percent of the excess of such amount over $1,000,000
Over $1,250,000 but not over $1,500,000	$448,300, plus 43 percent of the excess of such amount over $1,250,000
Over $1,500,000 but not over $2,000,000	$555,800, plus 45 percent of the excess of such amount over $1,500,000
Over $2,000,000 but not over $2,500,000	$780,800, plus 49 percent of the excess of such amount over $2,000,000
Over $2,500,000 but not over $3,000,000	$1,025,800, plus 53 percent of the excess over $2,500,000
Over $3,000,000	$1,290,800, plus 55 percent of the excess over $3,000,000
Beginning 1993: Over $2,500,000	$1,025,800, plus 50 percent of the excess over $2,500,000

There is an extra 5 percent for taxable estates between $10 million and $21.04 million.

Many people wonder about state death taxes. Generally these are not relatively high, and there is a credit against the federal estate tax for state inheritance taxes paid up to a specified amount. In most states a close relationship exists between the state inheritance taxes and the amount of credit allowed against the federal estate tax. The net effect in many states is that there is no state inheritance tax at all, except for the amount of the federal state tax credit.*

Against this backdrop of estate tax rates, there is a lifetime credit, called a *unified credit,* for every taxpayer under the present law. We will talk more about the "unified" nature of this credit later, because it includes gifts above $10,000 per individual donee, except for gifts to a spouse, which are tax free. The net effect of this credit is to shield the first $600,000 of assets from federal estate taxes.

The way the credit works is that you compute what the estate tax would be without the credit. Then you determine from the tax table the credit for $600,000 (assuming you had made no prior gifts subject to gift tax), which is $192,800. You then subtract the credit from the preliminary figure to compute the final tax.

In the case of a married couple, each partner has a $600,000 unified credit. Sophisticated estate planners know that there is a relatively simple way to use each individual's separate $600,000 unified credit so that a couple can shield up to $1,200,000 from federal estate taxes and save approximately $235,000 in the process. This is done through the use of the vehicle of a trust, rather than outright distributions of property.

This forms the foundation of a basic rule for tax planning for married couples with combined net worth of more than $600,000: You can save tens of thousands and in many cases hundreds of thousands of dollars by avoiding the traditional estate plan of leaving everything to your spouse.

Here is a specific example. A husband and wife have a total net worth of $1,200,000 and all of their property—home, savings accounts, stocks, bonds—is held in joint tenancy so that, on the death of either the husband or the wife, the surviving partner will get all the property. If the husband dies first, there is no federal estate tax, *regardless of the size of the estate,* because everything that you leave to your spouse goes tax free. However, on the death of the surviving spouse—in this case, the wife—there is a federal estate tax on the entire $1.2 million because all the property is in her name. The

---

*In this book, I am going to ignore the impact of state inheritance taxes and gift taxes and leave that for you to discuss with your own advisers. However, in some states, such as New York, these can be significant.

federal estate tax computation would show a preliminary figure of $427,800, less a credit for the first $600,000 of approximately $192,800, leaving a net tax to pay of $235,000.*

All of this tax could have been avoided through sound estate tax planning. Instead of holding all their property in joint tenancy, half the property could be transferred (without federal gift tax) to outright ownership by the wife and half the property transferred to outright ownership by the husband. Each partner would then have a taxable estate of $600,000. Their individual wills, instead of leaving all property outright to the survivor, could leave the property in a trust that would provide that all of the income go to the surviving party, who would be the beneficiary. In addition, the trust could give the survivor access to the principal, if needed, through the power of the trustee to invade principal for the proper care, support, and maintenance of the beneficiary.

On the death of the first to die, the taxable estate would be $600,000, and there would be no federal estate tax at all because the value of the estate did not exceed the $600,000 base.

Similarly, on the death of the survivor, assuming no increase in the value of the survivor's estate above the $600,000 level, there would be no federal estate tax because the survivor's estate was within the $600,000 base.

Each will would provide what would happen to the trust on the death of the survivor. The property would go to whomever the husband and wife selected. Thus, through the combination of dividing property between the parties and the use of basic trusts, all federal tax on a combined estate of $1.2 million, or less, can be avoided.

In order to avoid the tax, the property must be owned outright by individuals rather than in joint tenancy, which as we have seen transfers ownership directly to the joint tenant who survives. In many families the equity in a home represents a substantial portion of net worth and can have a value of several hundred thousand dollars. If the home passes to the survivor because of joint tenancy, and the survivor already has several hundred thousand dollars of

---

*This assumes there are no other deductions and that the taxable estate equals $1.2 million.

property in her or his name, federal estate tax problems can arise. Therefore, it is important to integrate all ownership of property with sound estate planning.

Life insurance can also have a major impact on federal estate taxes, if the policy is owned by the decedent. One practical way to avoid any federal estate tax is to transfer the ownership of the policy to a third party or a trust. Of course, this means giving up control over the policy, including the right to change beneficiaries and the right to borrow against any cash values. On the other hand, the new owner may voluntarily concur with your suggestions in changing beneficiary designations.

If you have a potential federal estate tax problem, you should bring your life insurance agent into your estate-planning team and consider alternatives that can remove the proceeds of life insurance from the federal estate tax bite.

Even in estates that are larger than $1.2 million, tax benefits can be obtained by dividing property between a husband and wife because the Unified Rate Schedule is "graduated." The top tax bracket at the $3,000,000 level is 55 percent. At the $750,000 level, extending to $1 million, the tax bracket is 39 percent, and it goes to 41 percent at the $1 million level. Obviously, there are opportunities to save federal estate taxes by balancing the size of the estates between husband and wife.

This often poses a dilemma for the couple to consider, since everything that is left to a spouse is tax free. Many people take the position that the differences in tax brackets should be ignored and the only item to consider should be the first $600,000 of estate tax exemption that each taxpayer has.

The rationale for this position is very simple. Every dollar above $600,000 (that is not left to a spouse) will be subject to federal estate tax. If the tax is paid, at the very least it will be at the 37 percent bracket and will quickly go to the 39 percent bracket and higher. Paying federal estate taxes takes assets that would otherwise be available to produce income. After two or three years, the cumulative loss of income is greater than the amount saved by adjusting the difference in estate tax brackets. Therefore, many tax advisers do not put a lot of weight in the differential of tax brackets.

If you are married, you can avoid all federal estate taxes if your spouse survives by setting aside the first $600,000 in a trust, taking advantage of the $600,000 exemption and leaving everything else to the surviving spouse.* (Obviously, second marriages and blended family situations will influence decisions about how much to leave a surviving spouse.)

But taxes are not the only issues of concern. Although some people are content to leave property outright to their surviving spouse, with no concern that some of the property may ultimately go to a second spouse on the survivor's marriage, there are many other people who are extremely concerned about what will ultimately happen to their property after their death and the death of their surviving spouse. "If I leave everything above $600,000 to my husband (or wife), and after I die he remarries, how can I prevent his second wife from having at least a 'dower' one-third interest in my property and giving that to her family?" Fortunately, there is a relatively easy way to meet this problem. It is through the use of what is known as a *marital deduction trust*—one of the basic vehicles for leaving money wisely.

But before examining the marital deduction trust in greater detail, it is important to discuss two other important provisions that can be incorporated in an estate plan for both married and unmarried people—the "five and five" power and the special power of appointment. After you have an understanding of these unique estate-planning tools, I will make some specific recommendations that I generally offer to clients who ask me for suggestions to help them reach their own decisions.

*Opportunities to take advantage of the $1 million per person generation-skipping tax exemption affect decisions in this area, as we will see in Chapter 26.

16

The "Five and Five" Power: A "Double Check" on the Trustee

"But what happens if the trustee and my children do not get along?"

"What happens if my trustee is too tight when it comes to distributing principal to my children?"

"Why should I try to dictate from the grave what happens to my property?"

"I am single and want to leave property to my brother and sister, and I want there to be liberal trust distribution provisions for them. What special provisions should I have?"

These are common concerns raised by people weighing the pros and cons of whether to leave property in trust. They often arise because most people have had no experience in dealing with trustees.

As a practical matter, trustees are in the business of trying to encourage people to bring funds to a trust department for management because the trustee's income is usually based on a percentage of the amount of property that is being managed. If trustees are difficult to deal with in matters involving distribution of income and principal, and if they give little credence to reasonable suggestions or requests by beneficiaries, word of mouth will lead potential customers to go to other trust departments or fund management companies.

The management fees of trust departments for medium and large trusts usually aggregate between .4 of 1 percent and .8 of 1 percent of the principal that is being managed and administered. Sometimes the fee is a lower percentage of principal, but there is an additional percentage of income added. For instance, the fee might be 5 percent of trust income and .3 percent of trust principal. The highest fees do not necessarily reflect the best management. The investment performance record of a trust department is far more important than whether its fees may be one-eighth of a percent a year more than a competitor.

Some people wonder whether it is worthwhile to retain an independent corporate trustee. "Why not have a member of my family be the trustee?" There are several considerations. Sometimes family members do not know how to invest money well, and occasionally some family members engage in self-dealing and other forms of mismanagement. Tax considerations also weigh strongly against having a family member as a trustee, if that family member also has power to distribute property to himself or herself as a beneficiary. This can create income tax problems and also estate tax problems when that beneficiary dies.

If a person has the power to direct the distribution of income or principal to herself or himself, the property may be treated for federal estate tax purposes as belonging to that person at death, even if the power was never exercised. This is sometimes called *constructive ownership.* If this occurs, the fact that the property is in trust may not keep it out of that beneficiary's estate for federal estate tax purposes. The person might also be charged with having received the income from that property for income tax purposes, even though in actuality the income went to someone else, such as her or his child.

As a practical matter, in order to take full advantage of the tax savings features of trusts, a beneficiary who is also a trustee must not have a decision-making power to distribute property to himself, his estate, his creditors, the creditors of his estate, or someone whom he is legally obligated to support.

Accordingly, decision-making powers that are discretionary in invading principal and income should generally be exercised by an independent trustee. The family member can be a co-trustee so far as management of assets is concerned, but the family member should generally not have any power to distribute income or principal to himself, his creditors, his estate, etc.

However, there is one important exception that has been drafted into the law and is generally not very well known: The so-called *"five and five" power.*

The "five and five" power allows a beneficiary to withdraw up to either $5,000 or 5 percent of the principal of the trust each year (whichever is greater), without any substantial adverse constructive ownership consequences under either federal estate tax law or federal income tax law.

In other words, if a trust has $50,000 of principal and the beneficiary has a "five and five" power, the beneficiary can withdraw $5,000 a year until the trust is exhausted (assuming the trust principal did not appreciate). By the same token, if a trust contains $500,000 in principal, the beneficiary could initially withdraw 5 percent of $500,000, or $25,000. If the principal did not increase, at the end of the next year the beneficiary could withdraw 5 percent of the remaining principal of $475,000, or $23,750. If the trust eventually fell below $100,000, the beneficiary could withdraw $5,000 because the "five and five" power is 5 percent or $5,000, whichever is greater.

By statute, the power has to be exercised on a "noncumulative" basis. In other words, if you do not exercise the power in any year, you cannot exercise the power twice in the next year—once for the current year and once for the previous year.

Even if the beneficiary might be prone to excessive spending, it will take a while through the exercise of the 5 percent or $5,000 power of appointment for the principal to be exhausted. In the meantime, the beneficiary might very well change his or her excessive spending habits and still have principal left in the trust to continue receiving long-term benefits.

The "five and five" power, in essence, is a leavening device that helps overcome the concern of many people about whether they are trying to exercise too much control from the grave.

If the beneficiary is very young, I usually suggest putting in a minimum age before the "five and five" power can be exercised. In other words, instead of having the power automatically exercisable when a beneficiary attains the age of twenty-one, the trust instrument might state that the beneficiary must have attained the age of thirty. In the case of large trusts, the instrument might suggest that the exercise can be made beginning at age twenty-five, but it will only be to a maximum amount of $5,000 or 3 percent of the value of the trust at the end of the year, whichever is greater, and the 5 percent maximum will be permitted when the beneficiary attains a later age, such as twenty-eight, thirty, or thirty-five.

The "five and five" power is a very important estate-planning tool to integrate with the basic trust plan for distribution of income and principal. It provides for added flexibility. I generally recommend that it be included in long-term trusts, so long as there is a substantial degree of confidence in the judgment of the beneficiary.

17

Special Powers
of Appointment:
Post-Death Flexibility

"I want to leave property in trust, but I don't know exactly how my grandchildren are going to turn out. What can I do to give some discretion to my children to modify the basic trust plan I have established?"

"I don't care where my property goes after my wife and children are no longer living, as long as it goes to either my grandchildren, nieces, or nephews, or to some charity. What I don't want is to have it go to my in-laws."

"I am not leaving any money to my son-in-law, but I like him very much, and I would like to find some way to let my daughter leave some of the money to him, if she wants to do so. What can I do in my will to give her the discretion?"

"I am a single person, without children, and I want to leave property in trust for a very close friend. On the death of my friend, I would like to have my property divided among four charities, and I would like to give my sister the right to allocate whatever funds there are among those charities. Can I do this in my will when I am not leaving any property to my sister?"

These are typical questions. Fortunately, an excellent tool exists that can be used to accomplish most of these objectives: the *special power of appointment.*

The great advantage of a power of appointment is that it lets the donor give to someone else the ability to change the course and direction of a trust instrument. The person creating the power is known as the *donor*. The person who has the right to exercise the power is known as the *donee*.

We have already discussed the natural concern that arises when money is left in trust: whether the trustee will be flexible enough or the terms of the trust sufficiently flexible to take into consideration the hundreds of possibilities that can arise in the course of family circumstances. One way to add flexibility, as we have seen, is through the use of the "five and five" power. It can be used by children. If the trust continues into the next generation, the power can also be given to grandchildren, once they attain an appropriate age.

But if the trust is to continue, what can be done to take into consideration changing family circumstances that were unknown at the time the will or inter vivos trust* was executed? Suppose family circumstances call for unequal treatment among grandchildren? Suppose the parents of the grandchildren might want to have the trust terminate on their deaths, instead of continuing into the next generation? The best way to provide for these contingencies is to include in the will or living trust a wonderful vehicle for flexibility known as the special power of appointment.

Powers of appointment are divided into two categories: general and special. The tax treatment is entirely different. If we ignore the impact of the generation-skipping tax, there are almost no adverse tax consequences where there is a special power of appointment, unless the donee can exercise it in his or her favor. On the other hand, with a general power of appointment, the property that is subject to the general power of appointment is subject to tax in the estate of the person who was given the general power.

The most common use of a general power of appointment is where property is left in a marital trust for the benefit of a spouse. If there are no potential conflicts from blended family situations,

---

*An *inter vivos trust* is one that is created by a person during his lifetime, such as a revocable living trust or an irrevocable trust. A *testamentary trust* is created under a will and does not take effect until death.

husbands and wives often each leave property in trust for the benefit of the other and let the survivor have the unrestricted right on her or his death to direct where the property goes.

But sometimes, because of tax reasons or personal reasons, people do not want to give a general power to appoint. The special power of appointment is an excellent alternative to consider.

The underlying difference between a general and a special power of appointment is that the person granting the special power of appointment limits the group in whose favor it can be exercised. The most typical special powers of appointment state that the recipient has the right to appoint to anyone in the world, other than himself, his estate, his creditors, or the creditors of his estate, so long as the person for whose benefit the property is appointed is in a particular class or group, such as a lawful descendant of the donor.

The reason you include the phrase "other than himself, his estate, his creditors, or the creditors of his estate" is that if a person had any of these rights, the property would be includable in the donee's estate for federal estate tax purposes and thus defeat one of the primary purposes for which the property was put in trust.

Often the class can be enlarged to include not just the descendants of the donor but the descendants of the donor's parents, so this will get collateral relatives into the group. Another possibility is to include appointment to a spouse of a lawful descendant, although some donors are reluctant to do this. A charitable institution is often included as a permitted donee, but here there can be some concerns. As the donee ages, will she or he be able to remain free from excessive influence by representatives of a particular charity?

I have seen many situations where powers of appointment have been used wisely, the most common of these arising where the grandparent has left property in trust for the benefit of children and grandchildren, but the children have the right to appoint the property on their death as long as the appointment is made to lawful descendants of the donor. This gives the children (the donees) the opportunity to see how their own children (the donor's grandchildren) are going to turn out—both personally and financially—an opportunity that may not arise during the lifetime of the donor.

I have seen situations where one grandchild needed a lot more money for medical care. I have seen situations where there have been two grandchildren—one an extremely successful business person and another a government employee without a large income but with several children who, down the line, would need college education help. On the other hand, I have seen situations where a grandchild has become hooked on drugs, has used trust income to support his habit, and has refused treatment. The availability of the special power opened up the possibility of some adjustment in light of these circumstances, which were unknown at the time the trust was created.

The special power of appointment enables the donee to have the flexibility to make such adjustments. It may even enable the donee to terminate the trust if she or he does not want to have the trust continue to its maximum length. It can also allow the donee to disinherit someone if circumstances warrant.

My general counseling in this area is very simple. Leave the property in trust for the benefit of your children and grandchildren, but consider giving your child the opportunity to terminate the trust at the child's death, if she or he so desires, or to change the allocations among the child's children. If you don't leave it in trust, you will never have that opportunity.

What you can do is to "have your cake and eat it, too"—have all the advantages of a trust but yet give the child the opportunity to terminate the trust if that seems the best decision to make under the circumstances that exist at that particular time. This offsets many of the concerns that people naturally have about being perceived to exercise too much control from the grave. In short, the special power of an appointment is an added plus with very few minuses.

One other variation can be adopted through the use of a special power of appointment. The donee can be given the opportunity not only to appoint the property outright but also to appoint the property in trust for the benefit of children, putting into place a trust with new terms of trust distributions and trustees' powers. In essence, this provides another opportunity to create a new trust with terms that are particularly adaptable to the needs of the family at the time of the exercise of the power of appointment.*

Ordinarily, the exercise of a power of appointment takes place in a person's will. In other words, a parent gives her or his child the right to exercise the power of appointment in that child's will. This gives the child the opportunity from time to time to make changes in that will (if the child wants to exercise the power). But one can also give the right to exercise the power of appointment "by deed"—in the donee's lifetime. Of course, if the power is exercised and property is distributed outright, that ends the use of the power. But a power to exercise by deed can also be used to create another trust. It is just another element of flexibility to be considered when mapping out one's estate plan.

There is one major limitation on how long the property can stay in trust under the exercise of a power of appointment. This is a general rule that governs all noncharitable trusts: the rule against perpetuities. It is a rule that was adopted centuries ago in Great Britain to limit the duration of trusts, and it is still applicable in most jurisdictions today. We will look at this in Chapter 25 when we talk about the fountainhead for transfer of wealth.

Special powers of appointment are unique tools. Unfortunately, they are not used nearly as often as they might be. Any person who has a substantial amount of property in her or his estate and wants to leave money wisely should consider incorporating special powers of appointment in wills and living trusts.

---

*There are tax restrictions under what is known as the *generation-skipping tax,* which are applicable where the amount left in trust is more than $1,000,000 per settlor, or donor. This is discussed in Chapter 26.

18

The Marital Deduction Trust: A Unique Vehicle

"I know that whatever I leave to my wife goes tax free. But I'm afraid if I leave everything to her outright she won't know how to handle the funds. What can I do?"

"I really want to take care of my husband, but if something happens to me and he should remarry, I don't want his second wife to have any of my property."

"I really love my wife, but she is not the mother of my children—my first wife died. What can I do to protect my wife, let the property ultimately go to my children, and still have the property go tax free?"

"I would like to leave everything to my wife in a way where she will get all of the income and can have access to the principal, and I would then like to have it go in equal shares to my children. However, I am not quite sure how they will turn out, and I would like to find a way to give my wife a second opportunity down the road to redivide it among my children, if she thinks this might be better. Can I do this and still get the federal estate tax deduction?"

The *marital deduction trust* is a unique vehicle that can help resolve all of these questions. The underlying concept of the marital deduction trust is that it is an alternative way to leave property to one's spouse but still receive the benefits of a tax-free marital deduction. In order to qualify for the marital deduction, there must be a mandatory distribution of income to the surviving spouse. This does not necessarily mean capital gains income. It means the interest, dividends, rents, etc.—the ordinary income from the property.

The trustee may be given (but does not have to be given) a right to invade principal for the benefit of the surviving spouse. In addition, the surviving spouse can be given the right to invade principal. When this right is given, it is usually limited by a stated standard, such as a maximum dollar amount, or a maximum percentage of the principal each year. This is generally a discretionary item in planning an estate.

On the death of the surviving spouse, a number of alternatives are available. One alternative is to provide that the property will go to the estate of the surviving spouse and have the disposition of the property be governed by the surviving spouse's will. Another alternative is to give the surviving spouse a general power of appointment, which permits the surviving spouse to treat the property as if it were his or her own, with complete discretion as to where the property will eventually go. At one time these two alternatives, plus outright distribution, were the only alternatives available if someone wanted to take advantage of the marital deduction provisions of the Internal Revenue Code.

More recently, the law has been amended to permit a more restricted structure for disposition of property where the surviving spouse gets the income for life but on the death of the surviving spouse the disposition of the property can be governed by the will or living trust that established the marital trust. The concept is known as *qualified terminable interest property* or, in the jargon of estate-planning experts, the *Q/tip trust.*

Under a Q/tip trust, the surviving spouse can have a very limited right of discretion—a special power of appointment—or the surviving spouse can have no discretion at all upon her or his death, to determine where the remaining property in the marital trust will go. Generally, wills or living trusts direct that this property is transferred (or poured over) to a residuary trust under the will of the spouse who was the first to die.

A very simple illustration will show that the Q/tip marital deduction trust is a relatively easy concept to understand.

Harry has an estate of $1 million. He wants to take care of his second wife, Mary, with a trust that will reduce his estate below the $600,000 level, so there will be no taxes to pay on his death. But he does not want to give Mary a general power of appointment to distribute the trust principal to her estate. Rather, on Mary's death he wants the property to go to the children of his first marriage. Harry divides his estate plan into two trusts. One of these trusts, a Q/tip marital trust, is for the primary benefit of his wife, and the second trust, a residuary trust, is for the benefit of his wife and his children from his first marriage.

The terms of the marital trust are straightforward. Mary will get all of the income, as long as she lives, and the trustee will have the right to invade the principal to provide for her proper care, support, and maintenance. On her death, the property will pour over to the residuary trust, but before this can happen, estate taxes must be paid out of the marital trust. If Mary has no other property, and if the principal of the marital trust has not increased above $600,000, there will be no federal estate taxes to be paid on her death.

The terms of the residuary trust are also very straightforward. Mary is to have the income as long as she lives. On her death, there are several common alternatives that Harry can consider:

1. The property can be distributed outright to Harry's children.

2. The property can continue to be held in trust for Harry's children until they reach specified ages, and in the meantime income and principal can be distributed to them.

3. The property can continue to be held in trust for the lifetime of Harry's children, distributing income and principal to them each year, and on their respective deaths the property will be distributed outright to their children (Harry's grandchildren)—except it will be held in trust for those grandchildren under age twenty-one until they reach legal age. Regardless of the size of the residuary trust, it will not be included in Mary's estate on her death, and there will be no additional federal estate taxes to pay because of the residuary trust.

If Harry desires, he can grant the trustee the right to invade the principal of the residuary trust to provide for the needs of both Mary and his children. However, he probably will include a clause directing the trustee that, before she or he invades the principal of the residuary trust for Mary's benefit, the trustee should first consider resorting to the principal of the marital trust. There is a practical tax reason to do this. The marital trust is the only trust that will be taxable at the time of Mary's death. Since Mary will get the income from both trusts, if there is a choice of which principal to invade, the choice should be made on the basis of cutting down the possibility of federal estate taxes.*

By using the vehicle of the marital trust, Harry was able to avoid all estate taxes, give Mary the income from all of the property for as long as she lived, and then ensure that, on Mary's death, the property went to his children.

Many variations can be made within the framework of a marital deduction trust. For instance, in the residuary trust, there is no requirement that the surviving spouse have any income interest in the property. The income could be left solely for the children. One rationale for this is that, if there had been no will at all, under the laws of many states Mary would have received just one-third of the total property. By giving her the income from the marital trust, plus access to the principal of that property, she receives a more favored treatment than the law would otherwise allow.

Another way to approach the situation is to give the independent trustee the right to "sprinkle" or "spray" income from the residuary trust among the members of the family group consisting of Mary and the children of Harry. Because Mary was not the mother of these children, conflicts might arise, but the independent

---

*Estate taxes could be levied if the principal of the marital trust increased above $600,000. Moreover, someday Congress could reduce the threshold to less than $600,000, and this could create additional liability. Also, the federal estate tax applies against the total of the property in the marital trust plus the property owned by the surviving spouse. Therefore, before taking principal out of the residuary trust for the surviving spouse, principal is taken out of the marital trust because it reduces the amount of property that would be subject to federal estate tax upon the death of the surviving spouse.

trustee would have the discretion to resolve such conflicts.

The marital trust is also a fine vehicle for saving estate and inheritance taxes where the spouse with most of the property does not want to make outright gifts of property to the other spouse in order to equalize estates. Thus, in the case of Harry and Mary, there would be no estate taxes to pay on Harry's death, as long as Mary survived Harry. Harry could definitely avoid all federal estate taxes if he were to give Mary $400,000 outright. He did not want to do this, however, because Mary, then, would control the ultimate distribution of that money, and it would not go to Harry's children. By not making that outright gift to Mary, Harry incurs a major tax risk if Mary does not survive him. In that contingency, there would be no marital deduction, and on the death of Harry there would be a $1 million estate, with federal estate taxes of $345,800, less the credit for the first $600,000 of $192,800.* This difference of $153,000 is the penalty that Harry's children are going to have to pay because their father did not want to leave enough property outright to his wife to avoid the imposition of any federal estate tax.

Generally speaking, the structure of the marital trust in large part depends upon the nature of the marital relationship. In a first marriage where the only children are those of the couple, it is very common to give the surviving spouse either a general power of appointment or a special power of appointment to distribute property among the children and grandchildren of the parties. This means that the partner who lives the longest will have a second look to determine the needs and circumstances of the children and grandchildren.

Sometimes the exercise of this power may be limited, depending upon how old the surviving partner is. In other words, either partner may fear that if the surviving partner is too far along in years, someone may exert undue influence to create favoritism on the part of one child or another. Should this possibility be of major concern, the estate plan can be structured to provide that, if the power of appointment is exercised, it has to be exercised in a will that was executed prior to a certain date or prior to the surviving

*Credit for state inheritance taxes is ignored in these computations.

partner attaining a certain age. This may be arbitrary, because some people are very competent at ninety and others begin to lose competency at an earlier age. However, if one has these concerns, it is better to have an arbitrary date than none at all.

In a blended-family situation, it is very common that the surviving spouse does not have a general power of appointment, because that could be exercised in favor of the children of the surviving spouse, rather than the children of the person who left the property in trust, or to collateral relatives or others whom he or she favors, including a new wife or husband.

Problems can also arise in second marriages where the second spouse has no children. I was asked to provide counsel to try to resolve a major disagreement between two people of middle age who were about to be married, Sam and Judy. Sam was a widower of substantial wealth who had three children. Judy had been married but had no children. In their discussion about a premarital agreement, Sam told Judy he wanted to divide his property four ways and leave her a full one-fourth share under his will, but he wanted it to be left in trust. Judy would receive the income for her life, and on her death the property would go to the residuary trust, which was for Sam's children. The income from Judy's one-fourth share would have been around $125,000 a year.

Judy was adamant that this was "not fair." She insisted that she should have the freedom to decide where the property in the trust for her should go after her death. She might leave it to Sam's children, but she might want to leave it to her sister, or possibly to charity. Sam voiced strong disagreement, particularly since Judy's parents had some degree of wealth. Eventually they compromised by dividing the marital trust into two parts. On Judy's death, one part would go to Sam's children, and the other part would go wherever Judy directed in her will.

This is just one of many examples of how a marital trust can be drawn with a wide range of options. The requirements are that income must be distributed, at least annually, to the surviving spouse for life, and no one else has the right to any principal as long as she or he lives.

Here is a summary of some of the most common alternatives that can be selected:

1. The surviving spouse has the right to invade the principal of the trust during her or his lifetime—sometimes without a limitation, or sometimes with a limitation such as a dollar limitation or a percentage of principal limitation.

2. The surviving spouse has a general power of appointment to decide where the property is to go on her or his death—to anyone (or any entity, such as a charity) in the world.

3. The surviving spouse has a special power of appointment, to be exercised in his or her will. The power can be limited among a group, such as lawful descendants of the testator or settlor, or, if the testator wants to include nieces and nephews, the lawful descendants of the testator's mother or father. The testator can even broaden the group to include charities.

4. The general or special power can be broken down so it applies to only a portion of the property, such as one-half.

5. The marital trust can specify that, on the death of the surviving spouse, the trust assets will be distributed to persons designated by the testator at the time the marital trust was created.

6. The marital trust can be structured so that, on the death of the surviving spouse, it will go ("pour over") into the residuary trust.

7. The marital trust can be structured so that, on the death of the surviving spouse, the trust assets can be distributed to a new set of trusts, which may be for the settlor's children or grandchildren.

These are just examples of the choices to consider in creating a marital trust. These choices are influenced by tax considerations, including the provisions of the generation-skipping tax exemption discussed in Chapter 26. The key is to know that these choices exist and then decide which selection best fits the family situation.

Sometimes the decision-making process can lead to friction. However, if a couple recognizes that reasonable minds can differ and if each partner has understanding for the other partner's perspective, conflicts can be resolved within the framework of good tax planning.

The amendments to the Internal Revenue Code that allow a Q/tip marital deduction trust are constructive, particularly in light of the increased incidence of divorce and remarriage. These flexible, tax-saving provisions are important for people of moderate (or greater) wealth to understand.

My general recommendation for married couples is to take advantage of the tax-saving features of the marital deduction trust. I usually recommend two trustees, one of whom would be independent and the other the surviving spouse. Ordinarily, the independent trustee should have the power to invade principal to provide for the proper care, support, and maintenance of the spouse. Whether or not the surviving spouse alone should have the right to get at principal each year is an option to be considered. It is more common in first marriages than it is in second and third marriages. Sometimes a "five and five" power is incorporated into the trust instrument, giving the surviving spouse a limited right of direct access to trust principal.

In the case of first marriages, where there are children, I generally recommend giving the surviving spouse either a general or a testamentary special power of appointment, which can be exercised if she or he feels in later years some further adjustment should be made. Even when the property has been equally divided between the spouses to minimize the federal estate tax, special powers, rather than general powers, are often included in the marital trust because the survivor still has the general power to decide where the property in her or his name will go.

If substantial wealth is involved, I recommend including as a part of the overall estate plan the generation-skipping tax exemption discussed in Chapter 26.

Where there are no lawful descendants, I recommend that the parties decide ahead of time how they want the property distributed upon the deaths of both husband and wife. Such decisions can be incorporated in the marital trust. In a long-term marriage, if the property is not evenly divided between husband and wife, I suggest that they consider giving the party who has less than half the property a general power of appointment for at least a portion of the marital trust. This is not only fair, but it also gives the emotional satisfaction of having the parties share in the power and control over the ultimate destiny of part of the property that has been accumulated during the marriage. After all, equality in the relationship between the husband and wife should include equality in the overall control of the ultimate destination of the property accumulated during the marriage.

The marital deduction trust is a unique vehicle for those who want to leave money wisely. It can be sculpted to achieve tax savings and at the same time fit the particular needs of almost every family situation. Married couples should consider taking advantage of this opportunity.

19

The Residuary Trust: For Spouse or Children?

"How much should I leave my wife as compared with how much I leave my children?"

"What happens if my husband, who now has a high income, should become incapacitated?"

"What happens if my husband remarries and his new wife has substantial funds of her own?"

"What happens if my wife lives to be ninety—should my children have to wait until they are sixty or sixty-five to get any of my property?"

These are difficult questions. When clients ask for my opinion, I begin our discussion from the perspective of what would happen if there were no will. In many states the surviving spouse would receive only one-third of the property, if there are also children. In harmonious marriages, most husbands and wives want to leave more than one-third of their property to the survivor. How much more is influenced in large part by the family finances.

Suppose the amount of property involved is $250,000, which might produce an income of approximately $15,000 a year (using an average return of 6 percent). If the surviving spouse does not have much outside income, then most of the property is usually left outright or is left in trust, with the entire income to go to the surviving spouse.

On the other hand, if the amount of property involved is $1 million, and a two-trust estate plan is adopted, the residuary trust will be funded with $600,000 to take full advantage of the unified credit. The surviving spouse would receive all of the income from the marital trust of approximately $400,000. This would (at 6 percent) yield $24,000. In this scenario, the parties may decide that the surviving spouse should not automatically receive all of the income from the residuary trust, particularly if the surviving spouse also has a substantial amount of income from retirement plans, insurance benefits, or other property that produces income. Social security benefits also have an impact.

Some people are concerned that if everything is left to the surviving spouse, and she or he lives to age ninety, there will be nothing distributed to children until they are in their sixties. Yet the children might need financial help earlier, particularly if they, in turn, have children who need help during college years.

I have a general suggestion as a starting point. In the case of a happy marriage, the major concern of husband and wife is for each other. If there is not sufficient money to take care of both spouse and children, then the primary use of the funds of any trust should be for the benefit of the surviving spouse.

One way to give the surviving spouse priority but still maintain flexibility to meet the needs of children is to provide in the residuary trust that all of the *income* goes to the surviving spouse. However, the trust can also provide that the trustee has the power to invade principal for the benefit of both the surviving spouse or children, if either needs additional money. This can be integrated with the provision that where the surviving spouse needs principal, it should first come from the marital trust.*

If there is any concern about providing for children, the surviving spouse can have a special power of appointment to appoint by deed (during his or her lifetime) or by will to lawful descendants.

There are other possibilities. One variation is to designate that

---

*See the discussion in Chapter 18 concerning federal estate taxes.

only half of the income from the residuary trust go to the surviving spouse and the other half be distributed to the children.

Another common structure is the sprinkling or spray trust. The independent trustee has the right to apportion income from the residuary trust among the members of the family group consisting of a surviving spouse and children (and possibly grandchildren). At one time this was a common provision in larger estates, but its use has been diminished because of the generation-skipping limitations of the Internal Revenue Code that are now in effect.

Generally, the larger the estate, the less reason to give all of the income from the residuary trust to the surviving spouse. Also, the larger the net worth and the larger the earning power of the surviving spouse, the less need there is to give that spouse all of the income from the residuary trust.

It is possible, too, to provide for the contingency of the surviving spouse's income dropping substantially. For instance, where a husband is earning $75,000 a year, his wife might not feel that he needs all of the income from her property and might want to leave a portion of the residuary trust to her children. This can be accomplished by providing in the trust instrument that the income will go to the children until such time as the surviving spouse has a net income of less than $75,000 a year (as adjusted by inflation), including income from any marital trust. If that event should occur, the income could then be divided equally between the surviving spouse (who would get one-half of the residuary trust plus, of course, all of the marital trust) and the children. There would be a further proviso that, if the income of the surviving spouse, including income from the marital trust, ever dropped below $50,000 (as adjusted by a Consumer Price Index clause), then the surviving spouse would get all of the income from the residuary trust, or, alternatively, receive sufficient income to bring her or his total income back to $50,000.

This is just one of many ways a trust can be tailor-made to meet the circumstances of most families. One thing is clear: There is no perfect or "right" solution, and there are many alternatives to consider. The best resolution is invariably one of compromise, and the terms of the compromise will depend upon the unique factors in each family.

What happens in situations where there is no surviving spouse—a widowed or divorced person or someone who never married?

Whether the property goes to children, grandchildren, or younger collateral relatives, a basic question exists concerning how long property should be tied up in trust. In larger estates, sophisticated planners take advantage of the generation-skipping tax exemption, to the extent it is available ($1,000,000 for each individual).

Whether people do or do not have surviving spouses or children, some want to tie up property as long as they can, even in the case of smaller estates. A majority of my clients have chosen not to do this. It is a matter of philosophy and preference.

> "Let them have it now—if they blow it, that's their tough luck."

> "Let them have it now—I don't want to control it from the grave."

> "I spent thirty years of hard work putting together what property we have. I don't want to see it go out the window because my kids don't know how to handle money yet."

> "I know my kids can handle money, but I still think they'd be better off if the money stayed in trust for a while."

> "I don't know what to do—I don't know what future tax laws will be—but to play it safe, I think I ought to leave the money in trust."

Where the amount is not large, and the children are responsible, most people do not tie up their property beyond their children reaching forty. But the fact that the majority acts in a certain way does not mean that this is appropriate for you and your family. Ultimately, it is a personal decision.

What do attorneys usually recommend? The most common suggestions are distributions at relatively early ages, such as half at twenty-five and half at thirty, or one-third at twenty-five, one-third at thirty, and one-third at thirty-five. Others prefer a later age, such as half at thirty-five and half at forty. In all cases, as long as a portion of the property is still being held in trust, the income could be distributed and the principal would also be available for distribution, in the event of need.

When I am planning an estate with a couple, I suggest that they might want to integrate the ages of distribution in both wills to cover the possibility that they will die in an accident together or within a relatively short time of one another. In the wife's will, there might be an age of distribution set at one-third at thirty, one-third at thirty-five, and one-third at forty, while in the husband's will the age of distribution may be one-third at thirty-two, one-third at thirty-seven, and one-third at forty-two.

I also recommend to people of moderate wealth that the greater the amount of their estate, the more they consider giving their children some interest in the residuary trust and not necessarily wait for the death of the surviving parent, who may live to be ninety or more. My personal preference is a sprinkling trust, with an independent trustee in whom the family has confidence to exercise discretion in light of changing family circumstances from one year to the next. I recommend combining this with a grant of special powers of appointment to the surviving spouse.

When the surviving spouse dies, or where there has never been a surviving spouse (including, of course, single persons who have never married), the question then becomes: At what ages should beneficiaries receive distributions from the residuary trust? My recommendation is that distributions not start before beneficiaries attain the age of thirty. There is too great a chance of younger beneficiaries making irrevocable and disastrous mistakes in handling large sums of money. And if the estate is more than $500,000, I always raise the possibility of having the trust continue for the lifetime of the beneficiaries, but integrating this with a "five and five" power as well as a special power of appointment. This gives maximum flexibility.

Another problem to consider is what to do if the trust assets are relatively small. This can happen in the early years of a trust, and it can also happen in a generation-skipping trust when, after the death of a child, the trust is divided among several grandchildren. I recommend giving the independent trustee the power to distribute the entire principal of the trust if the amount is relatively small. This has worked out well in practice—in part because the independent trustees often look to the wishes of the beneficiaries, in part because a corporate independent trustee is happy to shed the burden of administering a small trust, which may not be very profitable, and in part because trustee charges may be too large when considered in the context of the income from a small trust.

The decisions about the residuary trust are important and difficult. Give a lot of thought and care about what you want to do. You have many options. To help you resolve your doubts, remember Basic Rule Number Two: Consider what advice you would give to your best friend under similar circumstances. If this still leaves you in doubt, then make the decision that seems to have the greatest appeal to you, comforted by the knowledge that there may be no perfect answer, but there is more than one right way.

20

Picking the Right Trustees and Executors

"Just what does an executor do?"

"What's the difference between an executor and a trustee?"

"Do I have to use a bank?"

These are common questions clients ask.

Many people do not understand the difference between an executor and a trustee. The executor's job is relatively short and more limited in scope. To the executor is delegated the responsibility to make the decisions; collect and gather together all of the assets; sell assets when advisable or necessary; pay all of the debts of the decedent and all taxes, costs, and expenses of the estate; and execute all documents that are necessary to complete the probate of the estate.

She or he then distributes what is left in accordance with the terms of the will. If trusts are created under a will, the executor will turn over the appropriate property to the trustee, who will take over and manage the property as directed by the language of the trust instrument.

Generally, the executor will work in consultation with a lawyer. If the lawyer has probate experience, the executor ordinarily will not need a great deal of technical skill. Family members can serve as executors, although problems may arise if the family members do not live in the same state where the will is probated. Another difficulty may develop if family members can give themselves preferences where they are beneficiaries and where the executor has discretion that can favor herself or himself as a beneficiary.

Executor fees vary from state to state. In some states they are relatively low, but there are some states where executors' fees can be as high as 5 percent of the value of the estate. In this situation, it is generally preferable to use someone other than a corporate executor, unless the testator or his attorney negotiates a lower fee with the corporate executor before the will is signed. Be sure to learn from your lawyer what executor fees will be under state law and what can be done to minimize these fees.

In some states it is important to have a provision in the will to permit a change of executors without the estate having any liability to pay a large percentage fee to the specific executor named in the will. Do not feel reluctant to speak to your attorney about flexible provisions in your will to minimize the costs of probate.

Sometimes people deliberately want to keep executors' fees high where family members are involved. For instance, if there is an estate of $1 million and no marital deduction, the top federal estate tax bracket will be at the 39 percent level (for that portion of the estate between $750,000 and $1 million, increasing to 41 percent for the next $250,000 of property above $1 million). At the present time, the top income tax rate is 28 percent (ignoring state income taxes and the possibility of a portion of income being taxed at the 33 percent level, depending upon tax brackets). To the extent that property in an estate is used to pay executors' fees, it is a deduction from the value of the estate, and at the $1 million level 39 cents of taxes would be saved for every dollar transferred to executors' fees, which would be taxed at the 28 percent level.

Of course, this ignores whether the person getting the executor's fees would otherwise share in the net estate after payment of taxes. In one big happy family, with no multiple branches, the problems may be minimal. But if the executor is just one member of a branch, and there are several branches of the beneficiary group, other heirs may not want the executor to draw a large fee, even though there might be savings in changing from the estate tax bracket to the income tax bracket.

Whenever an individual serves as executor (and the individual can be a spouse, a spouse and child serving as co-executors, one or two or three children serving as co-executors, etc.), it is wise to consider retaining an accountant to keep records and prepare income tax returns for the income that goes into the estate during the time of probate.

Should there be a bond to ensure the faithful performance by the executor? An executor can misappropriate funds. If the executor is a corporate executor, such as a substantial bank or trust company, the added expense of a bond is not generally necessary, because the net worth of the bank or trust company is often greater than that of the bonding company, and under banking regulations fiduciary bonds are required where there are trust departments. This can save hundreds or perhaps even thousands of dollars of bond premium.

On the other hand, if the executor is an individual who is not in the family (or if there is some question as to the character of the family member named), then a bond may be appropriate. If there is to be no bond, or a minimum bond, this should be specified in the will. State statutes affect these decisions, and a competent lawyer can offer helpful suggestions.

Generally, the executor has the power to sell assets; pay or settle debts; and, to the extent necessary (and to the extent powers are granted under statutes or in the will), borrow money; mortgage property; employ agents; sell real estate, stocks and bonds, and other property; and do all other things necessary to wind up the affairs of the estate and distribute the property as directed in the will.

Selecting an executor is generally not nearly as important as selecting a trustee, because the job of the executor normally will only last a year or two.* Selecting a trustee is much more sensitive because the trustee can have substantial discretion in managing the property and in distributing income or principal, if that discretion is granted in the instrument creating the trust. Moreover, the trust can last one hundred years or more. Therefore, the selection

---

*However, in complicated estates and in estates where the attorney is not very skilled in probate matters, the job of an executor can be very important.

of a trustee is one of the most important decisions to be made in planning an estate. The trustee must have the financial capability and judgment to make sound investments of trust assets or retain able investment advisers. The trustee must also have good judgment if the trust instrument gives discretion to distribute income, principal, or both. These tasks may lead one to choose an institution as a trustee, if there is no individual who can meet these requirements.

If the trust provides for a mandatory distribution of income, that is an easy direction to follow. If the trust instrument gives the trustee the discretion to distribute income and principal to provide for the proper care, support, and maintenance of one beneficiary, that is generally not a difficult task. Complications arise when the trustee has discretion to distribute income and principal among members of a group in equal or unequal amounts.

Here is a typical example:

> My trustee shall have the power to distribute such sums of income and principal as my trustee in my trustee's sole discretion may determine among the members of my family group, consisting of my surviving spouse and children and grandchildren, to provide for their proper care, support, and maintenance. Distributions may be equal or unequal among members of the family group.

That is a tall order to give to an independent trustee. Yet words of this kind give maximum flexibility to the administration of a trust, give the greatest opportunity for income tax savings (because of differing income tax brackets), and are well suited for use in closely knit families.

Sometimes there are conflicts among the beneficiaries, especially where second marriages or blended families are involved. If a surviving spouse gets all the income, she or he might want the assets of the trust invested in bonds, which pay the highest rate of return. On the other hand, the beneficiaries who might ultimately get the property, upon the death of the surviving spouse, might prefer to have the investment in stocks, to help keep up with inflation. However, the dividend yield on common stocks is usually much lower than interest-rate returns on bonds. In this situation it is important to have a trustee in whom you have confidence, and it may be helpful to leave specific directions to the trustee. You may want to consider including a provision specifying that, unless there are compelling economic reasons to the contrary, the investment portfolio should be diversified. One thing you cannot do is fund the marital trust with property that does not produce any income, such as stock in a closely held family corporation that does not distribute cash dividends. This could deny the deductibility of the marital trust for federal estate tax purposes.

Some people religiously avoid choosing a corporate trustee such as a bank trust department. Others avoid having any trustee other than a corporate trustee. Where there is a closely held family corporation, many people are afraid that a corporate trustee will create problems by voting stock in ways that may cause family dissension or by forcing the business to be sold because the trustee may feel the portfolio of trust investments should be more diversified. If this is a concern, be certain that the trustee powers in your will or living trust expressly allow the trustee to retain property in a closely held business without concern for diversification.

One of the first questions I ask clients is whom they might be favoring to serve as trustee, why they are considering that selection, and what provisions they would like to include for selecting successor trustees if the trustee they choose is an individual rather than a corporation.

If I am asked for a recommendation, I need to know a lot about the family, the assets, and the goals and desires of the person creating the trust. Generally, I suggest that if there is a corporate trustee, the will maker consider appointing one or two individuals to serve as co-trustees. Often co-trustees are family members, and this brings the family into a more personal relationship with the trustee. It also gives the family the feeling that someone is "looking over the shoulder" of the corporate trustee—which is usually beneficial from the family's perspective.

From a tax perspective, if there are decisions that have to be made concerning distributions of income and principal, it is important that those decisions be made by an *independent* trustee—someone who is not going to benefit by decisions made to distribute income and principal. As we have seen, if a person has the right as a trustee to direct the distribution of principal or income to herself or himself, the property might be includable in that person's estate for federal estate tax purposes, and there could also be adverse income tax consequences—except to the extent that the distribution is made under the "five and five" power.

Many clients are hesitant to use a corporate trustee because of horror stories they have heard about poor management of trust assets. They may ask: "If I have the ABC National Bank serve as trustee, can I have my children remove the trustee and put in another trustee if they are dissatisfied with the management performance of the trust?" One problem about having such a power is that it could conceivably be exercised if the beneficiaries did not think the corporate trustee was liberal enough in distributing income and principal. For instance, if the instrument gives the trustee the right to distribute such sums from the income and the principal as the trustee believes necessary to provide for the proper care, support, and maintenance of the beneficiary, the beneficiary should not have the absolute right to change the trustee. Otherwise, the government could claim that the beneficiary could indirectly control the trust by constantly changing trustees until she or he found a trustee who would do what the beneficiary wants. The government could assert that this power would result in income being personally charged to the beneficiary even if the beneficiary did not actually receive it. Even worse, the government could claim that this power would result in all of the trust's assets being included for estate tax purposes in the estate of the beneficiary. Therefore, it is not wise to give a beneficiary who is also a trustee these kinds of discretionary powers.

A common question is "But what can I do to remove the corporate trustee if it is doing an inadequate job of managing trust assets?" This sensitive area requires expert counsel to avoid potential tax problems. There are a number of alternatives, and the one I most often recommend is to designate as a trustee advisory selection committee a group of independent people who have no beneficial interest in the trust. The committee may include a relative, a lawyer, an accountant, or a family friend. This committee can be given the periodic power to change the independent trustee if the committee believes a change is warranted because of bad performance or other reasons. Some corporate trustees do not like such provisions. However, I have seldom seen a corporate trustee decline to serve because the trust instrument contains this protective language. The argument I give in representing clients is that the personnel in the trust department change from time to time, and the family has to have some protection in case new people are not competent.

On the whole, I have found that over the years the level of competence of individuals who work in corporate trust departments has increased. Corporate trustees offer a number of advantages, including technical expertise and experience in managing trusts. They also offer the advantage of being disinterested third parties to make decisions affecting members of a family group who might get into major disagreements if there were no independent third party.

Some experts suggest that clients talk to people in different trust departments to hear their "pitch" for selling trust department services. That can be helpful, although one should always recognize that the person who is making the pitch may not be there a year later and probably won't be there ten or fifteen years in the future when the tough decisions have to be made.

In many situations an independent corporate trustee is not needed if there are competent relatives, who are not beneficiaries, who can exercise the necessary discretion so far as distributions of principal and income are concerned, and who can select broad-based investments, such as the better mutual funds, or can select able investment advisors.

When individuals are named trustees or co-trustees, the will or living trust should provide how successor trustees are to be selected. There are many ways to deal with this. If the independent trustee route is followed, and one is looking at selecting successor co-trustees, one common device is to have each child serve as a co-trustee of that share of the trust that is for her or his benefit and give that child the power to designate a successor. Another common scheme is to pick one child to serve as a co-trustee for all shares, pick an order of succession, and then let the trustee named as the successor trustee, in turn, pick successor co-trustees, provided that there is approval by a majority of the adult beneficiaries of the trust.

The trust instrument can specify that, if no successor is named within a certain period of time, any beneficiary can apply to an appropriate court for the court to appoint a successor co-trustee.

Should the trustee have a bond? If there is any concern about mismanagement of property or self-dealing, then a bond would be appropriate. But if there is no such concern, then the bond premium might be an unnecessary expense.

However, be careful if the trustee is a small bank. Early in my career I represented a bonding company, headquartered in Chicago, that wrote fiduciary bonds for banks throughout the Midwest. The bonds protected banks from losses because of employee dishonesty. One day I received a cheerful call from the chief claims officer. Several months earlier, a young company salesman had tried to sell a $5 million fiduciary bond to a small bank in Northwest Iowa. The bond was designed to protect the bank from any loss caused by a dishonest employee. After the young salesman had made a long presentation, the controlling shareholder and president of the bank put his arm around the young man's shoulders and said, "You know, son, you really made a terrific presentation, because everything you said is right—except one thing. We don't need a bond for this bank because we have the finest and most honest bookkeeper in the world, Bernice—who has been with us for more than twenty years." A few months later the bank president found out that his trusted employee, Bernice, was not so honest after all and had embezzled over $2 million, almost bankrupting the bank.

Thus, I suggest a note of caution in deciding whether to dispense with a trustee's bond where the trustee is an individual or a small bank. However, if the bank is of medium or larger size, a bond-premium expense is usually not necessary.

If you decide to choose nonfamily executors and trustees, be sure to discuss with your attorney the potential costs and how these costs can be minimized. Where you have no strong preferences, I recommend using a bank or trust company as an independent trustee. I also suggest you consider having members of your family serve as a co-trustee, if they are capable, fair, and have good judgment. This has the benefit of "someone looking over the shoulder" of the corporate trustee, and it can also be a learning experience in the overall management of investments. And if you have a capable attorney with lots of probate experience, you may not need a corporate executor.

Picking the right trustees and executors is a very important part of leaving money wisely. This is particularly true in situations that involve blended families and in which the trust terms grant broad discretionary powers to distribute income and principal. Give careful thought about whom you select and how successors will be chosen.

21

Inflation Insurance:
The Need to Preserve
Purchasing Power

Current income is in some ways like a narcotic. You get hooked on the pleasures it brings. It can lull you into a sense of false security. And it's hard to give up.

But just because you have assets that provide enough income for a comfortable living today does not mean that you will have enough income five or ten years in the future. This is a critical concept to understand. It has many ramifications in personal financial planning, ranging from deciding when to retire to deciding how much you want to leave in trust for a surviving spouse or other members of your family.

Suppose all of your income-producing assets are in government bonds yielding 8 percent. I will assume $1 million because it is a round number and is easy for one to use as a unit of measurement.

If all of the $1 million is invested in 8 percent government bonds, you will receive $80,000 a year in interest, before taxes, and should have almost $60,000 after federal taxes, under the current rate schedule. To be sure, that's a sizable sum and should allow for comfortable living. But there is a major question that must be asked: How much will that $60,000 buy in goods and services five years from now? Ten years from now? Twenty years from now?

No one knows the answer, because no one can predict with

accuracy future inflation rates. Not too long ago, annual inflation was in double digits—10 percent a year, and more. An automobile that costs $20,000 now, or one-third of the $60,000 annual income, after five years of double-digit inflation would cost $30,000, or one-half of the available income.

But even if inflation were at what is today perceived to be a relatively low rate of 5 percent a year, in ten years that $20,000 automobile would cost $30,000. Meanwhile, the after-tax income from the government bonds of our hypothetical $1 million investment would remain at $60,000.

If you take the 50 percent increase in the price of the automobile and apply that to all other expenditures—food, clothing, housing, travel, utilities, medical costs, and everything else—it is clear that that $60,000 a year can move someone from upper-income levels to middle-income levels at best.

At worst, $60,000 a year could be considered a relatively low income ten years from now if the days of double-digit inflation return. What is the risk of this happening? No one knows. But even if it is only 5 or 10 percent, it is a potential catastrophe from a personal financial perspective. People buy insurance to cover economic disasters that are not very likely to happen. Each year, most American homeowners pay for fire insurance on their homes, and the premiums can be very substantial. Yet, how frequently do houses burn down?

If you believe in fire insurance to cover your home and liability insurance to cover the possibility that you will be sued and life insurance to cover the possibility of an early death, is it not wise to have what I call investment inflation insurance?

Wise investors diversify their assets, adding equity investments such as stocks and real estate. The most common real estate investment, of course, is a home. In many areas, home price increases over the long term have exceeded the rate of inflation. But a home investment does not produce income. Common stocks are the most widely used income-producing alternatives to hedge against inflation. The stock market, at times, goes down, but the general trend over several decades has clearly been upward.

Unfortunately, dividend rates from common stocks are generally far below interest rates paid by bonds. The yield—the dividends paid on common stocks as a percentage of their market value—can range from nothing to more than 8 percent. However, high-yielding stocks are often risky—or provide little chance of growth. A common assumption when planning how to invest money is for an average dividend return of 3 to 4 percent from common stocks. The average yield on the five hundred stocks comprising the Standard & Poor's Index on January 1, 1990, was 3.06 percent, and it was 3.74 percent on the thirty stocks making up the Dow Jones Industrial Average.

If you were to take your hypothetical $1 million portfolio and divide it into two parts—$500,000 in government bonds earning 8 percent, or $40,000 annually, and $500,000 in stocks earning 4 percent, or $20,000 annually, then the annual pre-tax income would be $60,000, or 6 percent of the total portfolio. The after-tax income would be approximately $45,000. The important principle to keep in mind is that, if you have a large sum of money to invest, you should not get hooked on a living style that assumes your income level will be measured in current bond rate yields. Think of an income stream from a balanced portfolio of stocks and bonds that may give you an average current yield of only 5 or 6 percent. In that way, current income will be reduced but future protection will be enhanced.

In our hypothetical portfolio, the wise investor would seek to have the $500,000 stock portion not only keep up with inflation, but grow at a rate at least double the rate of inflation in order to take account of the fact that the other half of the total investment portfolio, which is invested in bonds, will not increase with inflation.*

In other words, if inflation is 5 percent a year, or a $50,000 a year decline in purchasing power of the total hypothetical $1 million portfolio, the $500,000 invested in stocks must increase at least $50,000 a year, or at 10 percent (ignoring compounding), in order to have the total portfolio keep up with inflation.

Of course, if you are merely an income beneficiary of a trust and have a relatively short life expectancy, you might want a higher

---

*This ignores the possibility that sound strategic investment by sophisticated bond portfolio managers can provide capital gains.

percentage of the trust assets invested in bonds in order to give you more current income.

Another major consideration that has to be addressed is one of the most unfair provisions in our Internal Revenue Code: the taxation of fictitious capital gains.

Over the years tax policy has been often unfair and sometimes counterproductive from the perspective of what is best for the long-range future of our country. Philosophically, I am against the concept of high tax rates (which have often been avoided by the very wealthy through the use of tax shelters). I generally favor fewer permitted deductions and lower overall rates. Where overall tax rates are low, I do not favor special-favored treatment for *real* capital gains for relatively short-term investments in the stock market.

I emphasize the word "real." I do this because the dollar is not a fixed unit of measurement, like a yardstick or a measuring cup. It is variable in the terms of its real measurement: purchasing power—the amount of goods and services that a dollar will buy.

If you invested $100,000 in the stock market in 1980, kept those stocks, and your selection was so good that the stocks over the next ten years appreciated and became worth $400,000, you would not really have earned $300,000 in terms of real purchasing power. The actual change in the Consumer Price Index between 1980 and 1990 was approximately 50 percent, so in terms of 1980 purchasing power the $100,000 you invested is the equivalent of $150,000 in 1990.

Now let's apply the income tax laws to this hypothetical situation. Today the top income tax bracket for federal tax purposes is 28 percent (although there is a 33 percent bracket for one portion of the rate schedule). Most states also have a state income tax, so for ease of computation I generally ballpark the combined federal and state income tax rates at about one-third.

If we take our $100,000 investment in 1980 and sell it in 1990 for $400,000, there will be $300,000 of capital gain, which at a 33 percent tax bracket would result in about $100,000 of taxes, or net profit, after capital gain taxes, of $200,000.

A much more honest approach would be for our government to recognize that the $100,000 that was invested in 1980 is worth in

1990 dollars $150,000, so that the real gain in purchasing power was $250,000—$400,000 less the original cost adjusted by inflation ($150,000), or a net of $250,000, which at a one-third tax bracket would mean a tax of $83,000 instead of $100,000, or net profit, after capital gain taxes, of $217,000.

The taxation of fictitious inflationary capital gains compounds another problem for those seeking to invest money wisely. When an investor feels motivated to change investments in response to changes in market conditions and future prospects, the income tax consequences of portfolio management can be enormous.

If we go back to our hypothetical $1 million investment portfolio broken down to $500,000 in stocks and $500,000 in bonds, it is not enough for the stock portfolio to perform at a rate that is double the inflation rate to compensate for the fact that the bond portfolio will not increase because of inflation. The stock portfolio in a sense has to do much better than double the inflation rate, so that after taking into consideration capital gains taxes there will still be inflation protection for the overall portfolio.

How can an individual get good stock selection? For those who are not very sophisticated in the investment world, the best way is to seek first-rate financial management.

One way to get good financial management is through what is known as *mutual funds,* which are pools of money for individual investors that are under professional management. (Here I confess a bias. I am a trustee of one of the leading mutual fund groups, which manages nearly $40 billion in various funds, including money market funds, government funds, different kinds of stock portfolios, and even an international fund. Obviously, I believe this group of funds of which I am a trustee is well managed, but there are other well-managed mutual fund groups, and in addition there are investment advisers who have a very fine record of asset management.) The performance records of various funds and investment advisers can be obtained and compared. Whether you choose this as a possible investment is a matter of personal choice.

Many corporate trustees have internal investment portfolios that are like mutual funds. This is another alternative that can be explored. You should not hesitate to ask a prospective corporate trustee to spell out its investment record over the past five or ten years to help you reach your decisions. Also, you should find out what the costs are of fund management.

If you want to invest money wisely, one of your goals should be the preservation of purchasing power. Your portfolio should include investments that protect against inflation—the most common being corporate stocks. Therefore, when thinking of how much income will be produced by any property you leave outright or in trust, do not think in terms of bond interest rates alone. Think of a combination of stocks and bonds.

I also recommend that you do not invest exclusively in stocks. Protect yourself against the contingency of a disastrous fall in the stock market. A discerning investor should put a portion of her or his portfolio into quality short-term money market funds and government or high-grade corporate bonds. High-yield instruments that represent good credit risks are another possibility, but these require great expertise in credit analysis. High-income investors should consider tax-exempt bonds (which have lower pre-tax yields but may have higher after-tax yields).

The appropriate length of bond maturities, the balance between government and corporate bonds, and the question of whether there should be any high-yield or tax-exempt bonds are investment decisions that require expert counsel. You should obviously address these issues when you are planning your estate. One by-product is that a sound investment strategy can help educate the beneficiaries of your will and enable them to build upon your record. That can be an important part of your overall goal of leaving money wisely.

It is very important to preserve purchasing power in order to protect you as well as your loved ones. Do your best to develop an investment plan that takes into consideration the need for "inflation insurance."

Two final thoughts, which are directly related to the consequences and causes of inflation:

1. Whether you are a Republican, a Democrat, or an independent; whether you are a liberal, a conservative, or middle of the road in your political philosophy; whether you believe that capital gains in general should be cut or should not be

cut, I urge that you write your congressman and your senators to try to correct the fundamental unfairness that now exists in taxation of inflationary increments in capital assets. To levy a tax on so-called gains that represent the effect of inflation—a decreasing value of the dollar—is unfair and unsound. Moreover, in the event of great inflation, this tax on fictitious income could be disastrous to the social fabric of our democracy, since it could literally confiscate much of the net worth of millions of Americans. Federal (and state) tax laws that levy a tax based upon a decline in the value of the dollar are fundamentally unjust.

2. We are living in what I call the economic double time-bomb era of annual federal budget deficits of over $100 billion and annual trade balance deficits of over $100 billion. Our economy today is just as hooked on these deficits as is a drug addict on heroin. This is the worst legacy of the Reagan administration. If we do not address these issues promptly in meaningful rather than cosmetic terms, our whole economy can be turned into a shambles. We, our children, and our grandchildren will have to pay the piper to our economic taskmasters from the Far East and from Germany. So if you really want to leave money wisely, I would urge you to educate yourself and your friends about the critical consequences of our continued huge budget and trade deficits and let your congressman and senators know that these issues have to be faced with realism—not just rhetoric.

22

Stepped-Up Basis
to Reduce Income Taxes

Suppose you are fortunate enough to own real estate or common stock that has dramatically increased in value. For instance, assume that in 1970 you purchased for $50,000 a tract of land in Southern California that is worth $1 million today. Were you to sell that land, there would be a taxable gain of $950,000. Federal and state income taxes would take away around one-third of this amount, or something over $300,000.

On the other hand, if you did not sell the property and were to retain it until your death (and assuming no further change in its value), that property would be valued in your estate for federal estate tax figures at its fair market value: $1 million. If you had no marital deduction, a federal estate tax would be levied on the difference between $1 million and the $600,000 exemption (assuming your estate had no other property subject to tax). However, when the property was sold by your estate, its basis for computing gain would be the full $1 million. There would be no income tax to pay on the sale of the property, if it was still worth $1 million.

This is because of the doctrine of what is known as *stepped-up basis.* As we have previously discussed, gain on the sale of property is ordinarily determined by deducting from the net sales price the

159

cost of the property, plus any additions, less any tax-deductible depreciation or amortization. Because over the decades inflation has increased the price of most investment assets, their value at the time of an owner's death is usually greater than the acquisition cost. Federal estate taxes are levied on the current fair market value of the property, rather than its original cost. Concurrently, federal tax laws provide that, when a person dies, for income tax purposes there is a new basis, which is equal to the value of the property at the time of the death of the owner. Since this valuation is usually higher than the original "basis" of the property, the new basis is called a stepped-up basis.*

Over the years, there has been a long-standing argument between proponents and opponents of the stepped-up basis rule. Those arguing against the rule claim that it is unfair because it allows people to avoid paying income tax that they otherwise would be obligated to pay. Those favoring the rule say that, since the federal estate tax is levied on the fair market value of the property, it would be unfair and represent double taxation to impose a second capital gains tax.

One can argue on either side of the issue. However, it is indisputable that, as long as this beneficial tax provision is in the Internal Revenue Code, wise taxpayers should be aware of its benefits.

One of the most important decisions affected by the stepped-up basis provisions of the Internal Revenue Code relates to the selection of property for making gifts. If a person elects to make gifts to reduce the size of his or her estate and thereby reduce estate taxes, questions of tax basis are a very important consideration. Here is a typical example.

Abe has invested most of his money in the stock market. He is eighty years old and wants to start giving away some of his property to his two children.

Some of his stocks have done extremely well. For instance, twenty years ago Abe purchased some stock in XYZ Corporation, which is today worth many times more than he paid for it. On the other hand, he also owns some utility-company preferred stock,

---

*The Internal Revenue Code permits an alternate valuation date, which is six months after the death of the decedent.

which pays high dividends but is worth about the same as its original cost.

If Abe gives away the XYZ Corporation stock and his children sell it, they will have to pay a tax on the capital gains measured by the difference between the sales price less the net purchase price paid by Abe. On the other hand, if he gives away the utility company stock and his children sell that, there will be no capital gains tax to pay, assuming the stock has not increased in value. If Abe dies owning the XYZ stock, and the stock is then distributed from the estate to Abe's children and they subsequently sell it (and there has been no further increase in value since Abe's death), there will be no capital gains tax to pay. The stock will have a stepped-up basis for income tax purposes equal to its fair market value in Abe's estate. Of course, if Abe retains the XYZ Corporation stock and it continues to rise, it would increase the value of Abe's estate and make his federal estate tax even higher.

After weighing all of the pros and cons, Abe decided to keep his XYZ Corporation stock and have his family take advantage of the stepped-up basis provisions of the tax laws.

There was one additional factor that helped him reach his decision: concern for keeping up with inflation. In an era of budget deficits of more than $100 billion, year after year, there is no telling what future inflation rates might be. Abe knew that XYZ Corporation had outstanding management and that its stock had performed extremely well in the stock market. There is no guarantee that XYZ stock will continue to appreciate, but he felt that he needed to have some protection against the possibility of future erosion of the purchasing power of the dollar. He had done very well with XYZ Corporation stock in the past, and he felt that he would keep this in his stock portfolio and kill two birds with one stone: protect himself from future inflation and also take advantage of the stepped-up basis provisions of the Internal Revenue Code. Although its dividend yield was not as high as the utility stock, if Abe needed more cash he would sell a few shares of XYZ stock.

Of course, this decision could result in higher estate taxes. In addition, there is the risk that between the date that Abe made his gifts and the date of Abe's death, Congress could change the provisions of the laws to remove the stepped-up basis benefits. Abe recognized this risk, but he decided nonetheless to keep his XYZ Corporation stock.

Was this a wise decision for Abe to make? What would you have done?

One conclusion is obvious: The shorter a person's life expectancy, the more important it is to take into consideration the opportunities afforded by stepped-up basis.

23

The Family Business:
A Potential
for Family Disaster

"**D**angerous road ahead." That is the warning sign that should be placed on many plans for transferring ownership in a family business from one generation to the next.

There are hundreds of scenarios and thousands of answers, each depending upon the nature of the business and the dynamics of the family members. Sibling rivalry and jealousy are always potential problems. Complications often arise because of in-laws—directly, where they are involved in the enterprise, and indirectly, where they counsel their wife or husband, who is a member of the family that controls the business.

A typical example: Henry wants his son, Ned, to take over running the business. Henry is not sure how to divide the stock between Ned and Ned's two sisters, one of whom has a husband who works in the business. Initially, Henry's disposition is to split the stock three ways. But Ned is afraid that in the future his two sisters may "gang up on him," particularly if their husbands get together. Ned tells his father, "I don't want to work for my sisters and their husbands."

Henry then thinks about some alternatives, such as giving his son an opportunity to buy stock in the business because he is working full time in the business as his father's chief lieutenant.

When Henry discusses these plans with his daughters, they become upset. Why should their brother have more of the family business "gold mine" than they?

You can extrapolate this into all kinds of variations. The common denominator of most of these is acrimony—the very thing the parents don't want to happen.

Henry turns to his wife—what does she recommend? She thinks her daughters ought to be treated equally with her son. "But I don't want him to leave, and he says that he will leave if I don't give him voting control." Another potential for acrimony—between husband and wife.

Some of the most difficult challenges I have faced have been in working with families in the role of a counselor, trying to seek solutions to problems such as these. There are no clear-cut answers to these difficult problems that have both business and family components. Rather, there are alternatives that afford some kind of "ballpark" resolution.

My starting point is that doubts should usually be resolved in favor of equality among all children. I also suggest that if there is a potential deadlock that can cause family disharmony, one good way to resolve disagreements is through "liquidity"—giving family members a fair basis for converting into cash their interest in the business.

I also generally recommend that families avoid putting one child in the position of holding a majority of the stock of a closely held corporation. A majority shareholder can take advantage of his position in many ways. He can control the election of boards of directors, which set the compensation for key executives and also control dividend policy. Conceivably, a majority shareholder could take out most of the profits of the business in salary and bonuses, discontinue dividends, and leave the minority shareholders holding stock that might on paper represent a lot of net worth but yet have no income-producing value. Accordingly, from a practical perspective a minority interest in a closely held corporation is generally worth far less than its theoretical proportionate value.

In other words, if a corporation has a market value of $10 million, a person owning 25 percent of the corporation does not necessarily have stock that could be sold for $2.5 million. It might be worth only half as much, or conceivably even less, depending upon what the prospects are for selling the corporation and ultimately providing liquidity to all shareholders.

Some families have tried to come up with compromise solutions. In a family with four children where one of the sons was the executive vice president, the founder of the company, Ted, decided to split the stock in five portions, giving his son who worked in the business a double portion and his other son and his two daughters single portions. He had other assets that he divided among the other three children to try to even up the differences in stock distribution.

His rationale was that his son in the business had cast his lot to help make the business grow and should have an opportunity for more of the equity. He also felt comfortable because it would take at least one other child to give voting control to one side of the family. On the other hand, his daughters felt that they were not being treated fairly, because both of them had husbands in the business. Even though their husbands did not have as responsible a position as their brother, they felt hurt.

What should Ted do to avoid a family war? The easiest solution would be to sell the business. However, sometimes businesses have the potential to grow to be worth infinitely more to all shareholders, given another five or ten years of operation and growth. In these circumstances, I recommend to the parents that they get all their children together, sit down, and bluntly state that if the family cannot arrive at a general agreement on what is fair, the entire business will be sold. Then everyone will suffer, because the current sale price would probably be far less than what the business would bring in another five or six years of operations.

In situations of this kind, it can be important to bring in an outside consultant as a mediator or a facilitator to help the family reach a consensus that comes as close as possible to treating all family members "fairly."

Sometimes a parent who is the chief executive officer of a closely held company selects one of his children as successor and in his will or living trust leaves majority control in the hands of his designated successor. This is what industrialist Malcolm S. Forbes did, according to newspaper reports shortly after his death in

1990. Forbes had five children. His son, Malcolm S. Forbes, Jr. (who is known as Steve), supposedly was to receive 51 percent of the company voting stock, with the balance evenly divided among his three brothers and his sister. Although Steve Forbes will be able to control the company for a period of time, no single person will have majority control when he dies unless he leaves the entire block of 51 percent to one single person.

Sometimes, where family members are in the business, a type of arrangement known as a *phantom stock plan* can be developed as additional incentive compensation. Under a phantom stock plan, a key executive is given theoretical shares or units of percentage interest in the overall equity of the corporation under an arrangement that provides for substantial bonus compensation upon termination of employment or in the event the business is sold. The phantom stock plan might give the key employee a theoretical interest of an extra 5 or 10 percent of the value of the corporation, depending upon its performance over the years. At retirement, or when the company is sold, the incremental increase in value is paid to the employee, just as if he had received actual shares of stock and had sold them back to the company. The payments under the plan have an additional advantage of being deductible as compensation by the corporation. This area requires substantial expertise, and it is important to retain competent lawyers or accountants to help develop these plans, if this is the road the family members take.

Part of the resolution of these problems depends upon the overall philosophy of the family members. In some corporations the philosophy is to give key executives large incentive bonuses for performance but not give them any equity. In other companies cash compensation in the form of salaries and bonuses is kept low, and incentives are given through stock or phantom stock plans.

If the family can reach consensus on how to pass control from one generation to the next, there are opportunities to facilitate passing wealth from one generation to the next. One of the most important is known as the *estate tax freeze*. The basic concept is simple. A family takes the stock of a corporation and divides it into two parts. One part is in the form of preferred stock, which has a preference in dividends (if dividends are declared) and in liquidation if the company goes bad. The other portion involves common stock, which increases in value as the business net worth grows.

Often this division into common and preferred stock has taken place after the business prospered for a number of years, with continuing future growth prospects. The older generation would convert their stock interest into preferred stock, with little growth potential, and the younger generation would retain all of the common stock, which meant all of the future growth. Voting rights could be structured so the older generation could still have a significant voice in management.

The net result of this restructuring was that the older generation's interest in the business was "frozen" at the level when the restructuring occurred. Thus, the phrase "estate tax freeze." There would be no more additional estate taxes caused by further incremental growth of the family-owned business.

As you might expect, lawyers and accountants jumped at the opportunity to explain to their clients the great opportunities of "freezing" asset values for estate tax purposes. As you also might expect, the response of Congress was not long in coming. At the end of 1987, Congress passed the Revenue Act of 1987, which was substantially modified by the Revenue Act of 1988. The net effect was to diminish substantially the use of the estate-tax-freeze technique.

Limited estate-tax-freeze opportunities are still available, and if this is of interest to your family you should talk to your lawyers and accountants.

Another practical problem facing the family with a closely held business is how to pay federal estate taxes when the principal owner dies. If there is a surviving spouse and a marital deduction trust is used, payment of the tax can be postponed until the death of the surviving spouse. However, someday the tax will have to be paid, and the resources of the family might be strained if the primary asset is stock in a closely held business. The family may simply not have enough cash outside of the business to pay what could be an estate tax of hundreds of thousands, or perhaps even millions, of dollars. This may force them to sell the business or incur debt in amounts that will jeopardize the prospects for survival.

This problem is known as one of *liquidity*. There are two important provisions of the Internal Revenue Code that provide assistance. The first is known as Section 6166. If the gross estate of the decedent includes a closely held business whose value exceeds 35 percent of the adjusted gross estate, and either 20 percent or more of the voting stock was in the gross estate or the corporation has fifteen or fewer shareholders, a portion of the federal estate tax can be deferred for as long as fifteen years with an interest rate as low as 4 percent. The rules are technical, but they can be helpful, and careful planning can greatly increase the benefits from Section 6166. For instance, the owner of a major portion of the stock of a small business can, subject to certain conditions, transfer non-business assets to remove them from the gross estate, which, in turn, would make certain that the qualification tests under Section 6166 are met.

The provisions of Section 303 of the Internal Revenue Code are also often helpful. Ordinarily, in a closely held business where only part of the stock of a shareholder is redeemed by the corporation, the redemption is treated as a dividend, rather than as a capital gain. Moreover, even if all of the stock of a particular taxpayer is redeemed, it may not be treated as a complete redemption entitling the taxpayer to capital gain treatment if there are other family members or trusts for the benefit of other family members that own stock in the company. However, under Section 303 of the Internal Revenue Code, it is possible for stock to be redeemed to provide cash to pay federal estate taxes, without dividend treatment. One condition required is that the stock's value must exceed 35 percent of the gross estate (after certain allowable deductions). Once again, this is a technical area, and you should look to your lawyers and accountants for expertise.*

These rules, which give the family "breathing space" and reduce the pressure to sell the business in order to pay estate taxes, represent an important tax benefit that Congress has enacted to help the small business.

---

*Under the current law, where capital gains are taxed at the same rate as ordinary income, these differences are not nearly as important as they once were, but there are still advantages to capital gain treatment.

Unfortunately, Congress has not addressed the income tax problems of small businesses with the same spirit of support. Despite political rhetoric that the government is interested in helping small businesses prosper, our income tax laws do not give much of a break to the small corporation. Once $75,000 of earnings are reached, the corporate income tax rate is 34 percent. If a company earns $100,000 to $335,000, the marginal earnings above $100,000 will be taxed at a 39 percent rate. This supposedly takes into account the fact that earnings below $75,000 were taxed below 34 percent. The extra five percentage points between $100,000 and $335,000 bring everything below $75,000 to a 34 percent level of taxation. If a company earns above $335,000, the tax rate drops back down to 34 percent.

No matter how huge the earnings—they can be $1 billion or more—they will be taxed at the same 34 percent rate as the small businessman was taxed for earnings between $75,000 and $100,000.

It is my conviction that small business needs more effective spokespersons to publicize the unfairness of the present tax structure and offer some constructive solutions. For instance, the overall top corporate bracket could be increased to 35 percent with offsetting reductions for those portions of corporate earnings below $1 million. I believe that giving smaller corporations an edge over the corporate giants is sound policy from both a sociological and an economic perspective.

One additional recommendation in this area relates to buy-and-sell agreements and insurance. Most closely held businesses have contractual arrangements that provide that, if a shareholder wants to sell to a third party, the shareholder must first give the corporation the right to buy its own stock; if that right is not exercised, the remaining shareholders have a secondary right. This helps keep control of the corporation within the family. It can also have some positive benefits in the event of divorce. Without such protection, a court could arbitrarily divide family corporation stock between husband and wife. A portion of the stock might end up in the hands of a person who was no longer an in-law of the family.

Unfortunately, many buy-and-sell agreements are not updated to reflect the current value of the company, and often family members postpone executing any kind of a buy-and-sell agreement. This matter should not be postponed. It is almost as important as preparing a comprehensive will or living trust.

Insurance can often be helpful in funding buy-and-sell agreements. However, if the death benefits are payable to the corporation, the federal estate tax valuation will increase, thereby resulting in more tax liability. Structuring buy-and-sell agreements with insurance requires careful planning.

If there is concern for continuing family control in subsequent generations, a number of alternatives can be considered. One is a *voting trust,* whereby family members commit the voting control of all company stock to a small group of people who are representative of family interests. There are pluses and minuses to this approach. One big minus is the possibility of abuse by those voting trustees who may be active officers of the company and who do not want to see the company sold, even though an overall sale might be in the best interest of a majority of family members.

I have seen voting trusts used effectively. On the other hand, I have seen voting trusts become a source of great family disharmony. "It all depends on the situation and the terrain." If a potential exists for increasing acrimony, I recommend that the family consider the least complicated solution: liquidity—either selling the business or providing an opportunity for those people who want to sell their interest to get fair value and convert it into cash.

If the family cannot get together, and they do not want to adopt the answer of liquidity, then I recommend they seek an outside counselor to suggest one or more alternatives that would come reasonably close to meeting the competing considerations involved with the particular family and business. Counselors can use different approaches. One of the best I have found is a modification of Basic Rule Number Two: What advice would you give your best friend if she or he came to you with this problem and asked for your help? I ask each family member to assume that she or he was playing my role as a facilitator and come up with two or three alternatives for consideration.

Once these are listed, I then seek some common ground upon which to build consensus. Sometimes no common ground can be found, and the only practical answer seems to be to sell the business. On the other hand, I have seen a number of situations where plans were developed that did work out, with minimum family friction.

Many closely held businesses face an additional risk when management is passed on to the next generation: Will the second or third generation have expert management capabilities so the business will continue to grow and prosper?

Here is the kind of a problem that can arise. Phil founded a very successful manufacturing business. Only one of his children, Ben, worked in the business. Phil had a sudden heart attack and died. His desire was that his son, Ben, run the business. Phil left a $6 million estate, over $5 million of which represented the value of the business. Unfortunately, Ben sought to expand the business, incurred a lot of debt, and was unable to make debt payments. Within a matter of a few years, the business had to be liquidated for a price of less than $1 million. The net result was that Phil's widow lost most of her financial net worth and Phil's other children, as well as Ben, lost a potential inheritance that would have given them a very comfortable standard of living for the rest of their lives, had the business been sold at the time of Phil's death.

I have seen many variations of this story. Where a closely held business represents the overwhelming bulk of a family's net worth, it is risky to put most of the family's financial eggs into that one basket. If the business fails, not only will it be a financial disaster for the family but it will also be a social disaster, leaving great wounds of bitterness among siblings and also between the surviving parent and the child or children who were running the business when it failed. Because I have seen a number of family businesses turn into disasters, or near disasters, I generally recommend that the family make every effort to provide options of liquidity for those members of the family who may want to "cash in chips."

Wherever a closely held business constitutes the major source of wealth for a family, the road ahead is filled with potential disaster. However, it is far better to plan to avoid disasters than it is to close one's eyes and do nothing, leaving the problems to the executors and the trustees to try to resolve after the death of the founder. Inadequate planning on the future of closely held family corporations has often caused bitter family fights. It has been one of the most disheartening aspects of my law practice.

A successful business can be a blessing for all family members. It can also become a curse.

There are no perfect answers to these problems, but the best common denominator for most solutions is the option of liquidity.

24

Problems of Giving Away Too Much

How much is enough? A million dollars is a lot of money. But is it enough?

Clients often ask me, "How much should I give away to cut down my estate taxes?"

I respond with questions of my own: "How long will you live? What will be the status of your health in five years? Ten years? Fifteen years? What will be the inflation rate and will your investment portfolio keep up with inflation? What are your needs?

"Does 'need' include a two-bedroom apartment with a den instead of a one-bedroom apartment? Does it include an apartment with help, twenty-four hours a day, instead of a nursing home? Does 'need' include a Caribbean cruise in the winter or a summer trip to Europe?

"What happens if because of financial reverses, or family controversy, or whatever, the persons to whom you give the property no longer can or will help support you, should you ever be in need?"

Discussions go back and forth, with the focus being on the federal estate tax rates. People do not want to have their heirs pay to the government hundreds of thousands of dollars, which could be avoided if they gave away enough property during their lifetime. At the same time, people want to feel secure. These two goals are often inconsistent. When clients come for help, my general recommendation is Basic Rule Number Three: Financial and emotional security are more important than tax savings.

I look upon federal estate taxes as something akin to an insurance premium. They are the price you let your heirs pay to make sure you have financial independence, with all of the objective and psychological ramifications that financial independence means.

The first $600,000, as we have seen, is in substance exempt from federal estate tax. For many people $600,000 is a lot of money. But to a person age sixty-five who may live to be ninety or more, $600,000 means a base of principal that will produce income. And if part of that $600,000 is in a nonincome-producing asset, such as a house or condominium, the income-producing base is even lower.

Here is a typical example of the inner conflict faced by people of moderate wealth. Diane, a widow in her sixties with two children and four grandchildren, has assets of $800,000. Of that, $200,000 is represented by her home and furnishings. The remaining $600,000 is invested in stocks and bonds producing annual income of approximately 6 percent (8 percent on the bonds and 4 percent on the stocks). Between her income and social security, she has about $45,000 to spend annually.

In her initial estate-planning consultation, she asked a very common question: "What will the taxes be on my estate?" I reviewed the current tax table with her and estimated that her taxes would probably be in excess of $60,000, depending in part on the deductions for debts and costs of probate. "Sixty thousand dollars is a lot of money. Can't I give away some of my property to avoid these taxes?"

The answer was easy. Without incurring a gift tax, she could give $10,000 a year to each of her children, $10,000 a year to each of her grandchildren, and, if she had confidence in the stability of the marriages of her children, she also could give $10,000 a year to her daughter-in-law and son-in-law. Within a matter of a few years, she could get her estate down to the $600,000 level, and there would be no estate taxes at all.

The only problem was that her income base would be reduced from $600,000 to $400,000—about $12,000 less in annual earnings.

At first blush that did not bother her, because she said she could always start using principal. But there was another problem. As the principal became further reduced, the income would continue to fall. Moreover, as she grew older, she might have greater needs for medical expenses. Other costs could also rise. What would happen if there were a stock market crash or mini-crash, as occurred in October 1987? What would happen if inflation went through the roof? What if she would want to take several vacations a year? Should she be limited because she felt economically insecure?

Suppose she wanted to refurnish her house and spend an extra $25,000? Suppose she wanted a new car?

"But I know if I am ever in need, my children will take care of me." Generally, that may be true, but it does not always happen that way.

I have seen situations where parents gave money to children to avoid estate taxes. The children invested the money in a business that failed. The parents were subsequently in need of funds and the children had no funds available to help their parents.

I have seen situations where parents gave money to a son, which he invested in a house. The son died, leaving the house to his wife, who remarried and as the years went by became further removed from her first husband's parents. In later years the parents really needed some financial help—but the help was not forthcoming.

One of the worst experiences involved a young couple who received a substantial sum from the wife's parents. They used it to buy a house. Subsequently they divorced, and the house ownership was split between husband and wife. The husband went on to become a wealthy doctor. In later years, his former wife's parents developed major medical problems that required substantial expenditures. They really needed money, but their former son-in-law felt no obligation to help out.

What minimum net worth should you retain without giving away property to help reduce your federal estate taxes? Obviously, it depends upon how much you have to start. If you have $5 million, I would wholeheartedly recommend that every year you give $10,000 to those with whom you want to share your wealth. But if you are single and your estate is less than $1 million, or if you are married and your estate is less than $1.5 million, you should hesitate to give away much money unless, because of health conditions or advancing years, you have a life expectancy of less than five years or unless one or more of your children or grandchildren has great financial need.

Of course, there are some families whose personal relationships are very close and where there is little likelihood of potential problems arising because too much money was given away. Special circumstances apply to families of great wealth with multimillion-dollar estates, where giving away property will have little effect on life-styles. But, if there is any doubt at all, my strong advice is to resolve that doubt in favor of a greater margin of financial security and emotional security. Do not let the specter of increased estate taxes give you any feelings of guilt or lead you away from protecting your own security. After all, those taxes will not be due until after you have passed away.

I vividly remember one discussion involving a seventy-year-old widower, Russell, a man of thrifty background who could not accept the concept of having his children pay taxes on his estate. On the other hand, he was fearful that, if he got sick and needed extra money, he could become financially pressed.

"Russell, how much money did you have when you first got started?" I already knew the answer to that question—he had started on a shoestring.

"If it turns out that you don't need the money and that when you pass away you will have a million-dollar estate, with about $150,000 of taxes, what will it mean to your two children that they ended with $850,000 instead of $1 million?" I waited a few seconds and then answered my own question.

"Your children will get annual income of six percent of $850,000, or $51,000 a year, instead of getting six percent of $1 million, or $60,000 a year. And, Russell, they will get that for life, assuming they invest the money wisely and have the principal keep up with inflation. That's pretty good compared with where you started, isn't it?

"And by the way, Russell, if you give away $400,000 to get your estate down to $600,000, with no tax, you will have lost the income on all of the money that you will have given away. Who knows— even as thrifty as you are, you might someday have a need for that income.

"And, Russell, one final point—for your children, the difference between $60,000 a year and $51,000 a year is not really $9,000, because they have to pay taxes on the income they receive. If there is a tax rate of one-third, that will mean a net difference of $6,000. So, Russell, think about all of these factors before you decide to give a large hunk of your property away."

When I put it in those terms, the answer was clear: Better to be financially independent than to be insecure because you have given away too much.

There is one additional comment that I often make to clients who are somewhat insecure about their future needs. When they vacillate about whether they should give away more money so their heirs will have less tax to pay, I remind them of a cartoon I once saw in the *New Yorker* magazine. It showed children gathered with great expectation around the desk of the family lawyer as the will of the family patriarch was removed from the sealed envelope. The lawyer read the will: "Being of sound mind and disposing memory, I spent all of it."

Special Opportunities
for People
of Great Wealth

25

The Fountainhead
for the Transfer of Wealth

There is no need to read Part IV of this book unless you are very wealthy, expect to be very wealthy, dream of being very wealthy, hope to marry someone who is very wealthy, or are just plain curious about some of the unique problems very wealthy people face and some special opportunities wealthy people have to leave money wisely. However, some of the comments in these chapters, and in particular the last portions of Chapters 26 and 31, may be of interest to you, regardless of your financial status.

The fountainhead for the transfer of wealth today is the *long-term generation-skipping trust.* This type of trust developed centuries ago under English common law. At one time, people sought to have such trusts extend hundreds of years, but a complex common law doctrine was developed that limited how long people could leave property in trust. The doctrine is called the *rule against perpetuities.* Its essence is simple: A noncharitable trust could continue for no longer than "lives in being plus twenty-one years." The rule, or variations of the rule, applies in most, if not all, jurisdictions in the United States.

A noncharitable trust could be much more limited in its term, if one so desired, but if you wanted to have it continue for as long as legally possible, you had to provide that the trust would end no later than twenty-one years after the death of the last member of the particular group you named. If the trust did not end by that time, it was void from its inception.

Once the rule was adopted in England, people sought out families with a history of longevity. They would list young members of that particular family as a part of a named group of "lives in being," which governed the maximum length of the trust, even though those people named were not beneficiaries under the trust. The sole purpose was merely to try to maximize the length of the trust. If a member of the group was five years old at the time the trust was created and lived another ninety years to age ninety-five, the trust could go on for one hundred eleven years (ninety plus twenty-one).

Today, when longevity is more common, few people search for families with a history of longevity. Instead, one can look to a group of people within her or his own immediate or collateral family and use this to govern the length of the term of the trust.

One easy way to do this is to use as a measuring standard the descendants of grandparents or great-grandparents—i.e., "those lawful descendants of my great-grandmother, Mary Smith, who are living at the time of my death" or "who are living at the time I executed this living trust."

One very important technicality to understand is that the term of a testamentary trust must be measured by people who are *living* at the time of the death of the testator. They are what is known as *lives in being.* One cannot just say "the lawful descendants of my grandmother" because some of those descendants could be born generations in the future, and this would subvert the very intent of the rule against perpetuities. Rather, the will must say, "the lawful descendants of my maternal grandmother who are living at the time of my death." Or, if a trust is being established during one's lifetime (an inter vivos trust as contrasted with a testamentary trust, which is created under a will), the measuring stick must be "the lawful descendants of the settlor's maternal grandmother who are living at the time of the creation of this trust."

Unfortunately, many lawyers do not fully understand the subtleties and complexities of the rule against perpetuities. In hundreds, and perhaps even thousands, of cases, trusts have been thrown out by the courts because the term of the trust extended beyond the maximum limit allowed by the perpetuities rule. A very practical way to avoid this problem is to be certain that every will or trust has what is known as a *rule against perpetuities savings clause.* Depending upon the specific law of each state, the language will go something like this:

> Notwithstanding anything else in this instrument, every trust established will terminate no later than 21 years after the death of the last to survive of the following group who are living at the time of the death of the testator (or, in the case of an inter vivos trust, "who are living at the time of the creation of this trust").

Many people complain about the length of wills and trust instruments. But part of the reason for the length of these documents is the necessity for having "boilerplate" provisions, such as a rule against perpetuities savings clause.

Prior to 1976 the tax laws did not limit the amount of money that could be left in a long-term trust that went on from one generation to the next. Of course, the property would be initially subject to federal estate tax, which could take away more than half of the estate, depending upon its size.

Once this tax bill was paid, the balance could be insulated from any further federal estate taxes for more than one hundred years. Meanwhile, the principal could be invested and reinvested from one generation to the next, throwing off income to the beneficiaries. If the principal were invested wisely, it could conceivably increase in value to the original amount and perhaps even double or triple that amount.

But this was only one part of the financial advantage that was available to people of great means. The other part was that these trusts could be used as vehicles for placing investments that had great opportunity for appreciation.

Here is a typical example. In 1972 two brothers, John and Jim, organized a company that they felt offered great opportunities for financial reward. They divided the stock into common and preferred stock and funded some generation-skipping inter vivos trusts. Each made a taxable gift of $250,000 in cash to a generation-skipping trust. The trustees used the cash to buy common stock. (If John and Jim had given common stock directly, rather than cash, it would have been easier for the government in later years to question the valuation of the gift for gift tax purposes. To cut down this possibility, the cash was given, which, of course, had a definitive value.)

The brothers invested additional sums in preferred stock, but preferred stock does not generally increase in value. Bank borrowings were also made to help provide working capital for the new company. In less than ten years, the value of the common stock of the company was nearly $10 million. Eventually the company was sold, and the net profits after capital gains taxes remained in the trusts, insulated from any estate tax liability on the death of John and Jim. Of course, had the company gone bankrupt (and many start-up companies do), John and Jim would have been unable to deduct the losses of the common stock on their own personal tax returns.

Many people, and I count myself among them, felt that it was really unfair to have an unlimited window of opportunity to put huge amounts of funds in trusts that could go on for more than one hundred years without payment of any estate taxes from one generation to the next. I firmly believe in the importance of incentives for people to accumulate wealth with the idea of passing the wealth on to their children. Such incentives motivate people to work harder and also motivate people to risk capital by investing in businesses. These investments, in turn, create jobs. Therefore, I am strongly against confiscatory estate and inheritance tax rates, such as 70 percent or more. On the other hand, I believe that each generation should be obligated to pay a tax on wealth that is transferred to it, above a certain limited amount. I therefore supported the movement in Congress in 1976 to put a ceiling on the free transfer of wealth from one generation to the next. The vehicle Congress chose was known as the *generation-skipping tax,* and it was substantially rewritten in 1986.

Today the fountainhead for the transfer of wealth is still the long-term trust established within the limitations of the rule against perpetuities. Even though its use has been severely limited because of the generation-skipping tax, many opportunities are still available. In the next several chapters we will explore some of the most important ways one can benefit from these opportunities.

26

The Generation-Skipping Tax Exemption: A Million-Dollar Opportunity

Vast fortunes have been handed down to grandchildren, great-grandchildren, and great-great-grandchildren through the use of long-term trusts. Legendary American families like Rockefeller and Du Pont have taken advantage of this opportunity to transfer wealth, and hundreds of other families who are not as well known have followed the same route by leaving property in trusts that extend to the maximum length permitted by the rule against perpetuities.

Sometimes it is almost impossible to comprehend the magnitude of this wealth. Two personal reminiscences stand out in my mind exemplifying the wealth of the Rockefellers. The first time I was in the Rockefeller brothers' suite of offices at Rockefeller Center, I was astounded by the extent of magnificent art that adorned the walls. It was akin to having one's own art museum.

A number of years later, I had an opportunity to work closely with Nelson Rockefeller. It occurred in the first half of 1975, when President Ford appointed me executive director of the Commission on CIA Activities Within the United States, which became known as the Rockefeller Commission because Vice-President Rockefeller served as chairman. (Ronald Reagan also served on the commission.)

Rockefeller would generally go to his family estate in New York during the weekends. On Easter Monday he returned to Washington with a big smile on his face and told me what a wonderful Easter he had had with Happy (his second wife) and their two children, who were at that time around eight and ten.

"We had a terrific Easter egg hunt."

"Did the boys enjoy it?" I asked.

"Oh, yes. They really had a close battle to see who got the most Easter eggs. The final score was 382 to 374."

"Governor," I said (he preferred to be called "Governor," because he felt that his former position as governor of New York carried a lot more power than vice-president), "may I make a modest suggestion. During your press conference this morning, do not disclose the actual results of the family Easter egg hunt competition. Some people might feel it is somewhat gross to have those kinds of numbers." (He thanked me and followed my suggestion.)

Today one could not leave an entire fortune in generation-skipping trusts without subjecting the trusts to huge tax liabilities. As we have seen, current law limits the generation-skipping tax exemption to $1 million per taxpayer. Of course, a spouse also has a $1 million generation-skipping tax exemption, so together a couple could leave $2 million in long-term generation-skipping trusts. Technically, it is possible to leave more than $1 million in a generation-skipping trust, but the surtax rates when the tax applies become almost confiscatory.

Suppose a couple with enormous wealth did not want to leave any money to their children, who were already well provided for, but instead desired to leave money in a trust directly for grandchildren? That's also banned. The generation-skipping tax not only applies to a trust with more than one generation of beneficiaries, but it also applies to transfers from an individual to his grandchildren or great-grandchildren, which the government sees as an attempt to avoid having any property taxed in the estate of the children. (However, money can be left directly to grandchildren if their parent—your child—has already passed away.)

In essence, the generation-skipping tax "exemption" is *not* an exemption from federal estate tax. Rather, it is an exemption from a confiscatory tax called a *surtax*. All the estate tax rules that we previously discussed are still applicable. If a wealthy person wants to take advantage of the maximum $1 million generation-skipping tax allowance, she or he should understand that everything above $600,000 will be subject to tax. Therefore, in order to fund a generation-skipping trust for the full $1 million, it is necessary to leave an amount substantially higher, which will take into consideration (and provide for the payment of) the federal estate taxes that would be levied.

As a practical matter, you can "ballpark" this at $1.25 million. (The precise amount is approximately $1.26 million.)* If you are married and want to avoid paying any more federal estate taxes, then leave everything else either outright to your surviving spouse or in a marital deduction trust or to a charity.

One can argue that the $1 million generation-skipping surtax exemption is too large or too small. I happen to believe that the exemption is at the low end of the spectrum and should probably be increased somewhat, particularly for families where one spouse has already died and the surtax exemption has not been used. Perhaps I am somewhat influenced by the fact that I am a widower with five children. If I were drafting the law, I would make the exemption somewhere between $1.5 million and $2.5 million per taxpayer, and I would have a provision increasing the exemption for single people who have never married and for widows and widowers where the deceased spouse did not use the exemption. I would also definitely include an automatic Consumer Price Index adjustment in the ceiling to take into consideration inflation and the depreciating value of the dollar. Concurrently, I would also put a 50 percent ceiling in estate tax rates. It seems to me that 50 percent for the government and 50 percent for the family heirs is about right.

Some people might argue that the entire exemption should be

---

*The basic computation is relatively simple. The federal estate tax payable for an estate of $1.26 million is $452,600. The maximum amount of unified credit available for a $600,000 estate (assuming the unified credit has not been previously used for taxable gifts) is $192,800. If you subtract this maximum credit from $452,600, the net difference is $259,800, which represents the actual federal estate tax payable, and if you in turn subtract this from a $1.26 million generation-skipping bequest, the net difference approximates the $1 million exemption.

abolished. I strongly disagree. In our capitalistic system, incentives play a major role in encouraging people to work hard to accumulate wealth—in part so it can be passed on from one generation to the next. In recent months Americans have become more aware of the virtues of the capitalistic system as compared with the state-controlled economic systems in Russia and the Eastern bloc.

On the other hand, I stand with those who believe there should be some limitation on the amount of wealth that can be transferred from generation to generation, free of successive levies of federal estate tax. In a family with three or four children, the combined exemption for husband and wife of $2 million should produce an income of approximately $120,000, assuming a combined 6 percent rate of return for stocks and bonds. If you divide this income among three or four children, it is not an astronomical amount for each child. That is one of the reasons I believe the surtax exemption should be somewhat higher than its current level.

Wealthy individuals can still leave the property outright to their children, who will have 45 percent left (after paying the maximum 55 percent federal estate tax). Each child, in turn, will be able to take advantage of the generation-skipping tax exemption and leave $1 million in generation-skipping trusts to her or his descendants, after the payment of federal estate taxes in their respective estates. If they are married and have property transferred to their spouses, there would be another $1 million generation-skipping tax exemption for the spouse.

For the very wealthy, there is a threshold question that should be considered: Should I merely incorporate appropriate generation-skipping tax provisions into my will or living trust, or should I establish during my lifetime generation-skipping inter vivos trusts and transfer property into these trusts right away?

If you are very wealthy, I strongly urge that you establish these trusts now. There are three basic reasons:

1. It is conceivable that Congress could eliminate the generation-skipping tax exemption in the future. Generally, when Congress takes away tax benefits of this kind, the laws do not apply retroactively. In other words, if such legislation is enacted in 1993, it will not normally apply to generation-skipping trusts that were in existence in 1992.

2. If property is placed in a generation-skipping trust, under current law any accumulated income that is not distributed but rather is added to the base of the trust would not be subject to additional federal estate or generation-skipping tax.

3. If property placed in trust appreciates in value, under current law that appreciation in value will be free of any additional federal estate tax.

There is one additional aspect of using the generation-skipping tax exemption to its maximum value. Generally speaking, the assets placed in this trust should be assets that have opportunities for future appreciation, rather than fixed income securities such as government bonds. Asset selection is a very important consideration.

For wealthy people, the generation-skipping tax exemption is a million-dollar opportunity. I strongly recommend that it be included as part of an overall intelligent estate plan. And because Congress could further restrict this opportunity, I recommend that wealthy people consider taking advantage of this opportunity while they are living by establishing generation-skipping inter vivos trusts.

Even if you are not ready right now to transfer substantial assets to the trusts, at least consider establishing those trusts while the opportunity still exists. Once the trusts are established, you can later think about possible ways to create investment opportunities for those trusts. But if you don't establish them today, and if within the next two or three years this existing window of opportunity is closed, you will regret that you missed the opportunity.

You may not have the assets of a Du Pont. You may not be able to leave your assets in generation-skipping trusts the way John D. Rockefeller did. But wealthy people can still set aside $1 million per taxpayer and pass this free of estate taxes for as long as one hundred years, or more. Not only is this protection from the current federal estate tax bracket of 55 percent (which for estates between $10 million and $21 million can increase to 60 percent), but it is also insurance against potential higher rates in the future.

As a matter of fact, although the generation-skipping tax exemption is an obvious planning device for very wealthy people, it is also an opportunity that people whose assets exceed $600,000 should consider. Because estate and inheritance tax rates could conceivably go to a 70 percent bracket, or higher, and the $600,000 unified credit could be reduced, people of moderate wealth who desire to use family trusts and have these trusts continue after the death of their children should consider incorporating into their wills or living trusts provisions to take advantage of the generation-skipping tax exemption, even though their assets may be less than the current $600,000 unified credit.

Under current law, the generation-skipping tax exemption is a million-dollar opportunity. If you take advantage of this opportunity and establish trusts with flexible provisions, including special powers of appointment, from a family-planning standpoint the downside risk is minimal. The upside potential is great. Whenever you can make a bet on those kinds of odds, go for it.

27

Opportunities
with Lifetime Gifts

For very wealthy people, there are only three basic ways to reduce potential liability for large federal estate taxes (other than the use of the marital deduction, which postpones the payment of the tax until the death of the surviving spouse): Spend it, give it to charity, or make lifetime gifts to donees, who are generally children and grandchildren.

The gift tax laws allow you to give away $10,000 per person per year without adverse tax consequences, provided that the gift is one of a "present interest" as contrasted with an interest placed in a trust. If you give more than $10,000 per donee, the excess will in substance reduce the lifetime unified estate and gift tax credit that insulates the first $600,000 from any federal estate tax liability. A husband and wife can each give away $10,000 a year per donee, so together they can make a gift of $20,000 annually to each child or grandchild without having it be charged against the lifetime unified estate and gift tax credit that every taxpayer has. However, questions of fairness sometimes arise in the case of gifts to grandchildren because of the per stirpes–per capita conflict that we discussed in Chapter 4.

Most people with a history of substantial family wealth make full use of these annual gift tax exclusions, unless particular family problems or other circumstances override the pure tax savings reasons for making a gift. As a matter of fact, sophisticated planners often make these gifts right after the first of the year, instead of waiting until the December holiday season. This covers the possibility that a death will occur before December and thereby preclude that year's gift.

In the case of multimillion-dollar estates, every dollar given away reduces the amount of federal estate tax by 50 or 55 percent. Therefore, I generally recommend that a gift program include any grandchild who is living. Almost always, questions of fairness arise because not every child has the same number of offspring. When those questions arise, I respond with Basic Rule Number Four, the "ballpark rule": Where there are differences in family group sizes, do not try to be exactly equal in the treatment of each individual; rather, seek as your goal something that is in the "ballpark" range of equality.

Here is a typical example involving grandparents who are concerned about being fair with their children. "Tom has three children, Virginia is not married and has none, and Fred has only one child. If together we give $20,000 to each of Tom's children, this will not be fair to Fred and Virginia, and if we go ahead and give $20,000 to Fred's child, this would be really unfair to Virginia."

To emphasize the "ballpark rule," I handed a pencil and paper to my clients, and together we did some projections. "If together you give $80,000 a year to your four grandchildren, in twelve or thirteen years you will have given away a million dollars, which will save half a million dollars in future federal estate taxes. Moreover, you would have transferred income from your estate to your grandchildren. Do you want the government to get the extra half-million dollars in estate taxes? Do you want to deprive your grandchildren of the income from this property—income that you don't need?"

Then, I suggested they consider a "ballpark" adjustment in their living trust to take into consideration differences because of gifts to grandchildren. For instance, in Virginia's case I suggested that her parents include a clause along the following lines:

I hereby will, devise, and bequeath outright to my daughter, Virginia, a sum equal to the aggregate amount of gifts made by my spouse and me to the children of my son Tom between the dates of January 1, 1989, and the date of my death; provided, however, that this amount shall be reduced by any gifts that my spouse and I may have made, prior to my death, to any children of my daughter, Virginia.

In the case of Fred, the amount of the special bequest would be reduced by any gifts made to any children of Fred over this period of time.

Technically speaking, this special bequest does not take into consideration the fact that the grandchildren who have been receiving gifts have been able to invest the money from the date of each gift. In other words, gifts made ten years ago might have doubled or tripled in value, depending upon the investments that have been made. On the other hand, there may be some offsetting reductions because of income taxes that have been paid during the interim period of time or losses incurred on account of investments that turned out to be unfortunate. Whether you want to make further adjustments to take into consideration the earnings that have been made on property that has been gifted to grandchildren is a matter of personal preference. When clients ask for my recommendation, I again generally apply the "ballpark rule." I suggest either forgetting the interest factor or, as an alternative, applying a simple 3 or 4 percent per year factor (which adjusts for a theoretical net effective interest rate after taxes) and include this factor in a simple practical formula in their will or living trust.

In addition, I suggest that the couple discuss the whole problem with their children and make sure their children understand what they are doing and why they are doing it. I also recommend that couples seek to have their children "sign on" to the concept of "ballparking" so they do not become upset with what they might perceive to be technical inequalities in treatment.

"After all, whatever you get is going to be far more than what we started out with, and, for goodness' sake, don't get upset about any relatively minor differences in your good fortune."

There are other ways to make adjusting entries in a will. For instance, Gladys had a three-carat diamond ring she wanted to leave to her daughter, Debbie. She asked if I thought this would be unfair to her son, Jeff. I suggested that she might consider having a special cash bequest to Jeff in her will and let both Debbie and Jeff know ahead of time what she was doing and why.

What do you do about gifts when the recipients are minors—not of legal age? Here a major problem arises because a minor does not have the capacity to contract. If you make cash gifts directly to a minor, and the money is to be invested with stock brokerage firms or money managers, they may state that they cannot do this because the minor does not have the legal capacity to buy or sell stocks and bonds. Therefore, it may be necessary to go to the expense of having a court appoint a legal guardian for the minor and have the minor's affairs conducted under the jurisdiction of the court. Fortunately, there is a way around this potential problem: the Gifts to Minors Act. Most states have adopted this statute. Instead of making the gift to a minor, the gift can be made to the minor's parent as custodian under the Gifts to Minors Act. When the minor attains the age of twenty-one, the property will be turned over to him or her.

Many wealthy people take advantage of the annual $10,000 exclusion to make gifts to children and grandchildren. However, although this is a very important way to transfer wealth, free of estate taxes, another potential problem arises. When children and grandchildren attain the age of twenty-one, large sums of money will be turned over to them. Their parents and grandparents may be concerned about whether they have the maturity to handle large sums of money and also whether there could be negative fallout, such as decreasing the incentive for leading productive lives.

One practical way to address this issue involves a two-step approach. The first step takes advantage of the one exception to the general tax rule that a gift in trust is not a gift of a "present interest" and therefore does not qualify for the $10,000 per donee annual exclusion. The exception permits you to use a trust to receive the gift if the purpose of the trust is to avoid a guardianship, if the trust provides for mandatory distribution of income to the beneficiary, and if it also provides that the trust terminates at the time that the beneficiary reaches the age of twenty-one and the beneficiary gets all of the principal and any undistributed income.

The second step adds to the general trust language an additional provision that the trust can automatically continue for another five, ten, fifteen, or more years (whatever figure is specified), if the beneficiary directs in writing within a period of sixty days of the time the beneficiary reaches age twenty-one. Concurrently, I prepare for the client a form where the beneficiary can direct the trustee (who is often the donor's spouse or a close friend or relative) to continue the trust.

The rest of the problem is up to the parents or grandparents. For instance, a grandparent can say to his grandchild, George: "Over the past ten years, we have given in trust for you over $100,000. Technically you are entitled to the cash now, but we would strongly advise that you consider continuing the trust for another ten years. In the meantime, each year the income will be distributed to you." George, like most grandchildren, will probably accede to the suggestion. If George were to say that he wanted the money outright, his parents might say something like this: "George, you can receive the money outright, but your grandparents would really prefer that the gift continue to be kept in trust because they feel that ten years from now you will be in a better position to handle the money. In the meantime, you can get the income. And, George, if you still insist on getting the money outright, and if it turns out you don't manage it very well, it could have an impact on what your grandparents leave you in their will."

Generally speaking, grandchildren have gone along with these or other informal suggestions and encouragements. If they do not go along, but handle the money well, the family gifts may continue. On the other hand, if they dissipate the money, that is an important fact for grandparents (and also parents) to know as they consider overall family estate planning.

Another important aspect of an annual $10,000 per donee gift program involves which assets to give. Should it be cash, marketable securities such as stocks and bonds, or other assets such as interests in real estate or stock in family corporations?

To maximize the benefit of an annual $10,000 per donee gift program, consider giving away assets that you feel will substantially appreciate in value, subject to tax-planning concerns involving stepped-up basis. However, as discussed in Chapter 23, if these assets include stock in a closely held family corporation, you should consider whether you want to have in place a buy-and-sell agreement and a first right of refusal, to make certain that the donee does not put the stock in the hands of unrelated third parties whom you might not want as stockholders and also to make sure that the donee does not give the stock away or sell the stock at a ridiculously low price. Restrictions can also be very helpful in the event of divorce, because people generally do not want the ex-wives or ex-husbands of their children or grandchildren to have nonrestricted stock in a closely held family company.

There are potential gift tax valuation opportunities where you give away stock in a closely held family corporation. You may be able to claim a discounted value because the stock is a minority interest in a closely held corporation. Your argument will be reinforced if there is no history of paying dividends. This is an area you should discuss in great detail with expert counsel, and there are potential gift tax problems if you are too aggressive with this approach. Obviously, if over a ten-year period you can make gifts of stock aggregating $500,000 based upon the valuation of the gifts at the time they were made and the stock continues to appreciate, the size of your estate will be much lower than it would have been if you had given away cash instead of stock. This, in turn, will result in a lower liability for federal estate taxes.

For wealthy people, there is another important option to reduce the size of one's estate. This involves making a large gift to a generation-skipping inter vivos trust. There are many advantages for making this gift and using the entire $600,000 lifetime credit that each taxpayer has against gift and estate taxes.

For instance, if you make the gift right away, the trust receives all of the benefits of ownership of the property, including any income the property produces as well as any appreciation in value.

Suppose you made the gift in tax-exempt bonds yielding 7 percent. If you had owned $600,000 of tax-exempt bonds and had kept them for yourself, each year your estate would grow by the amount of the annual income (assuming you did not need it and had other income to spend). Compounding factors over a period of fifteen years could add another million-dollar value emanating from the bonds, which, if you still owned them, could result in half a million dollars, or more, of additional estate taxes.

But it is possible to save even more estate taxes if you give stock in a closely held family corporation or stock in a public company that grows at a substantially greater rate. Any appreciation in the value of the stock would be insulated from any further estate tax liability after the gift.

Another reason that I urge clients to consider taking advantage of the $600,000 unified credit during their lifetime is that no one knows what the tax laws are going to be next year or the year after. Conceivably, Congress could make some radical changes in the law that would take away the $600,000 unified credit. Congress might also take away the $1 million generation-skipping tax exemption. Do not pass lightly over this possibility. In the scenario of an economic downturn, a Populist Congress and a Populist President, it could very well happen.

Here is one additional suggestion for the very wealthy: Consider the possibility of making a large gift, which would result in the payment of gift tax. The amount of the gift tax you pay will reduce the size of your remaining estate for federal estate tax purposes. This is particularly important advice for older people.

Here is a typical example. Margaret, a widow, is seventy-five years old and has an estate of $6 million. She has been making annual $10,000 gifts to each of her children and grandchildren and in addition has used her full unified credit to make additional gifts to her children. Now she is considering whether to transfer $1 million to a generation-skipping trust for her grandchildren. If she makes the gift now, she will pay a gift tax of approximately $408,000. Therefore, in order to transfer $1 million to her grandchildren, it will require approximately $1,408,000.

On the other hand, if she were not to make this gift, and instead were to leave $1 million in a generation-skipping trust under the terms of her will, it would require setting aside a portion of her estate equal to $2,222,222. The reason for this is that her estate would be taxed at the 55 percent level, and if you apply the federal estate tax rate to $2,222,222, the net amount remaining after taxes is approximately $1 million.

There are two primary reasons for this differential. The first is that the gift tax rate for a $1 million gift is less than 55 percent. The second, and most important, reason is that, if you make the gift during your lifetime and pay the gift tax, your estate is reduced by the amount of the gift tax that is paid, and this in turn reduces the amount of remaining property that is subject to federal estate tax. On the other hand, if you do not make the gift during your lifetime, a federal estate tax will be levied against the property that remains in your estate because it was not used to pay gift taxes.

Of course, when Margaret paid a gift tax of $408,000, she lost the use of the money that was spent to pay taxes. Offsetting this loss is the fact that, when property is given away, any further appreciation in value of the property is not subject to tax in the donor's estate. Also, the donor's estate is not increasing because of the accumulations of income not spent. In addition, if the gift is made, income from the property can be immediately distributed for the benefit of the donee, if needed.

This example illustrates the great opportunities that exist for very wealthy families to transfer wealth through reducing the size of their estates. An estate plan is like a tailor-made suit. It can be made to fit the circumstances of each family situation. Often the choices are difficult. But better to make difficult decisions now than to do nothing.

Lifetime gifts to charities are another important option to consider. Charitable gifts have a quadruple advantage. They can reduce income taxes, they can reduce estate taxes, they can provide help to others that is urgently needed, and they can give a lot of pleasure to the donor during her or his lifetime—the pleasure that comes from charitable giving and the opportunity to see the named charity put the charitable gift to very good use. Many times, clients have thanked me for the advice I gave to "make some of your major charitable gifts now, so that while you are living and in good health you can enjoy the real pleasure that comes from your generosity."*

The pleasure that one receives from making lifetime gifts goes far beyond the savings of tax dollars. Whether this pleasure comes from seeing the added opportunities financial security can give to children or to grandchildren, or whether the pleasure comes from the making of gifts to other family members or friends, or to charities, one can receive a wealth of psychological satisfaction

*Gifts to charity are discussed in greater detail in Chapter 29.

from giving away money. But there are potential hazards, also, particularly where young people may not act as responsibly as they might in later years. There are many families who have horror stories about what occurred when too much money fell into the hands of immature children or grandchildren. In recent years wealthy clients have become increasingly concerned about potentially adverse consequences arising from family wealth. If you are concerned about such problems, I strongly recommend that you weigh the balance between tax savings on the one hand and family values on the other. If you have any doubts, resolve them in favor of personal family considerations rather than tax savings.

One of my favorite sayings is that "money is the cheapest commodity." Anyone who has experienced family tragedy knows how true that is. And anyone who has reached emotional peaks of joy and satisfaction knows that the greatest of these come from things that money can't buy.

Lifetime gifts offer wonderful opportunities to save taxes. Wealthy people should take advantage of these opportunities, where appropriate, but they should also keep in mind the potential negative outcome of excessive generosity.*

*Legislation has been introduced in Congress to limit the total dollar amount of annual tax-free gifts that can be made. Before making any gifts, you should double-check with your attorney or accountant to determine if the gift tax laws still allow every taxpayer to give away $10,000 per person per donee each year. One proposal would limit the aggregate total of tax-free gifts each year to a maximum ceiling, such as $30,000, per donor.

28

Wealth Transfer Opportunities with Life Insurance

Life insurance policies offer one of the best remaining avenues for the transfer of wealth. Naturally, life insurance companies and agents encourage wealthy people to purchase insurance company products as a part of an overall program to lever the $1 million generation-skipping tax exemption into a $5 or $10 million exemption.

The current vehicle most in vogue among sophisticated estate planners is known as a *Crummey power trust.* The name stems from a 1968 court decision for the Ninth Circuit Court of Appeals involving a San Francisco taxpayer, Crummey. In 1962 Crummey established a trust for each of his four children, who were then twenty-two, twenty, fifteen, and eleven. Crummey wanted to use the annual gift tax exclusion, which in 1962 was $3,000, instead of today's $10,000 figure (which, of course, in terms of real value is not that much different from the $3,000 in 1962). Crummey had a very astute lawyer, who included this provision in the trust instrument:

Each child . . . may demand at any time (up to and including December 31 of the year in which a transfer to his or her trust has been made) the sum of $4,000 or the amount of the transfer from each donor, whichever is less, payable in cash immediately upon receipt by the Trustee of the demand in writing and in any event, not later than December 31 of the year in which such transfer was made. Such payment shall be made from the gift of that donor for that year. If a child is a minor at the time of such gift of that donor for that year, or fails in legal capacity for any reason, the child's guardian may make such demand on behalf of the child.

Therefore, Crummey's lawyer argued, this could not be deemed a gift of a future interest because the donee had the right each year to take out of the trust the amount of the gift that had been made. The Internal Revenue Service attacked the concept and won in the Tax Court, but Crummey successfully appealed the adverse ruling to the Ninth Circuit Court of Appeals.

The key in the Crummey case is that the person who has the power to withdraw must receive adequate notice that the addition to the trust has been made. The settlor who is transferring the property each year to the trust wants to make sure the technical rules are being followed so the gift transferred can qualify for the annual exclusion.

From the standpoint of the donor, she or he is vitally interested that all gifts to the trust qualify for the annual exclusion. If they do not, then they must be added together with all taxable gifts made since January 1, 1976, and reduce the amount of the unified credit available for the first $600,000 of gift and estate transfers.

Knowledgeable tax lawyers jumped on the bandwagon and started to integrate the use of Crummey powers with generation-skipping trusts. However, in 1988 further restrictions were made by Congress. Now the Crummey power can no longer apply to generation-skipping trusts with multiple beneficiaries. Rather, the power must be limited to generation-skipping trusts for single beneficiaries, and in addition the balance of the trust remaining at the beneficiary's death must be includable in the beneficiary's gross estate.

Here is a family situation that typifies the way a Crummey power trust can be used. Frank and his wife are each forty-five years old. They have two children who are both of legal age. Frank's lawyer drafts an irrevocable trust with a Crummey power for each of the two children. In 1988 Frank and his wife begin a gift program to transfer $10,000 to each of the two trusts. Notice is given to their two children, who naturally decide that they are not going to withdraw the $10,000. The cash in the trust is used to purchase a "last to die" life insurance policy on the lives of Frank and his wife. The insurance policy proceeds are paid when neither one of them is living. The incremental value of the life insurance policy under present tax laws is not subject to income tax, and at the death of Frank and his wife the proceeds payable to the trust would not be subject to estate tax because the policy was owned by the trust. The amount of life insurance that can be purchased with $20,000 of annual premiums depends in part upon the ages of the insured parties and the particular companies who write the insurance policies. Literally, millions of dollars of insurance policy proceeds can become part of Crummey-type trusts. Eventually, of course, the federal estate tax law will catch up with these funds because they will be taxed in the beneficiary's estate. However, thus far nothing precludes the beneficiary from doing the same thing for her or his children.

Other technicalities involved in Crummey-type trusts should be reviewed with a lawyer who has expertise in the area. I also recommend exploring these opportunities with a reputable life insurance agent who has the sophistication and expertise necessary to be part of the estate-planning team.

Other opportunities exist to include life insurance products as part of an overall estate-planning program to transfer wealth. Often these wealth transfers are accomplished by modifying the usual situation where the insured is also the owner of the policy. Instead, the beneficiary can be the owner.

However, making the beneficiary the owner can become a problem if disharmony arises between the insured, who is paying the premium, and the beneficiary-owner. Other circumstances can interfere with this type of plan. For instance, husbands not only often make wives the beneficiaries of their insurance policies, but they may also transfer ownership of the policies to their spouse. If the wife predeceases the husband, it is important to discuss with your attorney whether your will or living trust should contain a specific provision directing that ownership of insurance policies on your life be retained in a residuary trust, rather than being given to you or to a marital trust for your benefit, which, in turn, would be includable in your estate for federal estate tax purposes. On the other hand, you may for personal reasons want to own these policies, if your spouse predeceases you. Generally speaking, however, from a tax-planning standpoint, policies insuring your life should be owned by someone else.

If you consider purchasing life insurance products, be sure to investigate the performance record of the insurance company and its financial strength. Just because a company's name is well known does not necessarily mean that it has great financial strength, particularly in this modern era where so many companies invested large portions of their reserves in high-yield bonds and real estate that suffered substantial declines in market value.

When considering the purchase of life insurance products, I strongly recommend that you consult with your attorney to get the benefit of her or his objective advice and also to make certain that any purchase is integrated with your overall estate planning.

Finally, it is essential to update your estate plan to make certain that no new legislation has been enacted by Congress and no new regulations have been adopted by the Internal Revenue Service that undercut the tax benefits you hope to achieve. Life insurance is one area where tax law changes have had an impact on prior decisions made to purchase life insurance products. One of the best examples is a tax law change that affected literally millions of taxpayers. For many years billions of dollars of life insurance policies were sold on the basis of financial projections involving the deductibility of interest expense on cash value increases in life insurance policies. The financial projections were prepared in a table format that showed that, once you paid the initial premium on your policy, cash values automatically increased. You could borrow against this increase in cash value to get the money for the next premium, and you could deduct as an interest expense on your tax return the interest that accrued on cash value borrowings. The interest rate was generally a submarket rate, such as 5 or 6 percent.

The rise in cash value would also permit you to borrow to pay the interest on the policy loans, so in effect you could borrow from the insurance policy to make interest payments and not have to spend any additional cash of your own. In turn, the fact that you made interest payments gave you a deduction on your federal income tax return, which offset income and, in the days of 50 percent tax brackets, saved literally hundreds and thousands of dollars. On paper, everything looked almost too good to be true. It was. Congress changed the law and limited the amount of insurance-policy interest expense that could be deducted for income tax purposes. This is a vivid example of how the best-laid tax planning can be undercut by tax law changes.

Life insurance is still very important in providing protection for families in the event of the death of a principal wage earner. It has many more facets, particularly for wealthy people. Life insurance trusts remove insurance proceeds from the estates of both husband and wife. The Crummey power trust is one vehicle that should be considered. But do not forget: Congress can change the law, and it is very possible that, in the not-too-distant future, Congress will close the door.

Casey Stengel, who had great success as manager of the New York Yankees in their glory years of the 1950s, used to say: "Win today's game today, and don't worry about tomorrow's game until tomorrow." So it is with life insurance. Explore the options that exist today. But be prepared to change direction, if the law changes. Unique opportunities still exist to transfer wealth through life insurance. Consider taking advantage of it while you can.

29

Wise Charitable Giving and the Private Foundation Option

"**Y**ou know, David, everyone thinks giving away money to charity is very easy. That's just not true. It's really tough to give away money wisely."

This wisdom was shared with me by a wonderful client who was a community-minded philanthropist as well as an astute business-man. One of the most challenging and psychologically rewarding parts of my law practice has been to counsel with clients concerning wise charitable giving and the private foundation option.

Most people do not have the financial resources to make large charitable gifts. However, if you are wealthy and are considering the possibility of leaving a portion of your estate to charity, I would like to share some thoughts with you that may affect how much you want to leave the charity and also the form in which you want to leave the gift.

If your estate will be subject to federal estate tax on your death or, if you are married, on the death of your surviving spouse, consider the fact that the government in effect is going to help subsidize a major charitable gift because it will reduce the amount of federal estate tax that otherwise would be paid. You can do your own calculation by looking at the federal estate tax schedule in Chapter 15. For many wealthy people, a $500,000 gift to charity will cost their family heirs only $250,000.

Here is another way to look at it. Let us assume a potential $500,000 charitable gift and an estate tax bracket of 50 percent. If the gift were not made, there would be a $250,000 federal estate tax on the $500,000, and this would leave beneficiaries $250,000. Assuming a 6 percent rate of return on this amount, the beneficiaries would earn $15,000 a year more than they would have received had the charitable gift not been made.

You can then carry the projection further. There will be income taxes payable by your beneficiaries if they receive the additional $15,000 of income. Assuming a combined federal and state income tax rate of approximately 33 percent, this means there would be $5,000 of income taxes on the $15,000 of projected income, leaving a net after-tax income available of $10,000 a year.

On the other hand, if the $500,000 gift would have been made to charity, and the money invested with an overall yield of 6 percent, the charity would have received $30,000 a year. Therefore, the issue becomes whether you want to leave your beneficiaries with an extra $10,000, after taxes, or have $30,000 a year available for charitable purposes.

To all of this I would add another dimension: the intangible factors that stem from charitable giving. Your charitable bequest will not only be a perpetual memorial to you but a living memorial also, a part of the ongoing work of a worthwhile charitable organization that means a great deal to you and your family. That same feeling of psychological satisfaction will pass on to your children and grandchildren, who will be aware of your charitable generosity.

If you want to maximize the emotional satisfaction and pride for you and your family, you might consider establishing a family foundation. Members of your family could serve as foundation directors. If you were to fund the foundation with a major gift, such as $500,000, the annual income would provide $30,000 to give away, and the directors might have the option to give away more. You could direct that for a specified number of years the net income of the foundation be distributed to charities that you can specify in your will. Or, you could leave the distribution of the income from the foundation in whole or in part to the discretion of its directors.

By establishing a foundation, you would not only be establishing a permanent living memorial but also setting in motion a wonderful vehicle for your children and grandchildren to use to gain the pleasures and psychological satisfaction that comes from giving money to worthwhile charities.

Some clients have incorporated a foundation because they want to undertake a charitable gift program but are uncertain at the time of the gift which charities they might ultimately want to select. They make the initial gift to the foundation, take the allowable income tax deduction, and use the foundation as a vehicle for making future gifts to the particular charities they desire. The Internal Revenue Code requires that each charitable foundation distribute a certain minimum amount of its assets each year to charity, and you should review these requirements with your attorneys or accountants.

One more special benefit can come from a family foundation. It can be a practical means for helping keep brothers and sisters and their children in closer touch with one another. We live in a mobile society, where brothers and sisters often live in cities miles from one another. Sometimes their children (cousins who are your grandchildren) rarely see one another. A family foundation can be a wonderful vehicle for increasing personal contact within the family and helping keep people close.

If you are undecided whether you want the foundation to continue "forever," you can always insert in the instrument creating the foundation the authority for the directors at some particular time to liquidate the assets and give them to charities—either of your choice, their choice, or a combination.

If you want to go one step further, you can establish a private foundation during your lifetime and make contributions each year, making it possible to achieve important income tax benefits. An attorney with background and expertise in the tax and private foundation area can be of great assistance to you in discussing these possibilities. In addition, establishing a foundation during your lifetime may provide a sum for you to continue substantial charitable giving after you retire, when your income may decrease. Many clients, after they retire, spend increasing amounts of their time working on behalf of charitable organizations. Those with private foundations have found their pleasure enhanced by their ability to continue substantial financial support after retirement.

I have never known a client who established a private foundation and later regretted it. I have never known a wealthy family whose members did not take great pleasure in important gifts that have enriched their community—gifts to hospitals, gifts to enrich the cultural life of the community, gifts to enrich the educational life of the community, its public schools, its colleges and universities.

I have one additional suggestion to make to wealthy individuals with young children. When your children become of college age, consider giving them a sum of money each year that they can allocate to the charities of their own choice. You may want to give some general guidelines. For instance, if you give $1,000 to be allocated to the charity of your son's or daughter's choice, you might state that no more than 20 or 30 percent of the total amount should go to any particular charity. Or you might suggest that at least half the money should be given away this year, but half could be carried over and added to the money that would be received from you next year. Undertaking a program of this kind can result in a very important educational experience for the children of wealthy families. It can also help your children understand that giving money away to charity is not always an easy decision.

What is the purpose of acquiring wealth? I will not try to entirely answer the question for you, but I would suggest a part of the answer. Surely, one purpose is to help you be a happier person, a more fulfilled person, a person who can partake in the full spectrum of all that life has to offer. Wise charitable giving can be a wonderfully enriching experience—for you and for those you love most.

30

Charitable Lead Trusts and Charitable Remainder Trusts

Volunteerism has been one of the hallmarks of the growth and development of our country; in fact, the United States has been unique in this among all nations of the world. Citizen involvement has many benefits—the psychological and social benefits that come from personal involvement, the economic benefits that come from greater efficiencies, the social benefits that come from the work undertaken by charitable institutions.

But charitable institutions need financial support in order to sustain their work.

Although most executives who work with charitable organizations seek a broad base of financial support, they know that the financial viability of the organization often depends upon receiving substantial charitable gifts from wealthy individuals. They also know that tax laws have a major impact on charitable giving.

Because I am a strong proponent of volunteerism, I have generally supported tax incentives to encourage charitable gifts. However, sometimes tax incentives go too far, and at one time the *charitable lead trust* fell into this category.

The concept of a charitable lead trust is relatively simple. A lump sum of property is left in trust with a designation that the trust itself will be split into two interests. The first part is an income interest for a charity. For a certain period of years, the charity would receive all of the income from the property. After that term of years expired, the charity would have no further interest in the property, and it would go to another person (or persons), who was called a *remainderman*.

Here is a typical example.

I hereby leave $500,000 in trust with the provision that for the first ten years after my death $50,000 a year will be paid to the XYZ University for scholarship aid to students who show academic achievement and financial need. After the expiration of this ten-year period, the remaining property will be held in trust during the lifetime of my children and the income from this trust shall be paid to my children in equal shares in equal periodic installments, preferably quarterly but in any event not less than annually.

The underlying concept of the charitable lead trust is that if the $500,000 were left in trust for the children only, with no charitable interest in the beginning, it would be subject to federal estate tax. Assuming a federal estate tax bracket of 50 percent, this would leave $250,000 in trust for the children. On the other hand, if a charitable lead trust were to be formed and the principal invested in assets that actually earned 10 percent, at the end of ten years the charity would have gotten a total of $500,000 (ten annual installments of $50,000). There would still be $500,000 of principal left for the children, but the federal estate tax applicable would be far less than $250,000 because the children were not able to get the money for ten years. This involves the concept of what is known as *present value*.

In other words, if I were to have the right to receive $50,000 a year, starting tomorrow, and someone else were to have the right to receive $50,000 a year, starting ten years from now, I would have something far more valuable than the other person, who had to wait ten years before getting any money. In determining how to measure this difference, part of the computation depends upon what rate of interest is assumed.

At one time the federal tax tables for computing the present value of the remainderman's interest assumed an interest rate that was much lower than what a sophisticated investor could earn.

This offered great opportunity to project a low valuation for the remainderman's interest. If the charity received dollars that were in excess of what the tax table interest rate showed, the taxpayer was allowed to treat this as a reduction in principal, which in turn reduced the value of the remainderman's interest to a very low figure. In other words, the valuation for tax purposes depended on a tax table computation based on a theoretical interest rate and an assumption that, if the theoretical interest rate would not be enough to make the initial payments to the charity, a portion of these payments would come out of principal. In fact, the actual interest rate would be sufficiently high to take care of all of the payments, and there would be no reduction of principal.

Conceivably, it was possible to transfer millions of dollars to a charitable lead trust, provide for a rate of return substantially higher than the tax table rate, cover one's self with a high-interest coupon security, and have the federal estate tax apply to a very low valuation of the remainderman's interest. The tax tables assumed that a portion of the payout to the charity was a reduction of principal, even though that had not actually occurred. The charitable lead trust was then integrated with the $1 million generation-skipping tax exemption so that millions of dollars could be funneled into the generation-skipping trust, since the present value at the time of the gift (or at the time of death where charitable lead trusts were established under a will) was less than $1 million.

The government finally responded to what was happening. Recent amendments to the Internal Revenue Code and regulations have materially diminished the tax benefits of charitable lead trusts. Nevertheless, there is still an area of opportunity that wealthy people should explore with expert counsel.

Under current law it is not necessary for you, yourself, to name the charitable beneficiaries. The trustee or someone else may be given the power to designate which charity or charities will receive the money. Although the term of a lead trust is generally specified as a number of years, it can also continue for the life or lives of named people, but there can be no noncharitable beneficiaries during the term of the charity's interest. If excess income accrues, it can be paid to the charity during the term, but it cannot be paid to noncharitable beneficiaries.

The *charitable remainder trust* is the "flip-side" version of the charitable lead trust. In the scenario of the charitable remainder trust, the income for the initial years goes to the noncharitable beneficiary. Often, the trust terms provide that the noncharitable beneficiary, who may be the settlor, receives a certain specified annual sum for life. On death the trust terminates and the assets are paid to or held for the benefit of the specified charity or charities, known as the *charitable remainderman,* or remainderman.

Two common forms are known as *charitable remainder unitrust* and *charitable remainder annuity trust.* In each case the transfer of the asset is to a charitable beneficiary or to a foundation or trustee acting on behalf of the charitable beneficiary. In the case of a unitrust, the noncharitable beneficiary receives an annual amount equal to a specified percentage (which is not less than 5 percent) of the net fair market value of the trust assets, valued annually. In the case of the annuity trust, the charitable entity that is the transferee of the property is obligated to pay a certain sum each year to the noncharitable beneficiary that is not less than 5 percent of the initial net fair market value of the assets. In both cases, whatever assets are left after the death of the noncharitable beneficiary are retained by or paid over to the charity or charities. If payments are to be made for a term of years, the term cannot be greater than twenty years, unless the lives of the noncharitable beneficiaries extend beyond that time.

One advantage of creating these trusts is that there can be a deduction for federal income tax purposes at the time of creation of an inter vivos trust. These advantages can be enhanced by giving away property that has appreciated in value. If the property is sold after it goes into the trust, there will be no income tax under the present tax laws. There can also be deductions for federal estate tax purposes where the beneficiaries are people other than a surviving spouse, who would qualify for the marital deduction.

One major concern about establishing charitable remainder trusts is that, when you give the property away, it is no longer under your control. If the charity to which you give the property cannot afford to pay the annuity that is due you or the particular person that has been designated, there is often no recourse. The annuitant is left holding the bag.

Older people are particularly susceptible to being pressured to establish charitable remainder trusts. If the charity does not have sound financial management, it can dissipate the proceeds of the property transferred, and no funds will be available to pay the annuity to the person who gave the property away. If you are planning to use a charitable remainder trust, be sure to investigate the financial strength and capability of the charity you are contemplating selecting.

The law on charitable lead trusts and charitable remainder trusts has changed rapidly. If these are areas of interest to you, make certain that the counsel you select to help with your estate planning has personal familiarity with all the intricacies of the statutes and regulations, or that someone in her or his firm does.

What do I advise? "It all depends upon the situation and the terrain." The amount of wealth, the structure of the family, the goals of individuals are variable factors, all of which are important.

There is one other factor that also has a bearing, and that is the importance of volunteerism in our democratic society. There is no other country where volunteerism plays such an important part in the fabric of a society. If you believe in individualism, you should be supportive of volunteerism.

Charitable lead trusts and charitable remainder trusts are important alternatives to consider. There are others, including direct gifts.

How much should a wealthy person set aside? Some clients provide only a nominal amount, such as 1 or 2 percent of their estates. Some clients are very generous and set aside 10 percent or more. If there are no children, many unmarried clients and many married clients after the death of a surviving spouse will leave half and sometimes more of their estates to charity.

If clients ask what I have done, I tell them candidly that in younger years I had a figure of less than 5 percent. Today the figure happens to be 10 percent. But whether the figure is 1, 5, or 10 percent or more, the question is one of personal choice. One advantage of the charitable lead and charitable remainder trust is that you can make that choice during your lifetime and savor the pleasures that come from giving wisely.

31

Putting It All Together

When you begin to develop an overall plan for leaving money wisely, you have many choices. It is almost like going into a supermarket with a grocery cart and being able to pick and choose exactly what you want to meet your needs and tastes.

As you think about your own circumstances, you should understand that there are opportunities to mix and match approaches and strategies to help you achieve your goals. You can take a basic residuary trust and add special powers of appointment to give someone else a future opportunity to affect how the property is distributed. You can provide for mandatory distribution of income where you have great confidence in the beneficiaries. If you have a child who unfortunately has no work ethic, you can cover that situation as well. I have seen powers used to disinherit children who already have income from trusts established by their grandparents and whose parents believe their lives to have been very adversely affected because of too much money. On the other hand, there is always the possibility that the situation will improve, and the use of sprinkling powers in a trust instrument, coupled with judicious use of powers of appointment, can help meet these circumstances.

Once an estate plan has been developed and the final instruments signed, it should not be left on the shelf and forgotten. Family circumstances change, and tax laws change. I recommend to clients that they keep in their homes or offices copies of estate plan documents together with a letter from their attorney summarizing the salient provisions. I also recommend that each year on a particular date, such as a birthday or anniversary, the documents be reviewed. I analogize this to an annual physical examination. Most people are concerned about their physical health. They should also be concerned about their financial health—and that of their heirs.

One additional admonition: Do not fall into the trap of spending huge portions of time on the intricacies of tax savings and relatively little time on the particularities of what you want and what you believe to be in the best long-range interest of your loved ones.

I want to close my special advice for the very wealthy with some personal observations concerning priorities. I make these observations because my greatest satisfaction from the practice of law has not come from merely showing clients how they can save tax dollars. Rather, it has come from counseling clients and helping them work out their own solutions to what is the best for them and best for the long-range personal, psychological, and financial needs of those they love.

Almost everyone aspires to more wealth. Yet those who are wealthy know that great material riches can often lead to serious problems. How often have I seen intrafamily jealousies arise among the members of wealthy families. How often have I seen an excess of riches destroy that which is most precious: the social and psychological well-being of a child.

On the other hand, many families have handled immense wealth with outstanding judgment and foresight. One of my friends in New York has the good fortune of being a member of such a family.

Recently I asked him: "How did it happen that you and your siblings each turned out so well in the face of all of the family wealth that surrounded you—all of the possibilities that existed for laziness, squandering of money, and other unfortunate consequences that all too often are found in the presence of great wealth?"

"David, there are lots of reasons, but if I were to single out the most important reason of all, it is that we were raised as children in a middle-class family."

Those are very important words for people of wealth to understand. If you want to leave money wisely, a major factor to consider is the possibility of unhappiness resulting from the transfer of too much wealth, too fast, to your children and your grandchildren. Of course, children and grandchildren from whom transfers are withheld may become deeply resentful, which also can lead to problems.

To avoid the pitfalls, there is much that can be done—and most of this goes far beyond the drafting of legal instruments as a part of an overall estate plan.

When clients speak to me about such philosophical matters, I offer another Basic Rule, which includes one of my favorite techniques—the use of an acronym. In this case, the acronym is LUCK, and it stands for Love, Understanding, Caring, and Kindness. If you have a lot of LUCK, you have a fabulous combination, regardless of whether it is accompanied by great material wealth. If you have a lot of LUCK plus material wealth, you have an even more fabulous combination.

Most wealthy people I know constantly aspire toward acquiring additional wealth, even though they may already have more riches than either they or their children could ever possibly spend. However, from my professional experience, I suggest that wealth really should be regarded as a means toward happiness. If wealthy people really want to be happy, they would be well advised to spend a little bit less time accumulating more money and instead spend more time on the intangibles of life, of which Love, Understanding, Caring, and Kindness stand at the top.

All of this leads me to my final Basic Rule: Giving is receiving. When you give of yourself, you receive far more than you give. To understand and follow this rule is an even more important goal than leaving money wisely.

PART V

Potpourri

32

The Living Will

"**O**ld age is not for sissies" is a favorite saying of my mother, who was born in 1903. Thirty years of widowhood have not dampened her cheerfulness and optimism. But she is smart enough to know that there is no guarantee of continued mental and physical good health.

Like many other older Americans, she has become increasingly concerned about what might happen in the event of a serious accident or illness. She might require life-support systems in order to live but yet be unable to communicate competently. If she cannot communicate and there is no likelihood of recovery, she doesn't want her life extended for months or years through sophisticated life support systems. "That's not the way I want to live."

There is another factor that concerns her, a question of economics from both a personal and a public-interest perspective. She is not wealthy, in monetary terms, but she has accumulated a small estate that she wants to leave to her grandchildren. "It would be terrible to have all of my money used for life-support systems I don't want until I have nothing left and then have Medicare take over the burden. Why should I have to do this, if I don't want it? Why should Medicare money be spent on life-support systems to add two or three months to my life when it could be better used to care for younger people or for people who have a chance to get well or to help find a cure for cancer?"

She asked me many years ago to prepare for her signature a *living will* to protect her from the possibility of her having to spend the last few months of her life in a hospital bed, fed by tubes, unable to communicate. Her biggest concerns were about situations where she could not communicate intelligently with her doctors and her family to express her desire not to exist as "a human vegetable."

In consultation with her, I developed a family form, which has been adapted for use by many clients:

I hereby declare that the following Declaration shall become immediately operative if (1) I can neither speak coherently nor write coherently and should have what my attending physician believes to be an incurable or irreversible condition that will cause my death within a relatively short time, or (2) if I can neither speak coherently nor write coherently and am unable to feed myself and am generally confined in bed because of an incurable or irreversible condition that will cause me to die and where the judgment of my attending physician is that there is a less than 1% chance that I will either regain my capacity to speak coherently or to write coherently during the rest of my life.

In the event either of the foregoing circumstances occurs, it is my desire and I hereby express my desire that my life not be prolonged by administration of life-sustaining procedures.

I further declare that if either of the foregoing circumstances occurs and I am unable to participate in decisions regarding my medical treatment, I direct my attending physician to withhold or withdraw procedures that merely prolong my life under these circumstances or that merely prolong the dying process and are not necessary to my physical comfort or freedom from pain, and I further direct my attending physician not to force-feed me or intravenously feed me or force me to drink.

I hereby designate _____ to serve as my attorney-in-fact for the purpose of making all decisions pertaining to my medical treatment including, but not limited to, decisions relating to discontinuance of artificial life-support systems. This power of attorney shall remain effective in all circumstances including those where I become incompetent or otherwise unable to make medical decisions for myself.

The validity of a particular living will depends upon the laws of your state. Check with your attorney to see what provisions are valid in your state. In many states printed forms are available.

I spend a great deal of time in New York City, where there is an organization known as Concern for Dying (which is merging into the National Council on Death and Dying), which has forms of living wills. Often these forms provide for insertion of additional provisions relating to personal needs or desires, such as living out one's last days at home rather than in a hospital, if feasible.

Living wills are not just for old people. Life is tenuous. Tragedy can strike at any moment. When a thirty-five-year-old person makes a will, she covers the possibility, unlikely though it is, that she will never reach age thirty-six. Otherwise, she could wait until age thirty-six to write a will.

Why not also cover the possibility that a serious accident or illness could result in her requiring life-support systems, with no realistic possibility of recovery? Regardless of your age, when you are preparing a regular will or living trust, you should also consider preparing a living will.

These potential problems are vividly illustrated by the recent U.S. Supreme Court decision involving Nancy Cruzan, a young woman who has been in a vegetative-state coma since an auto accident in 1983 destroyed part of her brain. Even though family members asserted that she would never want to live as a "vegetable," the U.S. Supreme Court affirmed the decision of the Missouri Supreme Court that there was not "clear and convincing evidence" of Ms. Cruzan's own wishes. A well-drawn living will obviously would have provided that "clear and convincing" evidence.

One additional suggestion: If you do execute a living will, it may not be of any benefit to you unless you make sure that copies are given to your family physician and close members of your family.

These possibilities are not pleasant to contemplate. Yet if you want to leave money wisely, you will not ignore the laws of nature. As people reach their eighties, nineties, and one hundreds, it is only natural that they have a greater likelihood of incurring physical and mental infirmities. The wise person will be prepared for such contingencies.

A wise nation will also encourage living wills, for our economic resources are not unlimited. Many older people concur with my mother's feeling that society should not spend thousands or tens of thousands of dollars to extend the life of people in their late eighties or nineties, or in their one hundreds, for another few months, where they may be sustained only by life-support systems, unable to move, unable to communicate. Legislators may find it difficult to agree on the wording of statutes, for broad questions of morality and human values are involved, but this situation calls for undertaking every effort to reach consensus.

The starting point should be a national campaign to educate the public about choices that can be made. One of those choices is the execution of a living will by people who have a philosophy similar to that expressed by my mother. It makes a lot of sense.

33

Statements of Custody

When our children were young, Connie and I faced the decision of whether to travel in the same airplane. If we flew in separate planes, we would lessen the possibility of orphaning our children. If we flew in separate planes, we doubled the exposure to serious injury or death.

Being optimists, we felt that we would never be in an airplane crash, so we always flew together. In the 1960s, on a trip to the Yucatán, we narrowly escaped a serious accident when upon landing our plane struck two cows that had roamed onto the runway.

After that, we began to think about where we would want our children to be raised in the event we were both killed. We were sure that we did not want our children separated in different households. We also concluded that we did not want to place our children with either set of grandparents, because we felt they were too far along in years to have the responsibility of raising several grandchildren that might be thrust upon them.

Fortunately, we had several good choices, including my brother and sister-in-law, Connie's brother and sister-in-law, a wonderful uncle and aunt who had five children of their own, and some close friends. Unfortunately, not everyone has these choices. But parents should recognize that, if they do not make the choices they feel are best, someone else will make those choices, and they may not necessarily be good ones. Moreover, if surviving members of both families do not agree on which choices are to be made, court battles can ensue.

One set of grandparents can fight with another set of grandparents. A brother or sister on one side of the family can fight with the other side of the family. Meanwhile, it may have been best for the children to be raised in the household of family friends, particularly if they live in the same city, so the children would not face the disruption that occurs when a geographical move is made.

Therefore, I urge every client with young children to consider preparing a statement of custody that will direct where the children should be raised in the event of the death of both parents. Although it is not a legally binding instrument, it carries a great deal of weight should there be family controversy. The actual document is ordinarily not part of a will or living trust. Rather, it is a separate paper that can be changed as circumstances warrant.

I recommend that the instrument be flexible, with provisions for changes in custody in the event of a change in circumstances. For instance, suppose custody of the children were placed with two close friends, and subsequently a divorce occurred in that family?

I also recommend that the instrument specifically provide that funds available for the care of the minor children can be used by the family having custody to provide for extra household help and even possibly for helping move into a larger home or apartment to meet the burden of one or more extra people in the household.

Here are areas I believe should be covered in a statement of custody:

1. At the outset, you should state that the primary consideration is the welfare of the children.

2. You should include a general outline of the funds that will be available to help with the care of the children, in addition to funds from social security. Ideally, the social security payments plus income from life insurance or other assets should take care of the added financial burden of raising the children.

3. When naming specific custodians, you should include a qualifying clause to cover contingencies that might arise, such as changes in health or marital status.

4. You should name a person or persons who can review changes in circumstances and who have the right to make custody changes. In our case, we directed that the custody committee consist of my brother, Connie's brother, and one of my uncles. Connie passed away when the youngest of our five children was in the fifth grade. I then added to the group those children who had attained legal age and provided that a vote of the majority should determine custody of the minor children.

5. If there are children who have only one or two years left in high school, you should give consideration as to whether those children should remain in the same high school. If that were to happen, you then have the question about what to do to avoid the splitting of children. There are no easy answers.

6. You should consider some special provisions that may be uniquely applicable in your family situation. For instance, you can spell out a desire that the children visit their grandparents at least once a year or that the children have certain educational and cultural activities and experiences. You can also spell out your desire about what the funds are not to be used for, such as the purchase of an automobile for a high school student.

7. You should also consider stating your desire that available funds should be used to help pay for the living costs in the home where your children will reside, including not just direct items such as money for extra food, but also indirect items such as a share of household maintenance and money for extra household help so the person having custody will have more time available to spend with your children and help take the place of their mother and father.

8. You should include an overall general paragraph or two expressing some personal thoughts and philosophy so that the statement of custody becomes more than just a formal docu-

ment. Here is an example of a portion of a document that I helped prepare and that incorporates a number of these ideas:

We realize that whoever has custody of our children will have thrust upon them many added burdens and responsibilities. The value of proper care for our children, of course, cannot be measured in dollars and cents; it is beyond our power to compensate. However, we hope that part of the funds available for the proper care, support, maintenance, and education of our children will be used for such things as extra cleaning and household help so that the persons having custody of our children will be able to have more time available to spend with them and help take the place of their mother and father. In addition, these funds will help whoever has custody to maintain a house large enough so that the addition of one or two members to the family will cause no great physical inconvenience. Regardless of the circumstances, and regardless of who has custody of our children, we hope that all of the members of each of our families will do everything possible to facilitate the adjustment of our children in a new environment, just as we would do if any member of either of our families were to call upon us to help raise their children. We know that for our children to have neither parent living would be a very traumatic situation, and we would only hope that our families put the welfare of our children above any personal feelings pertaining to the custody of our children so that the best resolution possible can be made of a very unfortunate series of events.

These are some of the things that you should consider including in a statement of custody for young children. I can vouch from experience that it is not an easy decision to make. Most people are pretty certain, and rightfully so, that no one will be able to provide the love, care, and support that their children would have received had there been no loss of parents. Nevertheless, a statement of custody is a vital part of your estate plan.

One final area remains to be discussed, and that relates to what happens when a divorce has occurred and subsequently both parents die. Here the problems are not so readily resolved. However, if both parents really put the welfare of the children first, they can arrive at a mutually agreeable decision to cover the possibility of the death of both parties. If the parties cannot agree, I recommend that each parent designate a party to serve on a committee to determine custody, and the two parties named would together seek to find a third party to serve on a committee of three to help reach a final decision.

It is important to leave money wisely. But for those of you who have young children, it is far more important to do everything you can to assure that, if you are not living, you will have been very wise in your choice of the custodian for your children.

34

Disclaimers and Other Special Options

Many years ago, there was a couple in Des Moines who had everything going for them—a great marriage, five wonderful children, lots of friends, and professional and economic success. He was an attorney with rising reputation and increasing income. She was an educator who was elected to the school board and was eventually appointed to the Board of Regents governing the state universities. As part of family tax planning, the husband transferred assets into his wife's name, including the family home and all life insurance policies on his life. He never worried about divorce—one of the favorite family quips, with five young active children around the house, was that "we could never get a divorce because neither one of us would agree to take the kids."

Then, one day breast cancer struck, and the bubble burst. In little more than a year, the battle was lost. The children faced the trauma of the loss of their mother. Their father faced the trauma of the loss of his wife. And his psychological burden was made even heavier because he had to probate her estate.

I was that lawyer. It was by far the toughest professional task I ever faced. While Connie was sick, I did not want to encourage her to transfer her assets to a living trust, because that would have been psychologically devastating to her; until almost the very end she believed she could win the battle. But shortly after her death in June 1980, I transferred all of my assets into a living trust and became a strenuous advocate of clients taking steps to avoid probate. We all learn by experience.

When Connie's estate was formally opened in the probate court, one of the first decisions I had to make involved what is known as a *disclaimer,* which is a refusal to accept a bequest, thereby allowing the property to pass to someone else without any adverse tax consequences. Disclaimers provide a second look at estate planning. Connie's will left the house to me and also provided for a residuary trust that included me as a beneficiary as well as our children. For emotional reasons, I decided to keep the house in my name (which from a tax planning standpoint was not necessarily sound—but feelings are often more important than tax savings). However, I filed a disclaimer for all of my right, title, and interest in the residuary trust so it could be held exclusively for our children and their lawful descendants.

Disclaimers are often used in closely knit families where everything has been left outright or in trust for the surviving spouse, and the surviving spouse has independent means. If the surviving spouse accepts all of the property that has been left to her or him, it can create a much larger estate, which, in turn, will eventually mean more estate taxes. The survivor can decline to claim all of the property, or a percentage of the property. Whatever is disclaimed will then go to the remaining beneficiaries in the will, which may even be a trust where the surviving spouse is a beneficiary.

Sometimes, if there is a technical defect in the way certain clauses in the will are drawn, a disclaimer can be very helpful. If the estate is large enough to have a federal estate tax problem, there are technical Internal Revenue Code rules that must be followed. The disclaimer must be in writing, must be irrevocable, and must be made within nine months after the decedent's death. Generally, partial disclaimers are permissible under federal estate tax laws. Check with your attorney to see whether they are permitted under the laws of your state.

Another important question involves the tax apportionment clause: Who will pay the federal estate and the state inheritance taxes? In a large estate, taxes can consume more than half of the property. Generally, the testator is permitted to direct in the living trust or the will who must pay the tax. The problem can be exacerbated in situations where property passes outside of the terms of will, such as joint tenancy property. Sometimes, in taxable estates with large amounts of joint tenancy property, the tax apportionment clause can be an extremely important provision in a will.

Another important area for consideration concerns qualified retirement plans and IRAs. There are very technical rules involving options for distributions during the life of the participant and distributions after the participant's death. Many recent changes have been made in these rules, and it is important to understand their ramifications when you are planning your estate. Generally, distributions must commence by April 1 of the calendar year following the calendar year in which the participant attains the age of seventy and one-half, regardless of the actual date of retirement. If the required minimum distribution is not made, there can be a substantial excise tax of 50 percent of the difference between the minimum required distribution and the amount that was actually distributed.

Alternative options exist concerning how death proceeds are to be distributed. For instance, should a surviving spouse acquire a single life annuity for the amount of these proceeds?* I generally recommend against this, but it is one of the many technical matters involving qualified retirement plans and IRAs that you should discuss with counsel.

Another major problem that can arise, particularly in a blended family context, involves the selection of property to fund different

---

*An *annuity* is a fixed monthly or other periodic payment made over a person's lifetime. The precise amount is actuarially determined and depends upon the terms of the annuity contract, the age of the beneficiary, and the interest rate used. As compared with a *single life annuity,* one can purchase a *joint annuity,* which will make a periodic payment during the lives of two people and, after one person dies, continuing during the lifetime of the other person. When a joint annuity is purchased, the life expectancy of the survivor of two people is actuarially longer than the life expectancy of a single person, so the periodic payment is smaller because it is made over a longer period of time.

trusts under a will. If there is a second spouse, conflicts may develop between the second spouse and the children of the first marriage. And if there are also children of the second marriage, the problems can be compounded. The larger the estate, the greater the possibility for problems to arise.

Several years ago James B. Stewart, Jr., wrote a book about some of the elite corporate law firms in America. Stewart is a well-known journalist who once practiced with one of the major New York City law firms, Cravath, Swaine & Moore. One of the major revelations in Stewart's book, *The Partners* (Simon & Schuster, 1983), involved the Nelson Rockefeller family and the leading New York law firm of Milbank, Tweed, Hadley & McCloy.*

According to Stewart, Nelson Rockefeller's second wife, Happy, was not represented by her own legal counsel in the probate of his estate. There were problems of valuation and allocation of properties to the marital trust under the will. The inherent conflicts of interest were exacerbated because Nelson Rockefeller had fathered children by two wives. Happy's own children from her marriage to Rockefeller would probably be preferred beneficiaries out of the marital trust on Happy's death. Questions arose about how particular assets, such as art works, were to be valued and how these assets were to be allocated between the marital and the residuary trust. According to Stewart, "In short, the situation gave rise to a classic conflict of interest . . . 'Who's to know what these things are really worth,' the Milbank source continues. 'I can tell you that some of the decisions were adverse to Happy.' " (P. 322.)

If the assets of the estate include property that cannot be readily divided on a pro rata basis, and if there is a blended-family situation, or a nonblended-family situation where conflicts exist between surviving spouse and children, it is important to consider independent representation for the different parties.

Another major option involves the alternate valuation date election for federal estate tax purposes. Ordinarily, assets are valued as of the date of death. However, the federal estate tax laws do

*When I served as counsel with the Warren Commission investigating the assassination of President Kennedy, I worked with John J. McCloy, who was a member of that commission.

permit an alternate valuation six months after the date of death. Sometimes fluctuating market conditions affect the value of stocks, bonds, real estate, and other assets during this six-month period. The decision is usually made to choose the date that results in the lowest overall values for federal estate tax purposes. However, there is an income tax matter to consider.

The Internal Revenue Code, as we have seen, provides that where property passes through an estate (including, of course, a living trust), its tax basis for capital gains purposes becomes the value used for the federal estate tax valuation. If you are the beneficiary of particular property from an estate that has little or no federal estate tax liability, it may be wise to seek the highest possible valuation of that property in order to increase its tax basis, so if you sell the property in the future, your federal income tax liability will be reduced. On the other hand, if a surviving spouse or other beneficiary is to get a fractional portion of the estate, increasing the value of the total estate increases the amount of property that beneficiary will receive.

Other valuation conflicts can also arise. For instance, if a will specifies that the surviving spouse gets half the estate, including the house, the surviving spouse might want the house to be valued at a lower valuation date because she or he is getting the house anyway, and the lower the valuation of the house, the more additional property the surviving spouse would receive to make up the balance of the one-half.

This leads into the most widely known option: the right of the surviving spouse in most states to elect against a will if she or he is not satisfied with the provisions that have been included. In most states, if not all, one can disinherit a child. But it is not possible to disinherit a spouse, unless a valid prenuptial agreement permits this. In the absence of such an agreement, if you try to disinherit your spouse, in most states, if not all, she or he can elect to take against the will. The statutes of the state in which the decedent lived will declare exactly what portion of the estate will be set aside for the surviving spouse.

These are all examples of rights and options that are available and also potential areas of conflicting interests. There are a number of other areas of potential conflicts that can arise in larger and more complex estates, and your own advisers can discuss these with you. Unfortunately, the trend of development of the Internal Revenue Code and regulations is to create more complexity, requiring expert counsel and advice from lawyers and accountants.

This is one major reason why from time to time amendments to the Internal Revenue Code have been called the Lawyers' and Accountants' Relief Act for 1986 (or 1988 or . . . you can probably name almost any year in the future when there is new tax legislation).

Disclaimers, tax apportionment clauses, allocation of assets, and alternate valuation date selections are examples of some of the special options that are available under the Internal Revenue Code. Each year the law seems to become more complex. Therefore, if you have any possible doubts about how you should proceed, seek expert advice—the sooner, the better. And if you are involved in a blended marriage situation, whether as a surviving spouse or a child, you should be especially sensitive to potential conflicts of interest and make certain that your rights are well protected.

35

Special Advice for Women

"**D**avid," a client of mine said to me, "I don't know what to tell my cousin. She doesn't understand what's going on in her family's business, she doesn't understand the documents she's being asked to sign, and she doesn't know what to do."

"She should not sign anything she does not understand," I replied. "She should take enough time to find the answers to her questions, and if she is still not satisfied, she should consider getting outside help from a lawyer. If she has confidence in the family lawyer, she can go to her or him. If not, she can retain independent counsel."

"But if she goes to another lawyer, the family will be angry."

Therein lies a problem. It is good to be sensitive to the feelings of others, but not at the expense of good judgment. All too often women (and men, too) have come to me for help after they have signed documents they should never have signed. They could have avoided so many problems if they had come earlier, so important changes could have been made that would have given them greater protection.

Many people put off seeing a lawyer, just as they often put off seeing a dentist or a doctor about a dental or medical problem. Yet the earlier one consults a dentist or doctor about a potential problem, the more readily that problem can be resolved. Similarly, the sooner one sees a lawyer, the more readily good results can be obtained.

Unfortunately, women today have not achieved equal status with men in hierarchies of business, government, and other institutions. Because of this, they have less experience in dealing with lawyers, and I would therefore offer what I believe is very important advice for women:

1. Do not be intimidated by any lawyer—particularly by a male lawyer who may be somewhat overbearing.

2. Do not assume that a female lawyer representing other people is going to do you any favors because you are both women.

Related to these admonitions is another warning: Do not take as gospel truth the pronouncements of someone else's lawyer. Here is an example of what can happen. In 1986 Phyllis was divorced from Bob, whose family left multimillion-dollar trusts for the benefit of Bob and his children. The court awarded custody of the minor children to Phyllis. On December 28, 1989, the attorneys for Bob's family thrust before Phyllis a legal document concerning the division of trust assets between Bob and the children. The lawyers claimed the document had to be signed by Phyllis as the children's guardian by the end of the year because the trust term expired on December 31. Phyllis was in near panic because of the severe time pressures, and one of her business colleagues recommended that she call me in Des Moines.

What Phyllis didn't know—what the lawyers hadn't explained to her—was that, although the trust term expired at the end of 1989, there is a general grace period for winding up the affairs of an expired trust. Accordingly, there was no necessity for her to sign any documents that day. I suggested that she politely but firmly tell the lawyers that she was going to retain outside counsel for help, and I recommended the names of two firms in her community. One month later she wrote me a thank-you note and said that the law firm she had hired had been "of great help."

When Phyllis was confronted by Bob's lawyers, she had no idea where to turn for legal help. "How can I find a good lawyer?" Most often, lawyers are selected on the basis of friendship or acquaintance or through word-of-mouth recommendation by friends. Yet there are no assurances that the attorney you or a friend knows is competent in estate planning and family counseling. Your goal should be to pick the best attorney you can find, and you should not feel pressured to hire an attorney immediately upon a first consultation. If the attorney has competence and expertise in the area, he will understand your hesitancy and will not pressure you to make an immediate choice. If the attorney states that this is not his primary field of expertise, he may recommend someone else in his firm or attorneys in other firms.

Often lawyers are selected on the basis of recommendations from co-workers. In many cases, the higher the position that is attained in an organization, the more contact one has with attorneys. Unfortunately, women have not had as many opportunities to attain high managerial positions, and therefore many women do not know where to go to seek legal counsel.

Local bar associations often have referral services and provide names of attorneys in specified areas of the law. You can generally obtain these names by telephone. However, regardless of whether lawyers actually have competence in a particular area, they can often simply register with the referral service and represent that they have expertise. They are then automatically put on the list.

Another source is the Martindale-Hubbell Law Directory—one of the best-kept secrets about the legal profession. The directory is intended for the use of lawyers, but it is often available in public libraries. Included are listings for lawyers in almost every city and town of substantial size in the United States and some communities abroad. The front of the directory contains alphabetical listings. There is a rating system that in large part is based on the opinions of other lawyers in the community. The two highest ratings are *a v* and *b v,* and if the lawyer you retain has either of these ratings, this is a fairly good indication of competence.

An absence of rating should not necessarily be construed as unfavorable, because the publishers do not undertake to cover all lawyers and some lawyers have requested not to have any rating published. Also, for younger lawyers a rating may not have been developed because of their relatively few years of practice, particularly in big cities where the bar is so large that it is difficult for an individual to make his competence known.

The directory also contains paid listings, which give additional background information about law firms and their members. This can be helpful in assisting you if you have no other source of information.

When planning their wills or living trusts, many people, usually women, face limitations imposed by prenuptial agreements they have signed. It is common for women to feel pressured during prenuptial agreement negotiations because they fear that arguments can lead to a breakdown of the entire relationship. It is difficult to give general advice in this area because "it all depends upon the situation and the terrain." If you face this problem, be aware of the fact that, under the laws of most states, if there is not full disclosure of *all* assets by the husband, including their fair market value, the prenuptial agreement may not be binding on the wife.

If you feel very pressured by prenuptial agreement negotiations, where one of the major areas of conflict involves what happens to property upon the death of a spouse, you may want to consider going further than what you feel is fair. The practical experience of many women is that, if the relationship develops into a very happy marriage, husbands in their wills often provide more generously than what the prenuptial agreement requires. However, there is obviously risk in this area, because the husband may choose to do no more than what the prenuptial agreement requires. Sometimes it is helpful to get outside professional help from someone other than an attorney, such as a psychologist or a family counselor.

In a second marriage, conflicts of interests can arise between the surviving spouse and other beneficiaries. Theoretically, the lawyer probating the estate should be fair to all beneficiaries. Nevertheless, it helps for the widow to retain independent counsel to make certain all of her rights are protected. Under the laws of many states, a surviving spouse is entitled to a widow's allowance. Issues can arise concerning the amount of the allowance, income tax considerations, and estate tax considerations. These issues can require independent counsel.

The division of assets can create conflicts of interests between a surviving spouse and the children of the decedent who may not be children of the surviving spouse. Do not hesitate to retain independent counsel because you are afraid other members of the family might be upset. You have your own rights to protect, and you can discuss with your attorney how you can best soothe the overall family situation.

Another word of advice: When an estate is opened for probate, act promptly. In many states a surviving spouse can decide to "elect against the will" and take one-third, or possibly more, of the property, regardless of what provisions are made in the will. However, this decision must be made within a limited period of time— usually a matter of months. If you fail to assert these rights within the required period, you will lose them.

Many widows face a major problem because their husbands never made them full partners in the family financial affairs and in particular in matters involving how best to invest money. For lack of experience, many women leave money invested in bank certificates of deposit or savings accounts. This does not necessarily give protection against inflation (nor does it necessarily give the best rates of return). If you lack sufficient confidence to make your own investment decisions, then consider getting professional money management help. You may also want to enroll in one or more investment courses in an adult education program.

Women who lack investment experience are susceptible to the ploys of securities sales people who work on a commission and who sometimes seek to peddle investments that are not necessarily sound. A rule of thumb is that you should avoid purchasing securities that are not "liquid." Start with publicly traded stocks, publicly traded bonds or publicly traded mutual funds. If you invest in limited partnership interests that are not on the public market or corporate bonds from corporations of relatively small size, you run a greater risk of loss, particularly if you want to dispose of the investment before its maturity.

One final observation: Even though we are now in the 1990s, many men still have difficulty giving their wives equal voice in family money matters. This reluctance has a direct adverse impact on overall estate planning. Many women have come to me and asked—sometimes in near exasperation—what they can do. My reply is that there is no ready answer, except that anger and hostility are counterproductive. What works best, of course, is communication and understanding, coupled with patience. Fortunately, there are an ever-increasing number of men who are becoming sensitized to the need for equality and the benefits that can come when women participate fully in all aspects of the family's estate planning.

If you have daughters, one way to help sensitize your husband is to ask him what he would recommend that his daughters do when they are adults. Generally, most men want their daughters to assert full equality and believe that their daughters have just as much to contribute as their sons-in-law. You can then use that positive response as a base to help build understanding of the importance of full equality in your own relationship.

Equality for women is a principle that, although becoming more accepted in theory, is not yet fully implemented in practice. Women need to become more aware of how to assert their rights and gain greater financial independence and security. Fortunately, as the walls of discrimination are gradually falling, women have increasing opportunities for attaining full participation in our society.

Equal rights are very important for all women. Equal rights for all women are very important for all men.

36

Some Final Thoughts: "When There's a Will, There's a Way"

"Which way is the right way?"
"There's more than *one* right way."

"What do you think I ought to do?"
"If your best friend was confronted with the same type of a problem, what advice would you give?"

We all have different perspectives from which we view the wonders of life and the troubles of life; the joys, the sorrows; the highs, the lows. My perspective has obviously been shaped by my family, my friends, my experiences, and the problems that clients have shared with me.

My own law partners who work in this area have differing points of view. Jeff Lamson—an outstanding attorney, a Harvard Law School graduate with broad expertise in business counseling and estate planning—recently said to me, "David, I think you lean a little bit more toward getting property to grandchildren, and I lean a little bit more toward just worrying about getting it to children. If they blow it, they blow it." His views are somewhat shared by Jon Staudt, one of the finest tax lawyers in the Midwest who spends a great deal of time in estate- and tax-planning work. However, Jon believes there is virtue in keeping property for children in trust for longer periods of time.

My partner Chuck Harris—a Fellow of the American College of Probate Lawyers—with great experience in estate planning and probate work as well as general corporate work, cautions that the benefits of a living trust can be overstated. "It can serve a useful purpose, but it is not a panacea." My partner Steve Zumbach, a superb lawyer who is also a CPA and has a Ph.D. in economics, combines broad expertise in the business world with broad expertise in estate planning. In many areas his views are similar to mine, but there are times where we do not always agree. Many lawyers who work in firms where a number of partners become involved in estate-planning work often find varying perspectives.

These differences underscore the fact that you, yourself, are capable of making the decisions that best suit you and your family. To be sure, where you have a complex situation, you may need outside advice. But it is the application of that advice to your own philosophy and circumstances that is ultimately most important.

In writing this book, my overall perspective has not been that of an estate tax or probate specialist familiar with all the intricacies of the law. Rather, I write from the viewpoint of a generalist who has a broad range of experience in dealing with clients in a legal way, a business way, and a personal way, and who has knowledge of some of the opportunities and pitfalls that confront people as they think about these problems.

I have not tried to ask all of the questions, nor have I sought to provide all of the answers. Rather, my goal has been to help open the door for you and help you formulate your own philosophy to meet your particular personal and family situation.

You have within yourself the ability to make the kinds of personal decisions that will be best for you and your loved ones. I hope that after reading this book you will feel more confident in making choices that will be good for you and for them.

In the beginning, I emphasized the importance of focusing on these problems, unbundling them, confronting them, dealing with them psychologically and emotionally, understanding the choices you have, and finding the wisdom that's inside yourself.

I close with a final plea. The worst thing you can do is to do nothing. If you care about all of the sweat and toil that have gone into accumulating whatever estate you have, if you care about your loved ones and want to make it a little bit easier for them in the sorrow of your death, if you want to take advantage of the tax-saving features that the laws allow, then undertake the effort to plan how you want to leave your property. Don't just give it cursory attention. Block out sufficient time to do the job well.

The road you will travel is not necessarily an easy one, for there are many junctions with many alternate routes. At times you will be perplexed and will not know which path to take. At times you may be frustrated with your attorney, with your family, and with yourself. But with the help of expert counsel, you can prepare a will or living trust that will be specifically tailored to your personal wishes. You probably already feel that someday you are going to want to do this. If eventually, why not now?

I have found that no matter how unique and how complicated a family's situation may be, no matter how large the family's wealth may be, it has almost always been possible for me, working together with clients, to develop an overall estate plan that will accomplish most goals and meet most concerns that they share with me. "When there's a will, there's a way." (One of my vices—I do like puns.) That way is invariably far better than dying intestate or with a will or living trust to which you have not given sufficient thought.

Choosing the way you leave your property is indeed a very important part of choosing your destiny. One thing I can promise you: When a first-rate job of counseling and planning has been completed and the final drafts of instruments have been signed, you will have a wonderful feeling of relief and even exhilaration that something important to you and your family has been accomplished.

Do not be scared by the legalese. Do not be afraid to disagree with your lawyer. You know yourself best. You know the potential beneficiaries of your will or living trust better than any attorney. Seek whatever outside counsel you desire, but when the time comes to make the final decisions, have the confidence in your own capabilities that you can make good decisions. There is no single right answer, and sometimes there are problems that have no solutions. Reach the decision that you think is best, and do this with the understanding that there is more than one right way.

Appendixes

The forms of wills and living trusts in the Appendixes are samples prepared under the laws of the State of Iowa for fictitious persons and are for illustration only. Individuals should consult with their own attorneys regarding the preparation of wills and living trusts for themselves.

Appendix A

Example of a Basic Will for a Single Person (with or without Children) with an Estate of Less Than $600,000, with a Contingent Trust for Any Beneficiaries Under Twenty-one

Last Will and Testament
of
Jennifer L. Stewart

Executed the _____ day of _____, 19 ____

Table of Contents

Last Will and Testament
of
Jennifer L. Stewart

When Wills are signed, it should be done in the presence of at least two other persons, neither of whom is a beneficiary, executor, or trustee.

The sample Will for the fictitious person named "Jennifer L. Stewart" is for an unmarried person who may or may not have children. The heart of the Will is in Article 5, which specifies how the residue of the estate will be distributed. If any beneficiaries are under the age of twenty-one, then trusts are established to hold the property in trust until the beneficiary attains the age of twenty-one. The trustees, as well as the executors, are appointed in Article 1. The sample form appoints co-executors, one of whom is a bank, with a proviso that if the individual named does not serve, the bank will serve alone. Two co-trustees are appointed, one of whom is a bank, with the proviso that if the individual named does not serve, a successor person is named.

There are annotated comments in boldface preceding some of the articles to help explain the purpose of these articles.

I, Jennifer L. Stewart, of _____ County, Iowa, being of sound mind and memory, declare this my Last Will and Testament, and revoke all my former Wills or testamentary instruments.

ARTICLE 1. APPOINTMENTS

The provisions of this Will shall be supplemented by and, when necessary, subject to this Article.

1(a) Executor.

I hereby appoint _____ and XYZ Bank as executors. If _____ is unable or unwilling to serve, XYZ Bank shall serve alone.

1(b) Trustee.

I hereby appoint _____ and XYZ Bank as trustees of each trust under this Will. If _____ is unable or unwilling to serve, I appoint _____ as successor co-trustee.

ARTICLE 2. EXPENSES, DEBTS, AND LIFE INSURANCE

I authorize my executor to pay all my expenses of last illness and burial, and next to pay all my just debts, requiring the filing and proof of any claim in its discretion; provided, however, that this Article shall not subject any of my exempt property to the requirements thereof, unless my executor waives any exemption.

ARTICLE 3. SPECIFIC BEQUESTS

3(a) Personal Property.

If I leave any children surviving me, all personal automobiles, household furniture and furnishings, and other articles of domestic use or ornament which I own at my death shall be distributed to my then living children, or sold and the proceeds disposed of under the remaining Articles of this Will, as my executor shall determine.

My executor shall make any such distribution as fairly as possible, but in all events, my executor shall resolve any disagreement and shall determine whether the property be sold or distributed and the method of distribution.

3(b) Memorandum of Disposition.

Notwithstanding the preceding section I direct that my executor and beneficiaries abide by any dated memorandum in my handwriting or signed by me which I leave indicating that a certain person should receive a specific article or articles of tangible personal property.

ARTICLE 4. PAYMENT OF TAXES

The federal estate tax is levied against the estate. In many states, there is an inheritance tax that has to be paid by the

beneficiaries. This paragraph provides that the estate itself will pay any inheritance taxes that may be levied and the beneficiaries will not have to pay these taxes.

All inheritance, estate or other similar taxes against my estate or the recipients thereof, including any taxes arising from the transfer or receipt of assets not part of my probate estate, shall be paid from my estate after complying with the foregoing bequests of this Will. Such taxes shall not be charged against any beneficiary and my executor shall not seek reimbursement therefor. This Article shall not require my executor to pay any tax on a generation-skipping transfer if such tax is not a liability of my estate.

ARTICLE 5. RESIDUE OF MY ESTATE

This article is the heart of the disposition of the estate. It provides in the first paragraph for a distribution to certain people to be named in the event there are no surviving descendants, and in the second paragraph, for a distribution to the descendants if there are surviving descendants.

Although the first paragraph of the sample Will uses distribution in equal shares, many people distribute their property in disproportionate amounts, giving some people more than others. The distribution is limited to those people who survive, with the proviso that if they do not survive but leave children, their children take their share. In the event any beneficiaries are under the age of twenty-one, the article uses the phrase "deferred distribution," which is covered in Article 6 and which establishes trusts to hold the property until the beneficiary attains the age of twenty-one.

The second paragraph of Article 5 provides in the event there are surviving descendants for "one share for each then living child of mine and one share for the then living descendants, collectively, of each child of mine who is deceased." This takes care of situations where a person may have a child who is no longer living but who, in turn, had children. Those children, together—i.e., collectively—take the share of their deceased ancestor.

If at my death I have no then living descendants, all of the rest, residue and remainder of my estate shall be distributed in equal shares to the following named people who survive me; provided, however, that if anyone named does not survive me but leaves children who survive me, such surviving children shall divide the share of their parents equally outright, subject to the provisions of Article 6 below pertaining to deferred distribution for beneficiaries under the age of twenty-one: _____

_____

_____ .

If at the time of my death I do have living descendants, then all of the rest, residue and remainder of my estate shall be divided into equal shares so as to create one share for each then living child of mine and one share for the then living descendants, collectively, of each child of mine who is deceased. Each share for a living child of mine shall be distributed outright to such child and each share for the then living descendants, collectively, of each child of mine who is deceased, shall be distributed outright, per stirpes, to such descendants, except that if any such child or descendant is under the age of twenty-one, that person's share shall be placed in trust and the property in such trust shall be held and administered subject to the provisions of Article 6 below pertaining to deferred distribution for beneficiaries under the age of twenty-one.

ARTICLE 6. DEFERRED DISTRIBUTION

This article is included in order to avoid conservatorship proceedings for minors under the age of twenty-one. It is much easier to have the property held in trust and the trust power provisions in Article 10 provide much more flexibility for the management of the property. Net costs are also generally lower than conservatorship proceedings. The second section of Article 6 covers the possibility that the beneficiary for whom the trust is held may, in turn, die before the age of twenty-one and directs that the property go to the beneficiary's descendants, if any, or if none, to the brothers and sisters, and also covers the possibility that one of the brothers or sisters may be deceased and provides that in that situation,

the share goes to the descendants of that brother or sister who is deceased.

6(a) Deferred Distribution.

Whenever a provision of this Will shall specifically subject a distribution of principal or income to this section, then if such distribution is to a person under age twenty-one, the trustee shall take or retain possession thereof in a separate trust while that person is under age twenty-one and shall pay such person so much of the net income and principal of such trust as the trustee deems advisable for the care, support, maintenance, education and hospital and medical expenses of that person. When such person attains age twenty-one, the remainder of the trust shall be distributed to such person.

6(b) Death of Individual.

If a person for whom a trust is held under this Article dies before age twenty-one, any remainder of such trust shall be distributed, subject, however, to this Article, per stirpes to such person's then living descendants, and if none, then per stirpes to such person's then living brothers and sisters and the then living descendants, collectively, of each deceased brother and sister, if any, or if none, to the then living descendants, per stirpes, of my mother.

ARTICLE 7. SPENDTHRIFT PROVISIONS

This paragraph is included in order to try and insulate the trust property from the claims of any creditors and also to preclude the beneficiary from trying to sell or dispose of any interest in the trust. Technically speaking, a beneficiary under the age of twenty-one should not be able to do this, although in some states legal majority is attained prior to the age of twenty-one.

No amount of any trust may be reached in any manner by the creditors of any beneficiary, and no beneficiary shall have any power to sell, assign, transfer, encumber or in any manner to anticipate or dispose of his or her interest in the trust prior to actual distribution by the trustee to the beneficiary.

ARTICLE 8. ABSENCE OF TAKERS

This article covers situations where none of the named beneficiaries survive and leave no descendants who survive to take the property. One example is a situation where the person making the Will has one child who was eighteen at the time the Will was probated and who died before age twenty-one without any children and without any brothers or sisters. Many people designate specific friends or relatives that they desire to have as beneficiaries, in the "absence of takers" contingency. Also, specific charities are sometimes named. This is a matter of personal choice.

If before final distribution of my estate or trust estate there is no one entitled to receive benefits under any other provision of this Will, then my estate or trust estate remaining shall be distributed subject, however, to the section entitled "Deferred Distribution," in such proportions and to those then living heirs of mine determined as though I had then died intestate, a resident of the State of Iowa owning such property, but in accordance with the laws of the State of Iowa on the date of execution of this Will relating to the descent of personal property of intestate decedents.

ARTICLE 9. RULE AGAINST PERPETUITIES

This paragraph is what is known as a "savings clause" and is used in most Wills where trusts are established in order to make sure that the trusts are not invalid because of a technical rule known as the "rule against perpetuities," which limits how long a noncharitable trust can exist.

Notwithstanding any other provision of this Will to the contrary, no trust under this Will shall continue longer than nor shall any interest created under this Will vest later than twenty-one years after the death of the last surviving of myself and my children and grandchildren living at my death. The property in any trust terminated under this Article shall be distributed to the person then living who is then entitled to the income or to have it applied for his or her benefit. If there is more than one such beneficiary, the trust shall be distributed to those beneficiaries in proportion to their income interests if definite, and if their income interests are indefinite, per stirpes to those beneficiaries as are descendants of mine, or if none, to those beneficiaries in equal shares.

ARTICLE 10. POWERS OF AND PROVISIONS RELATING TO TRUSTEES

This article gives general flexible provisions to the trustees to manage the property and gives rules for what happens when there is more than one trustee. The sample form specifies that no bond is required of any trustee, and this is a decision that people should discuss with their attorney. The second paragraph covers situations where there are closely owned businesses and gives flexibility to enable a trustee to serve as an officer or in another official capacity for the business. The fifth paragraph allows people dealing with the trustee not to have to inquire whether or not the transaction was valid. The subparagraphs include provisions that enable the trustee to have the flexibility to buy and sell marketable securities. There are provisions to allow the trustee to borrow money from a bank, if needed, to vote proxies, and to hold assets in "bearer" name to avoid complications in transferring title back and forth. There are flexible provisions allowing payment of distributions of income and principal as well as payment of costs and expenses. If there are several trusts, the trustee can manage them together as one trust, while dividing the income proportionately among the beneficiaries. There are provisions to allow the continuance of any business and other provisions to give the trustee flexibility in management without being concerned about potential litigation because a business was continued instead of sold. The key standard of care is in subparagraph (b), which is known as the "prudent person" rule, which declares that the trustee must exercise the judgment and care that people of prudence exercise in the management of their own affairs.

Each trustee is a distributee and need not qualify with or make any reports to any court. No trustee named in this Will need post bond.

A trustee may act in any official capacity for any business enterprise, any interest in which is owned (directly or indirectly) by the trust, and may receive compensation therefrom, and shall not be accountable to the trust or any beneficiary therefor. A trustee having an adverse interest to the trust or any beneficiary shall not be subject to removal solely on that account.

Whenever any person or corporation is acting as sole trustee, the action of the sole trustee shall bind the trust and whenever there is more than one trustee, the action of a majority of the trustees shall bind the trust. A trustee may delegate to the other trustee or trustees the exercise of any or all powers, discretionary or otherwise, and revoke any such delegation at will. Any of the powers so delegated may be exercised by the other trustee or trustees, with the same effect as if the delegating trustee had personally joined in such exercise. Each trustee shall be responsible only for his own willful neglect, default or misconduct.

Any trustee power may be disclaimed or released in whole or in part.

No person dealing with the trustee shall be bound to see to the application of trust property, or to inquire into the power or authority of the trustee, or into the validity, expediency or propriety of any action or transaction entered into by the trustee.

The trustee may do any act advisable in a fiduciary capacity for the administration of each trust. In extension of any power, right or discretion otherwise possessed said trustee shall have, without notice to or approval of any court or person, the following powers:

(a) To retain any asset which I own, even though it leaves a disproportionately large part of my assets invested in one type of property, and to sell, exchange, mortgage, lease or otherwise dispose of any asset, real or personal, upon such terms as the trustee deems advisable whether within or extending beyond the term of the trust and to receive from any source additional properties acceptable to the trustee.

(b) To acquire, invest, reinvest, exchange, sell and manage trust assets, exercising the judgment and care which persons of prudence, discretion and intelligence exercise in the management of their own affairs, not in regard to speculation but in regard to the permanent disposition of their funds, considering the probable income and safety of their capital. Within that standard, my trustee may acquire and retain every kind of property, specifically including corporate obligations, stocks and common trust funds operated by any corporate trustee, which persons of prudence, discretion and intelligence acquire or retain for their own account.

(c) To borrow money from the commercial department of any corporate trustee, or elsewhere, for the protection, preservation or improvement of any asset.

(d) To collect, receive and receipt for principal or income and to enforce, defend against, prosecute, compromise or settle any claim by or against the trust.

(e) To vote, execute proxies to vote and any other rights incident to the ownership of trust properties.

(f) To hold assets in bearer form or in the name of the trustee, or trustee's nominee, without disclosing any fiduciary relationship; provided, however, that all trust assets shall so appear on the books of the trustee.

(g) To make division or distribution in whole or in part in money, securities or other property, and in undivided interests therein, and to hold any remaining undivided interest. In any division or distribution, the trustee's judgment concerning the propriety thereof and the valuation of the properties concerned shall be binding and conclusive on all persons.

(h) To make payments (including distributions of personal property, if any) to or for the benefit of any beneficiary (including any beneficiary under any legal disability) either: (1) directly to the beneficiary; or (2) to the legal or natural guardian of the beneficiary; or (3) to anyone who has custody and care of the beneficiary; or (4) to, in the case of a minor, a custodian to be selected by the fiduciary under the Uniform Transfers to Minors Act. The trustee need not see to the application of the funds so paid, but the receipt of the person to whom paid shall be full acquittance to the trustee.

(i) To pay all expenses, taxes and charges incurred in administration of any trust, and to determine as a fiduciary what is principal and income of any trust.

(j) To employ attorneys, accountants and other agents whose services may be required.

(k) To hold the assets of the several trusts as a single fund for joint investment and management without physical segregation, dividing the income proportionately among them.

(l) To receive reasonable compensation for trustee's services.

(m) To continue, either as a going concern or for purposes of liquidation, without liability for errors in judgment, any business which I own or in which I am financially interested, for as long as trustee deems advisable and for any legal purpose and to exercise with respect to the management, sale or liquidation of any such business or business interest all powers which I could have exercised during my lifetime.

ARTICLE 11. EXECUTOR

This article grants the executor the powers of the trustees to enable the executor to deal with the assets of the estate. In particular, this can be important where the assets include real estate because it gives the executor the right to sell the real estate. The article also specifies that no bond is required. This should be discussed with your attorney.

I grant my executor all powers granted my trustee under the Article entitled "Powers of Trustees," all of which shall be in addition to those which my executor otherwise would have.

No executor named in this Will need post bond.

ARTICLE 12. CHANGE OF TRUSTEE AND SUCCESSOR TRUSTEES

This article covers situations where trustees are unwilling or unable to serve and provides that successor trustees have the same power and also provides for no bond. This should be discussed with your attorney.

Except where a successor has been designated under the section entitled "Trustee," each trustee, while acting as trustee, may by written instrument, revocable at any time prior to the installment of the successor trustee, designate a successor and/or provide for the method of appointment of a successor and the terms and conditions of such successor's service. If a trustee is unable or unwilling to serve and has not so designated or provided, the remaining trustee or trustees may either fill any such vacancy or serve alone, as they determine.

Every successor trustee shall upon taking office be vested with and subject to all the rights, powers, authorities, duties and obligations herein conferred and imposed upon the trustee without any transfer or conveyance of the trust property.

Any successor trustee need not post bond, unless the appointing person shall so require, and the approval of any court or person of the appointment shall not be required. The former trustee and the successor trustee shall exchange such accountings, receipts and documents as shall be reasonably required by either of them.

ARTICLE 13. NO GUARDIAN AD LITEM

No guardian ad litem or similar proceedings shall be required, and my executor and trustee shall be released from liability for acts occurring during a period for which they have received written approval of the then adult beneficiaries or of the court upon notice or waiver of notice to the then adult beneficiaries, or, in the case of a trust, for which period it has furnished a report and accounting to the adult beneficiaries if no such beneficiaries notify the trustee in writing of disapproval of such report and accounting within ninety days thereof.

ARTICLE 14. TERMINATION OF SMALL TRUST

This article allows there to be a termination of a trust if it is so small that it becomes economically unwise to administer or if for any other reason it is appropriate to terminate the trust.

If a trust shall, in the judgment of the trustee, be or become reduced in size, so that the administration thereof is not in the best interest of the beneficiaries, the trustee may, but need not, terminate such trust. If the trustee terminates any trust, the property held therein shall be distributed to such persons determined as if the trust were terminated under the Article entitled "Rule Against Perpetuities."

ARTICLE 15. USE OF TERMS

This article has miscellaneous provisions, including the designation of "per stirpes" rather than "per capita" distribution of property (see Chapter 4), and also covers adoptive children. There are conditions where a natural child has been adopted by someone else, and this is also covered in the sample form. However, these are matters that should be discussed with your own attorney.

The provisions of this Will, including the provisions of this Article, shall be supplemented by and when necessary shall be subject to the following:

(a) Each singular expression shall include the plural, and plural expressions shall include the singular, and the context of this instrument shall be read accordingly when the facts require it.

(b) "Trustee" shall refer to the trustee or trustees in office and shall include a successor trustee or trustees, whether so expressed or not.

(c) Whenever the phrase "per stirpes" is used, such phrase shall mean "per stirpes and not per capita."

(d) Whenever this Will provides for a distribution to or a division into shares for a person or persons described as "then living," such phrase shall mean those persons living at the time of my death if such distribution or division is from my probate estate, and shall mean those persons living at the time of the termination of the immediately preceding interest in the trust, if such distribution or division is from a funded trust.

(e) Whenever the term "parent," "child," "grandchild," "descendant" or "ancestor" is used, then for purposes of determining whether a person is a parent, child, grandchild, descendant or ancestor:

(1) An individual (including individuals other than such person) who has been adopted shall be deemed a child of the adoptive parent or parents.

(2) Except as provided in clause (4) below, an individual (including individuals other than such person) shall be deemed a child of his or her natural mother.

(3) Except as provided in clause (4) below, an individual (including individuals other than such person) shall be deemed a child of his or her natural father if his or her natural parents were at any time married to each other at law or at common law or if the paternity of the natural father was proven during the father's lifetime, or if the child was recognized by the father as his child if such recognition was either general and notorious or in writing.

(4) Notwithstanding the foregoing, an individual (including individuals other than such person) shall not be deemed a child of a natural parent: (A) If adopted during the life of that natural parent and if the parental rights of that natural parent were terminated in connection with such adoption proceedings; or (B) If adopted after the death of that natural parent unless, prior to the relevant division or distribution, the adoptive identity of such individual and such natural parenthood are actually known by my executor, by my trustee, or by any person (or by his or her guardian) whose share or beneficial interest in such division or distribution would be affected by such determination.

IN WITNESS WHEREOF, I have signed before the undersigned witnesses and declare this instrument consisting of _____ pages to be my Last Will and Testament.

Dated this _____ day of _____, 19 _____.

_____

Jennifer L. Stewart

On this _____ day of _____, 19 _____ , the above-named testator of the aforesaid County and State of Iowa, first exhibiting and declaring the foregoing instrument consisting of _____ pages, inclusive of this witness clause, to be such testator's Last Will and Testament and asking us to witness the execution thereof signed such testator's initials on the margin of the first to the last page, both inclusive of said instrument, in our presence, and signed such testator's name as it appears above at the end of said foregoing instrument in our presence; and as witnesses thereof, we, the undersigned, do now, at such testator's request, in the presence of such testator and in the presence of each other, hereunto subscribe our names and addresses, this clause having been first read to or by us, and we having noted and hereby certifying that the matters herein stated took place in fact and in the order herein stated.

NAME   ADDRESS

_____   _____

_____   _____

Appendix B

Example of a Basic Will for a Married Couple (with or without Children) with a Combined Estate of Less Than $600,000, with a Contingent Trust in the Event the Spouse Does Not Survive

Last Will and Testament
of
James L. Saunders

Executed the _____ day of _____, 19 _____

Table of Contents

Last Will and Testament
of
James L. Saunders

The sample Will for the fictitious person named "James L. Saunders" is for a married person who may or may not have children.

The heart of the Will is Article 5, which leaves everything outright to a spouse, if a spouse survives, but if not, the property is held in trust for any children with one-half of the principal distributed as each child attains the age of thirty and the other half at age thirty-five. In the meantime, the income and principal can be used to provide for the proper care, support, and maintenance of the child. In the event a child dies before age thirty-five, the property goes to her or his descendants, if any, or if none, to the other children and their descendants, if any. If no descendants survive and no spouse survives, under Article 8 one-half of the property goes to the heirs of James L. Saunders and the other half goes to the heirs of his wife.

There are typical provisions similar to those of the Jennifer L. Stewart Will, including the direction to pay inheritance taxes from the estate, rather than from beneficiaries (Article 4), provisions for a deferred distribution if a beneficiary is under the age of twenty-one (Article 6), spendthrift protection (Article 7), absence of takers (Article 8), rule against perpetuities savings clause (Article 9), provisions for flexible powers for trustees (Article 10), similar power provisions for the executor (Article 11), provisions for successor trustees (Article 12), provisions to avoid guardianship proceedings (Article 13), provisions for termination of a small trust (Article 14), and definition provisions, including those for adopted children (Article 15).

I, James L. Saunders, of _____ County, Iowa, being of sound mind and memory, declare this my Last Will and Testament, and revoke all my former Wills or testamentary instruments.

ARTICLE 1. DEFINITIONS AND APPOINTMENTS

The provisions of this Will shall be supplemented by and, when necessary, subject to this Article.

1(a) Spouse.

Julia J. Saunders.

1(b) Executor.

I hereby appoint my spouse and XYZ Bank as executors. If my spouse is unable or unwilling to serve, XYZ Bank shall serve alone.

1(c) Trustee.

I hereby appoint XYZ Bank trustee of each trust under this Will.

ARTICLE 2. EXPENSES, DEBTS, AND LIFE INSURANCE

I authorize my executor to pay all my expenses of last illness and burial, and next to pay all my just debts, requiring the filing and proof of any claim in its discretion; provided, however, that this Article shall not subject any of my exempt property to the requirements thereof, unless my executor waives any exemption.

ARTICLE 3. SPECIFIC BEQUESTS

3(a) Personal Property.

If my spouse survives me, I bequeath to my spouse all personal automobiles, household furniture and furnishings, and other articles of domestic use or ornament which I own at my death. If my spouse does not survive me, such property shall be distributed equally to my then living children, or sold and the proceeds disposed of under the remaining Articles of this Will, as my executor shall determine.

My executor shall, if my spouse does not survive me, make any such distribution as fairly as possible, but in all events, my executor shall resolve any disagreement and shall determine whether the property be sold or distributed and the method of distribution.

3(b) Memorandum of Disposition.

Notwithstanding the preceding section I direct that my executor and beneficiaries abide by any dated memorandum in my handwriting or signed by me which I leave indicating that a certain person should receive a specific article or articles of tangible personal property.

ARTICLE 4. PAYMENT OF TAXES

All inheritance, estate or other similar taxes against my estate or the recipients thereof, including any taxes arising from the transfer or receipt of assets not part of my probate estate, shall be paid from my estate after complying with the foregoing bequests of this Will. Such taxes shall not be charged against any beneficiary and my executor shall not seek reimbursement therefor. This Article shall not require my executor to pay any tax on a generation-skipping transfer if such tax is not a liability of my estate.

ARTICLE 5. RESIDUE OF MY ESTATE

All the rest, residue and remainder of my estate shall pass outright to my spouse, if my spouse survives me, and, if not, shall be divided into equal trusts to create one trust for each then living child of mine and one trust for the then living descendants, collectively, of each child of mine who is deceased. Each such trust shall be held and administered as follows:

(a) With respect to each trust, if any, for a then living child of mine:

(1) As such child attains age thirty, that child shall receive one-half in value of that child's trust; and as such child attains age thirty-five, that child shall receive the remainder of the trust. If a child dies before age thirty-five, the remainder of the trust shall be distributed, subject, however, to the section entitled "Deferred Distribution," per stirpes to that child's then living descendants, if any, or if none, then per stirpes to my then living children and the then living descendants, collectively, of any deceased child of mine.

(2) Until complete distribution of a trust, the trustee may pay such child such sums from the net income and principal of the trust as the trustee deems advisable after giving consideration to any other funds known to said trustee to be available to

such child, to provide for that child's proper care, support, maintenance, education and hospital and medical expenses.

(b) With respect to each trust, if any, for the then living descendants, collectively, of a child of mine who is deceased, that trust shall be distributed, subject, however, to the section entitled "Deferred Distribution," per stirpes to such descendants.

ARTICLE 6. DEFERRED DISTRIBUTION

6(a) Deferred Distribution.

Whenever a provision of this Will shall specifically subject a distribution of principal or income to this section, then if such distribution is to a person under age twenty-one, the trustee shall take or retain possession thereof in a separate trust while that person is under age twenty-one, and shall pay such person so much of the net income and principal of such trust as the trustee deems advisable for the care, support, maintenance, education and hospital and medical expenses of that person. When such person attains age twenty-one, the remainder of the trust shall be distributed to such person.

6(b) Death of Individual.

If a person for whom a trust is held under this Article dies before age twenty-one, any remainder of such trust shall be distributed, subject, however, to this Article, per stirpes to such person's then living descendants, and if none, then per stirpes to such person's then living brothers and sisters and the then living descendants, collectively, of each deceased brother and sister, if any, or if none, to my then living descendants per stirpes.

ARTICLE 7. SPENDTHRIFT PROVISIONS

No amount of any trust may be reached in any manner by the creditors of any beneficiary, and no beneficiary shall have any power to sell, assign, transfer, encumber or in any manner to anticipate or dispose of his or her interest in the trust prior to actual distribution by the trustee to the beneficiary.

ARTICLE 8. ABSENCE OF TAKERS

If before final distribution of my estate or trust estate there is no one entitled to receive benefits under any other provision of this Will, then my estate or trust estate remaining shall be divided and distributed, subject, however, to the section entitled "Deferred Distribution" as follows: One share consisting of 50% shall be distributed in such proportions and to those then living heirs of mine determined as though I had then died intestate, a resident of the State of Iowa owning such percent of such property, and one share consisting of 50% shall be distributed in such proportions and to those then living heirs of my spouse determined as though my spouse had then died intestate, a resident of the State of Iowa owning such percent of such property, in all cases in accordance with the laws of the State of Iowa on the date of execution of this Will relating to the descent of personal property of intestate decedents.

ARTICLE 9. RULE AGAINST PERPETUITIES

Notwithstanding any other provision of this Will to the contrary, no trust under this Will shall continue longer than nor shall any interest created under this Will vest later than twenty-one years after the death of the last surviving of myself and my children and grandchildren living at my death. The property in any trust terminated under this Article shall be distributed to the person then living who is then entitled to the income or to have it applied for his or her benefit. If there is more than one such beneficiary, the trust shall be distributed to those beneficiaries in proportion to their income interests if definite, and if their income interests are indefinite, per stirpes to those beneficiaries as are descendants of mine, or if none, to those beneficiaries in equal shares.

ARTICLE 10. POWERS OF AND PROVISIONS RELATING TO TRUSTEES

Each trustee is a distributee and need not qualify with or make any reports to any court. No trustee named in this Will need post bond.

A trustee may act in any official capacity for any business enterprise, any interest in which is owned (directly or indirectly) by the trust, and may receive compensation therefrom, and shall not be accountable to the trust or any beneficiary therefor. A trustee having an adverse interest to the trust or any beneficiary shall not be subject to removal solely on that account.

Whenever any person or corporation is acting as sole trustee, the action of the sole trustee shall bind the trust and whenever there is more than one trustee, the action of a majority of the trustees shall bind the trust. A trustee may delegate to the other trustee or trustees the exercise of any or all powers, discretionary or otherwise, and revoke any such delegation at will. Any of the powers so delegated may be exercised by the other trustee or trustees, with the same effect as if the delegating trustee had personally joined in such exercise. Each trustee shall be responsible only for his own willful neglect, default or misconduct.

Any trustee power may be disclaimed or released in whole or in part.

No person dealing with the trustee shall be bound to see to the application of trust property, or to inquire into the power or authority of the trustee, or into the validity, expediency or propriety of any action or transaction entered into by the trustee.

The trustee may do any act advisable in a fiduciary capacity for the administration of each trust. In extension of any power, right or discretion otherwise possessed said trustee shall have, without notice to or approval of any court or person, the following powers:

(a) To retain any asset which I own, even though it leaves a disproportionately large part of my assets invested in one type of property, and to sell, exchange, mortgage, lease or otherwise dispose of any asset, real or personal, upon such terms as the trustee deems advisable whether within or extending beyond the term of the trust and to receive from any source additional properties acceptable to the trustee.

(b) To acquire, invest, reinvest, exchange, sell and manage trust assets, exercising the judgment and care which persons of prudence, discretion and intelligence exercise in the management of their own affairs, not in regard to speculation but in regard to the permanent disposition of their funds, considering the probable income and safety of their capital. Within that standard, my trustee may acquire and retain every kind of property, specifically including corporate obligations, stocks and common trust funds operated by any corporate trustee, which persons of prudence, discretion and intelligence acquire or retain for their own account.

(c) To borrow money from the commercial department of any corporate trustee, or elsewhere, for the protection, preservation or improvement of any asset.

(d) To collect, receive and receipt for principal or income and to enforce, defend against, prosecute, compromise or settle any claim by or against the trust.

(e) To vote, execute proxies to vote and any other rights incident to the ownership of trust properties.

(f) To hold assets in bearer form or in the name of the trustee, or trustee's nominee, without disclosing any fiduciary relationship; provided, however, that all trust assets shall so appear on the books of the trustee.

(g) To make division or distribution in whole or in part in money, securities or other property, and in undivided interests therein, and to hold any remaining undivided interest. In any division or distribution, the trustee's judgment concerning the propriety thereof and the valuation of the properties concerned shall be binding and conclusive on all persons.

(h) To make payments (including distributions of personal property, if any) to or for the benefit of any beneficiary (including any beneficiary under any legal disability) either: (1) directly to the beneficiary; or (2) to the legal or natural guardian of the beneficiary; or (3) to anyone who has custody and care of the beneficiary; or (4) to, in the case of a minor, a custodian to be selected by the fiduciary under the Uniform Transfers to Minors Act. The trustee need not see to the application of the funds so paid, but the receipt of the person to whom paid shall be full acquittance to the trustee.

(i) To pay all expenses, taxes and charges incurred in administration of any trust, and to determine as a fiduciary what is principal and income of any trust.

(j) To employ attorneys, accountants and other agents whose services may be required.

(k) To hold the assets of the several trusts as a single fund for joint investment and management without physical segregation, dividing the income proportionately among them.

(l) To receive reasonable compensation for trustee's services.

(m) To continue, either as a going concern or for purposes of liquidation, without liability for errors in judgment, any business which I own or in which I am financially interested, for as long as trustee deems advisable and for any legal purpose and to exercise with respect to the management, sale or liquidation of any such business or business interest all powers which I could have exercised during my lifetime.

ARTICLE 11. EXECUTOR

I grant my executor all powers granted my trustee under the Article entitled "Powers of Trustees," all of which shall be in addition to those which my executor otherwise would have.

No executor named in this Will need post bond.

ARTICLE 12. CHANGE OF TRUSTEE AND SUCCESSOR TRUSTEES

Each trustee, while acting as trustee, may by written instrument, revocable at any time prior to the installment of the successor trustee, designate a successor and/or provide for the method of appointment of a successor and the terms and conditions of such successor's service. If a trustee is unable or unwilling to serve and has not so designated or provided, the remaining trustee or trustees may either fill any such vacancy or serve alone as they determine.

Every successor trustee shall upon taking office be vested with and subject to all the rights, powers, authorities, duties and obligations herein conferred and imposed upon the trustee without any transfer or conveyance of the trust property.

Any successor trustee need not post bond, unless the appointing person shall so require, and the approval of any court or person of the appointment shall not be required. The former trustee and the successor trustee shall exchange such accountings, receipts and documents as shall be reasonably required by either of them.

ARTICLE 13. NO GUARDIAN AD LITEM

No guardian ad litem or similar proceedings shall be required, and my executor and trustee shall be released from liability for acts occurring during a period for which they have received written approval of the then adult beneficiaries or of the court upon notice or waiver of notice to the then adult beneficiaries, or, in the case of a trust, for which period it has furnished a report and accounting to the adult beneficiaries if no such beneficiaries notify the trustee in writing of disapproval of such report and accounting within ninety days thereof.

ARTICLE 14. TERMINATION OF SMALL TRUST

If a trust shall, in the judgment of the trustee, be or become reduced in size, so that the administration thereof is not in the best interest of the beneficiaries, the trustee may, but need not, terminate such trust. If the trustee terminates any trust, the property held therein shall be distributed to such persons determined as if the trust were terminated under the Article entitled "Rule Against Perpetuities."

ARTICLE 15. USE OF TERMS

The provisions of this Will, including the provisions of this Article, shall be supplemented by and when necessary shall be subject to the following:

(a) Each singular expression shall include the plural, and plural expressions shall include the singular, and the context of this instrument shall be read accordingly when the facts require it.

(b) "Trustee" shall refer to the trustee or trustees in office and shall include a successor trustee or trustees, whether so expressed or not.

(c) Whenever the phrase "per stirpes" is used, such phrase shall mean "per stirpes and not per capita."

(d) Whenever this Will provides for a distribution to or a division into shares for a person or persons described as "then living," such phrase shall mean those persons living at the time of my death if such distribution or division is from my probate estate, and shall mean those persons living at the time of the termination of the immediately preceding interest in the trust, if such distribution or division is from a funded trust.

(e) Whenever the term "parent," "child," "grandchild," "descendant" or "ancestor" is used, then for purposes of determining whether a person is a parent, child, grandchild, descendant or ancestor:

(1) An individual (including individuals other than such person) who has been adopted shall be deemed a child of the adoptive parent or parents.

(2) Except as provided in clause (4) below, an individual (including individuals other than such person) shall be deemed a child of his or her natural mother.

(3) Except as provided in clause (4) below, an individual (including individuals other than such person) shall be deemed a child of his or her natural father if his or her natural parents were at any time married to each other at law or at common law or if the paternity of the natural father was proven during the father's lifetime, or if the child was recognized by the father as his child if such recognition was either general and notorious or in writing.

(4) Notwithstanding the foregoing, an individual (including individuals other than such person) shall not be deemed a child of a natural parent: (A) If adopted during the life of that natural parent and if the parental rights of that natural parent were terminated in connection with such adoption proceedings; or (B) If adopted after the death of that natural parent unless, prior to the relevant division or distribution, the adoptive identity of such individual and such natural parenthood are actually known by my executor, by my trustee, or by any person (or by his or her guardian) whose share or beneficial interest in such division or distribution would be affected by such determination.

IN WITNESS WHEREOF, I have signed before the undersigned witnesses and declare this instrument consisting of _____ pages to be my Last Will and Testament.

Dated this _____ day of _____, 19 ____.

_____
James L. Saunders

On this _____ day of _____, 19 ____, the above-named testator of the aforesaid County and State of Iowa, first exhibiting and declaring the foregoing instrument consisting of ____ pages, inclusive of this witness clause, to be such testator's Last Will and Testament and asking us to witness the execution thereof signed such testator's initials on the margin of the first to the last page, both inclusive of said instrument, in our presence, and signed such testator's name as it appears above at the end of said foregoing instrument in our presence; and as witnesses thereof, we, the undersigned, do now, at such testator's request, in the presence of such testator and in the presence of each other, hereunto subscribe our names and addresses, this clause having been first read to or by us, and we having noted and hereby certifying that the matters herein stated took place in fact and in the order herein stated.

NAME   ADDRESS

_____   _____

_____   _____

Appendix C

**Example of a Marital Deduction Living Trust with Power
of Appointment Provisions for Married People with
Combined Estates of Over $600,000 and Less Than
$1,000,000 (Including Home, Life Insurance, and
Retirement Plans)**

*Trust Agreement of the
Jane L. Smith
Living Trust*

Executed the _____day of _____, 19 _____

Table of Contents

Trust Agreement of the
Jane L. Smith
Living Trust

The sample living trust for the fictitious person named "Jane L. Smith" is for a married person who has children. Jane L. Smith is the settlor who created the trust and she and her husband are the trustees, and on the death of "Jane L. Smith" a bank becomes a co-trustee. During Jane's lifetime, the heart of the trust instrument is in Section 3(a), which provides that she will receive such sums from the net income and principal as the trustee (one of whom is Jane) deems advisable for her proper care, support, and maintenance or as she may request. Article 15 expressly provides that the trust is revocable and that the settlor (Jane) may revoke the trust or alter or amend any term of the trust instrument. On Jane's death, the trust becomes irrevocable and operates in the same manner as a Will. There are provisions for distribution of personal property (Section 3(b)(2)), distribution of the house to the living trust of her spouse, if he survives (Section 3(b)(3)), and a direction that the balance of the living trust be distributed under the remaining articles of the living trust instrument. The principal provisions that apply at the settlor's death are Articles 4 and 5, which establish a marital trust, and Articles 7 and 8, which establish a residuary family trust. The amount of the family trust, assuming there has been no prior use of the unified credit, is the first $600,000 of net property. The marital trust is any amount in excess of this. Together this would insulate the entire estate from federal estate taxes.

If the spouse survives and the estate is more than $600,000, so that there is a marital trust, Section 5(b) provides that all of the net income from the marital trust will go to the settlor's spouse and, in addition, whatever principal is necessary to provide for proper care, support, and maintenance can be used, and on the death of the surviving spouse, any remaining property shall go to the family trust. If either there is no surviving spouse or the estate is less than $600,000, there is no marital trust.

The provisions of the family trust provide that the trustee has discretion to pay sums of income and principal to the surviving spouse and to any child or children as are necessary to provide for their proper care, support, and

286

maintenance. Optional language specifies that the spouse is to be preferred. On the death of the surviving spouse the property is divided into equal shares for each child (plus a share, collectively, for the descendants of any child who is not then living). Each trust is a generation-skipping trust that continues during the life of the child. During the child's lifetime, the trustee has discretion to distribute income and principal to the child as necessary for the child's proper care, support, and maintenance and, in addition, when the child attains the age of thirty, the child has a right to receive $5,000 or 5 percent of the value of the principal of the trust each year, whichever is greater, in the child's sole discretion. On the death of the child, there is a special power of appointment that gives the child the right to appoint the property to any one or more of the descendants of Jane L. Smith. If that power of appointment is not exercised, then the property automatically will be distributed to that child's descendants, if any, or if none, to the other lawful descendants of Jane L. Smith.

The remaining portions of the trust instrument have standard powers similar to the provisions of the James L. Saunders Will, except provisions for deferring distribution until age thirty-five (under Section 9(b)). There are additional articles allowing for transfer of additional property to the living trust (Article 14), specifying that the trust during the lifetime of Jane L. Smith can be revoked (Article 15), provisions relating to the exercise of the powers of appointment granted to the children (Article 17), broader provisions for changing of trustees and successor trustees (Article 18), provisions pertaining to insurance proceeds (Article 20), broader powers for the termination of a small trust in light of the federal estate tax laws (Article 21), and the priority of invading principal for the surviving spouse so that the marital trust is exhausted first (Article 22). The absence of takers clause (Article 11) divides the property equally between the wife's heirs and the husband's heirs.

THIS AGREEMENT entered into this _____ day of _____, 19 _____, by and between Jane L. Smith as settlor and Jane L. Smith and John L. Smith as trustee.

ARTICLE 1. DEFINITIONS AND APPOINTMENTS

The provisions of this trust shall be supplemented by and, when necessary, subject to this Article.

1(a) Name of Trust.

This trust shall be known generally as the "Jane L. Smith Living Trust," provided, however, any separate trust or share set aside hereunder may be known by such other name as provided for such trust or share herein.

1(b) Settlor's Spouse.

John L. Smith.

1(c) Trustee.

The original trustee shall be Jane L. Smith and John L. Smith. Upon the death of the settlor, the trustee shall be John L. Smith and XYZ Bank.

1(d) Trust Property.

The trust property or estate shall comprise the property hereinafter described and any other property which may hereafter be brought within the terms of this trust by gift, assignment, conveyance, transfer, purchase, devise, bequest or otherwise; and all substitutions for any of said property, which may be made by the trustee under the powers herein conferred, and the income to arise from all of the above.

1(e) Marital Bequest.

The bequest provided for the benefit of the settlor's spouse under the Article entitled the "Marital Deduction."

1(f) Marital Trust.

The separate trust or trusts created under the Article entitled "Disposition of Marital Bequest."

1(g) Family Trust.

The separate trust or trusts created under the Article entitled the "Family Trust."

ARTICLE 2. TRANSFER TO TRUST

The settlor does hereby by the execution and delivery of this instrument to the trustee sell, assign, transfer and deliver to trustee and trustee's successors in trust the following property, to wit:

As per Schedule A attached hereto and made a part
hereof

To have and to hold the same together with any other trust property during the term of the trust for the use and benefit of the persons herein set forth, for the purposes and uses and upon the trust terms and conditions herein set forth, and the trustee does hereby by the execution of this instrument accept the trusteeship hereunder.

ARTICLE 3. LIFE OF AND DEATH OF SETTLOR

3(a) Life of Settlor.

During the settlor's life, the trustee shall pay the settlor such sums from the net income and principal as the trustee deems advisable for the settlor's proper care, support, maintenance, hospital and medical expenses and also such sums as may be requested by the settlor from time to time.

3(b) Death of Settlor.

Upon the settlor's death, the trustee shall continue to hold all of the trust assets, as then constituted, including any property which may be added to the trust by the settlor's Last Will and Testament, which assets shall be administered and distributed subject to the following:

(1) The trustee shall pay all of the settlor's expenses of last illness and burial, and next shall pay all of the settlor's just debts, subject to the filing and proof of any claim in the discretion of the settlor's executor; provided, however, that this Article shall not subject any of the settlor's exempt property to the requirements thereof, unless the settlor's executor waives any exemption.

Proceeds of insurance on the settlor's life shall not be used for the above purposes except to the extent that other assets of the trust estate are insufficient, and in no event shall any asset not includable in the settlor's gross estate for federal estate tax purposes be used for such purposes. The trustee may make such payments directly or may make the payments to the executor of the settlor's estate.

(2) The trustee shall distribute to the settlor's spouse, if such spouse survives the settlor, all personal automobiles, household furniture and furnishings, and other articles of domestic use or ornament held in trust at the settlor's death. If the settlor's spouse has established a living trust, such distribution shall be made directly to such trust. If the settlor's spouse does not survive the settlor, such property shall be distributed equally to the settlor's then living children. If any of the settlor's children are not then living, the then living children of each such deceased child shall take the share of their parent.

If the settlor's spouse does not survive the settlor, and if the then living children and/or the then living children of a deceased child or children are unable to agree upon division of the above property, the trustee shall place a value on each item thereof. Thereafter, each child shall alternately select the items he or she desires (except that if any child of the settlor shall not then be living and shall leave children surviving, any spouse of said deceased child may select on behalf of said children, or if the spouse of a deceased child is not competent or living, the guardian of said children shall make the choice, or the children themselves, collectively, may make the choice if they are all adults), and when a child has selected items having an aggregate value of one share, the child shall have no further right of selection. The order of selection shall be determined by lot.

The items not selected by the above method shall be sold and the net proceeds shall be divided so that the cash plus the items selected by a child will total in value one equal share. The trustee shall have authority to group a number of related items and thus determine what shall constitute a single selection.

Notwithstanding the preceding paragraph, the trustee and any beneficiaries of this trust shall abide by any dated memorandum in the settlor's handwriting or signed by the settlor indicating that a certain person should receive a specific article or articles of tangible personal property.

(3) The trustee shall distribute to the settlor's spouse, if the settlor's spouse survives the settlor, any homestead or interest

therein held in trust at the settlor's death, including any lands adjacent thereto and used as a part thereof. If the settlor's spouse has established a living trust, such distribution shall be made directly to such trust.

(4) The balance of the trust estate shall be administered and distributed pursuant to the following provisions of this instrument.

ARTICLE 4. MARITAL DEDUCTION

4(a) Marital Deduction Bequest.

If the settlor's spouse survives the settlor, the trustee shall set aside for the benefit of the settlor's spouse, property to be held as set forth in the following Article, equal in value to the maximum federal estate tax marital deduction, less the aggregate amount of marital deduction, if any, allowable for property which passes or has passed to the settlor's spouse otherwise than under this Article; provided, however, that the amount of such bequest shall be reduced by the amount, if any, required to increase the settlor's taxable estate to the maximum amount that, considering the unified credit and the state death tax credit (except to the extent the use of such latter credit increases the state death taxes payable), will result in no federal estate tax payable.

4(b) Computation of Amount of Marital Bequest.

In determining the marital bequest, the final determinations and valuations for federal estate tax purposes shall control and property allocated in satisfaction of the marital bequest shall be valued at its value as finally determined for such purposes. Appropriate adjustments shall be made for all encumbrances on property passing to the settlor's spouse to ensure that the settlor's spouse receives the amount of the marital bequest.

4(c) Selection of Property to Satisfy Marital Bequest.

The trustee shall select the property to satisfy the marital bequest within the limitations of this Article.

4(d) Property Allocable to Satisfy Marital Bequest.

In no event shall any property or the proceeds of any property which would not qualify for the federal estate tax marital deduction be allocated to satisfy the marital bequest and in all events, in satisfying the marital bequest, property shall be allocated having an aggregate value fairly representative of the appreciation or depreciation in value from the date of estate tax valuation to each date of allocation of all property then available for allocation.

4(e) Distributions in Satisfaction of Marital Bequest.

Before final determinations and valuations in federal estate tax proceedings are had, the trustee may make distributions in satisfaction of the marital bequest upon estimates of values made by the trustee, subject to revision upon the final determinations, and in case of under or over distributions, the trustee and any distributee shall make all necessary adjustments and transfers or retransfers.

4(f) Disclaimer of Marital Bequest.

If the settlor's spouse (or the executor of the settlor's spouse) disclaims all or any portion of the marital bequest, such amount disclaimed shall be added to the Family Trust. If any provision of said Family Trust is inconsistent with a qualified disclaimer for federal estate and/or gift tax purposes, then such provision shall not be applied to the amount disclaimed, and the trustee shall, unless such inconsistent provision is also disclaimed, segregate the amount disclaimed in a separate trust, the provisions of which, except for such inconsistent provisions, shall be the same as the provisions of the Family Trust.

4(g) Survival of Spouse.

The settlor's spouse shall be deemed to survive the settlor for purposes of this Article if they die under such circumstances that there is no sufficient evidence that they died otherwise than simultaneously.

ARTICLE 5. DISPOSITION OF MARITAL BEQUEST

5(a) General Provisions of Marital Trust.

The property bequeathed in satisfaction of the marital bequest shall be held and administered in trust (which trust may be called by the settlor's name and the words "Marital Trust"), as provided in this Article. It is the intention of the settlor that this trust shall meet the requirements of the Internal Revenue Code so the marital deduction will be allowed with respect thereto. To accomplish this, this instrument shall be construed and this trust administered to meet such requirements, and the settlor's executor or the trustee shall make any election so required.

5(b) Life of Spouse.

During the life of the settlor's spouse:

(1) The trustee shall, commencing with the date of the settlor's death, pay all of the net income to the settlor's spouse at least annually or at more frequent intervals designated by such spouse.

(2) The trustee shall pay the settlor's spouse such sums from the principal as the trustee other than such spouse deems advisable after giving consideration to any other funds known to said trustee to be available to such spouse, to provide for the proper care, support, maintenance, hospital and medical expenses of such spouse.

5(c) Death of Spouse.

Upon the death of the settlor's spouse:

(1) The trustee shall distribute any accrued and undistributed income to the estate (or Living Trust) of such spouse.

(2) The balance of the trust, subject to the payment of the trust's pro rata share of all inheritance, estate, succession, or other similar taxes otherwise payable from such spouse's estate, or the recipients thereof, resulting from the inclusion of the trust in such spouse's estate, shall be distributed to the Family Trust.

ARTICLE 6. PAYMENT OF TAXES

All inheritance, estate or other similar taxes against the settlor's estate, this trust or the recipients of either, including any taxes arising from the transfer or receipt of assets not part of the settlor's probate estate or of this trust, shall be paid from this trust after complying with the foregoing bequests. Such taxes shall not be charged against any beneficiary and the settlor's executor and/or the trustee shall not seek reimbursement therefor, except to the extent such executor and/or the trustee shall be so entitled under

Section 2207 (relating to general powers of appointment) or section 2207A (relating to qualified terminable interest property) of the Internal Revenue Code. This Article shall not require the trustee to pay any tax on a generation-skipping transfer if such tax is not a liability of the settlor's estate.

ARTICLE 7. FAMILY TRUST

All the rest, residue and remainder of this trust (including any amount disclaimed under the section entitled "Disclaimer of Marital Bequest") shall pass in trust (which trust may be called by the settlor's name and the words "Family Trust"), to be held and administered as provided in the following Article.

ARTICLE 8. PROVISIONS OF FAMILY TRUST

8(a) Life of Spouse.

Until the death of the settlor's spouse, the trustee shall pay such spouse or any child of the settlor such sums from the net income and the principal as the trustee other than the settlor's spouse deems advisable after giving consideration to any other funds known to said trustee to be available to such spouse or such children, to provide for the proper care, support, maintenance and hospital and medical expenses of such spouse or children. In the making of any distribution the trustee shall prefer the settlor's spouse to the settlor's children.

8(b) Death of Spouse.

Upon the death of settlor's spouse, or upon the settlor's death, if the settlor's spouse predeceases the settlor, the trustee shall divide the Family Trust into equal trusts to create one trust for each then living child of the settlor and one trust for the then living descendants, collectively, of each child of the settlor who is then deceased. Each such trust shall be held and administered as follows:

   (1) With respect to each trust, if any, for a then living child of the settlor:
      (A) During the life of the child:

         (i) The trustee shall pay such child such sums from the net income and the principal as the trustee deems advisable after giving consideration to any other funds known to said trustee to be available to such child, to provide for the proper care, support, maintenance and hospital and medical expenses of such child.

(ii) The child shall have the power to invade the principal each calendar year on or after the child attains age thirty, by written direction to the trustee during such year, to pay such child amounts from the principal for such calendar year not to exceed Five Thousand Dollars or, if greater, five percent of the value of the principal at December 31 of such year. If such payment is not requested by such child for any calendar year, no payment shall be made in any subsequent calendar year on account of the amount not requested.

(B) Upon the death of the child:

(i) The trustee shall distribute the balance of the trust to or for the benefit of such one or more, exclusively of the others, of the settlor's descendants, for such estate and interests and upon such terms and in such proportions as such child may appoint by Will specifically referring to this special power of appointment.

(ii) The remainder of the trust not appointed under the preceding provision shall be distributed, subject, however, to the section entitled "Deferred Distribution," per stirpes to that child's then living descendants, if any, or if none, then per stirpes to the settlor's then living children and the then living descendants, collectively, of any deceased child of the settlor.

(2) With respect to each trust, if any, for the then living descendants, collectively, of a child of the settlor who is deceased, that trust shall be distributed, subject, however, to the section entitled "Deferred Distribution," per stirpes to such descendants.

ARTICLE 9. DEFERRED DISTRIBUTION

9(a) Deferred Distribution.

Whenever a provision of this instrument shall specifically subject a distribution of principal or income to this section, then:

(1) If such distribution is to any individual under the age of thirty-five, such property shall (except as otherwise provided in subsection [2] of this section) be held in trust as provided in section (b) of this Article; and

(2) If such distribution is to a child of the settlor for whom a separate trust of the Family Trust is being held, such property shall be added to that trust.

9(b) Deferred Distribution Trust.

If distribution of any share of a trust is deferred to any individual under age thirty-five pursuant to subsection (1) of section (a) of this Article, then:

(1) The trustee shall retain possession thereof in a separate trust while that person is under age thirty-five, and shall pay such person so much of the net income and principal of such trust as the trustee deems advisable for the care, support, maintenance, education and hospital and medical expenses of that person. When such person attains age thirty, fifty percent of the trust shall be distributed outright to such person and when such person attains age thirty-five, the remainder of the trust shall be distributed to such person.

(2) If such person dies before age thirty-five, the remainder of the trust shall be distributed, subject, however, to this Article, per stirpes to such person's then living descendants and if none, then per stirpes to such person's then living brothers and sisters and the then living descendants, collectively, of each deceased brother and sister, if any, or if none, to the settlor's then living descendants, per stirpes.

ARTICLE 10. SPENDTHRIFT PROVISIONS

No amount of any trust may be reached in any manner by the creditors of any beneficiary, and no beneficiary shall have any power to sell, assign, transfer, encumber or in any manner to anticipate or dispose of his or her interest in the trust prior to actual distribution by the trustee to the beneficiary.

ARTICLE 11. ABSENCE OF TAKERS

If before final distribution of the trust estate there is no one entitled to receive benefits under any other provision of this instrument, then the trust estate remaining shall be divided and distributed, subject, however, to the section entitled "Deferred Distribution" as follows: One share consisting of fifty percent shall be distributed in such proportions and to those then living heirs of the settlor determined as though the settlor had then died intestate, a resident of the State of Iowa owning such percent of such property, and one share consisting of fifty percent shall be distributed in such proportions and to those then living heirs of the settlor's spouse determined as though such spouse had then died intestate, a resident of the State of Iowa owning such percent of such property, in all cases in accordance with the laws of the State of Iowa on the date of execution of this instrument relating to the descent of personal property of intestate decedents.

ARTICLE 12. RULE AGAINST PERPETUITIES

Notwithstanding any other provision of this instrument to the contrary, no trust shall continue longer than nor shall any interest created under this instrument vest later than twenty-one years after the death of the last surviving of the settlor, the settlor's spouse herein named, and the children and grandchildren of the settlor living at the time of execution of this instrument. The property in any trust terminated under this Article shall be distributed to the person then living who is then entitled to the income or to have it applied for his or her benefit. If there is more than one such beneficiary the trust shall be distributed to those beneficiaries in proportion to their income interests if definite, and if their income interests are indefinite, per stirpes to those beneficiaries as are descendants of the settlor, or if none, to those beneficiaries in equal shares.

ARTICLE 13. POWERS OF AND PROVISIONS RELATING TO TRUSTEES

Each trustee is a distributee and need not qualify with or make any reports to any court. No trustee named in this instrument need post bond.

A trustee may act in any official capacity for any business enterprise, any interest in which is owned (directly or indirectly) by the trust, and may receive compensation therefrom, and shall not be accountable to the trust or any beneficiary therefor. A trustee having an adverse interest to the trust or any beneficiary shall not be subject to removal solely on that account.

Whenever any person or corporation is acting as sole trustee, the action of the sole trustee shall bind the trust, and whenever there be more than one trustee, the action of a majority of the trustees shall bind the trust. A trustee may delegate to the other trustee or trustees the exercise of any or all powers, discretionary or otherwise, and revoke any such delegation at will. Any of the powers so delegated may be exercised by the other trustee or trustees, with the same effect as if the delegating trustee had personally joined in such exercise. Each trustee shall be responsible only for his own willful neglect, default or misconduct.

Any trustee power may be disclaimed or released in whole or in part.

No person dealing with the trustee shall be bound to see to the application of trust property, or to inquire into the power or authority of the trustee, or into the validity, expediency, or propriety of any action or transaction entered into by the trustee.

The trustee may do any act advisable in a fiduciary capacity for the administration of each trust. No power shall be exercised with respect to the Marital Trust if its exercise would disqualify the trust for any federal estate tax deduction. In extension of any power, right or discretion otherwise possessed said trustee shall have, without notice to or approval of any court or person, the following powers:

(a) To retain any asset, even though it leaves a disproportionately large part of the trust invested in one type of property, and to sell, exchange, mortgage, lease or otherwise dispose of any asset, real or personal, upon such terms as the trustee deems advisable whether within or extending beyond the term of the trust and to receive from any source additional properties acceptable to the trustee. Unproductive property shall not be held in the Marital Trust unless the settlor's spouse is under no legal disability and consents thereto.

(b) To acquire, invest, reinvest, exchange, sell and manage trust assets, exercising the judgment and care which persons of prudence, discretion and intelligence exercise in the management of their own affairs, not in regard to speculation but in regard to the permanent disposition of their funds, considering the probable income and safety of their capital. Within that standard, the trustee may acquire and retain every kind of property, specifically including corporate obligations, stocks and common trust funds operated by any corporate trustee, which persons of prudence, discretion and intelligence acquire or retain for their own account.

(c) To borrow money from the commercial department of any corporate trustee, or elsewhere, for the protection, preservation or improvement of any asset.

(d) To collect, receive and receipt for principal or income and to enforce, defend against, prosecute, compromise or settle any claim by or against the trust.

(e) To vote, execute proxies to vote and any other rights incident to the ownership of trust properties.

(f) To hold assets in bearer form or in the name of the trustee, or trustee's nominee, without disclosing any fiduciary relationship; provided, however, that all trust assets shall so appear on the books of the trustee.

(g) To make division or distribution in whole or in part in money, securities or other property, and in undivided interests therein, and to hold any remaining undivided interest. In any division or distribution, the trustee's judgment concerning the propriety thereof and the valuation of the properties concerned shall be binding and conclusive on all persons, provided that the assets set aside for the marital bequest shall be valued as provided thereunder.

(h) To make payments (including distributions of personal property, if any) to or for the benefit of any beneficiary (including any beneficiary under any legal disability) either: (1) directly to the beneficiary; or (2) to the legal or natural guardian of the beneficiary; or (3) to anyone who has custody and care of the beneficiary; or (4) to, in the case of a minor, a custodian to be selected by the fiduciary under the Uniform Transfers to Minors Act. The trustee need not see to the application of the funds so paid, but the receipt of the person to whom paid shall be full acquittance to the trustee.

(i) To pay all expenses, taxes and charges incurred in administration of any trust, and to determine as a fiduciary what is principal and income of any trust.

(j) To employ attorneys, accountants and other agents whose services may be required.

(k) To hold the assets of the several trusts as a single fund for joint investment and management without physical segregation, dividing the income proportionately among them.

(l) To receive reasonable compensation for trustee's services.

(m) To continue, either as a going concern or for purposes of liquidation, without liability for errors in judgment, any business for as long as trustee deems advisable and for any legal purpose.

(n) To purchase, own and pay premiums on life insurance policies, except that insurance shall not be held in the Marital Trust unless the settlor's spouse is under no legal disability and consents thereto.

(o) To designate, in writing, any member of the settlor's family to actively participate in the management of any farm, to secure qualification of the same for any election or benefits under the Internal Revenue Code or to prevent disqualification for such benefits. The trustee may delegate any authority or responsibility to such person advisable to obtain such benefits, and is exonerated from liability for such delegation. The trustee may change or substitute such designee from time to time.

(p) Notwithstanding any other provisions of this instrument, no trustee shall have or exercise any discretionary power or authority to make any payments to or on behalf of the trustee or to distribute income or principal to or on behalf of the trustee, including any distributions to satisfy all or any part of any support obligations of the trustee.

ARTICLE 14. TRANSFER OF ADDITIONAL PROPERTY TO TRUST

The settlor may, at any time and from time to time, including any transfers under the settlor's Last Will and Testament, transfer and deliver to the trustee additional cash or other property acceptable to the trustee which shall thereupon become a part of the trust property and shall be held and disposed of by the trustee in all respects subject to the provisions of this instrument.

ARTICLE 15. TRUST REVOCABLE

This trust is intended to be and is hereby declared to be revocable during the lifetime of the settlor and the settlor may alter, amend, revoke or terminate this trust, or any of the terms hereof, in whole or in part, by an instrument in writing delivered to the trustee.

ARTICLE 16. DIRECT DISTRIBUTION TO TRUST BENEFICIARY

If under any trust any property would, upon receipt by the trustee from the settlor's executor or from the trustee of any other trust, be distributable immediately to any distributee, then such property shall not pass to the trustee but shall be distributed by said executor, or by the trustee of such other trust, directly to said distributee.

ARTICLE 17. PROVISIONS RELATING TO POWERS OF APPOINTMENT

Any power of appointment created under this instrument shall, subject to the provisions establishing such power, be subject to the following:

(a) The exercise of a power exercisable by deed shall not exhaust the power, but the same may be exercised repeatedly as to any trust property not affected by previous exercise.

(b) The trustee shall honor each exercise of a power promptly and make conveyances, transfers and payments on such interests, whether absolute or in trust, or continue to hold the same in trust, as directed by the donee of the power (the "donee").

(c) If the power be exercised by deed, said deed shall be delivered to the trustee during the donee's lifetime, and unless said deed is stated to be irrevocable, it shall be revocable by said donee by a written instrument delivered to the trustee during donee's lifetime, in which case further exercise of the power may be made by said donee; provided that any prior action taken by the trustee pursuant to an unrevoked power shall be valid and binding.

(d) The donee of a power may: appoint life estates to one or more objects of the power with remainder to others; appoint to children or more remote issue even though the parents of such appointees are living; impose lawful conditions, including spendthrift restrictions, upon any appointment; make appointments outright to an object of a power or in trust; create in any object of the power a new power to appoint, exercisable by Will or deed; establish administrative provisions for and determine the laws of what state are to govern any trust created by the exercise of a power.

(e) No donee of a power (whether a power given by this instrument or created by authority of a power given by this instrument) shall exercise the same so as to postpone the vesting of any appointed estate or property or suspend the absolute ownership or alienation of any property or interest therein later than the end of the trust period as defined in the Article entitled "Rule Against Perpetuities."

(f) Any donee may release wholly or partially any power of appointment.

(g) If the power is a testamentary power, the trustee may rely upon any instrument admitted to probate as the Will of the donee. If the trustee has no notice of any such Will within three months after the donee's death, the trustee may assume that the donee died intestate without exercising said power, and may make distribution of the property subject thereto accordingly without any liability whatsoever, which distribution shall not, however, affect any right which an appointee or taker in default of appointment may have against any distributee.

ARTICLE 18. CHANGE OF TRUSTEE AND SUCCESSOR TRUSTEES

Except to the extent a successor trustee has been provided for under the section entitled "Trustee," each trustee, while acting as trustee, may by written instrument, revocable at any time prior to the installment of the successor trustee, designate a successor and/or provide for the method of appointment, of a successor and the terms and conditions of such successor's service. If a trustee is unable or unwilling to serve and has not so designated or provided, the remaining trustee or trustees may either fill any such vacancy or serve alone as they determine.

If there is no trustee, and the appointment of a successor trustee is not otherwise provided for, then a majority of the legally competent adults then entitled to receive income, either outright or in the discretion of the trustee, under the Family Trust, may appoint a suitable trustee or trustees. If no such appointment is made within ninety days after a vacancy occurs, any beneficiary may apply to any court having jurisdiction for the appointment of a trustee or trustees to fill the vacancy or vacancies, and the court shall appoint a suitable trustee or trustees unless said persons above referred to shall have made said appointment before the court has acted.

Every successor trustee shall upon taking office be vested with and subject to all the rights, powers, authorities, duties and obligations herein conferred and imposed upon the trustee without any transfer or conveyance of the trust property.

Any trustee may resign by written notice to his co-trustees, or if none, to any adult beneficiary, or if none, to the parent or guardian of any minor beneficiary. It shall not be necessary for any trustee to apply to any court to have his resignation accepted, but such resignation may be accepted by the remaining trustee or trustees, or if none, by the successor trustee.

Any successor trustee need not post bond, unless the appointing person shall so require, and the approval of any court or person of the appointment shall not be required. The former trustee and the successor trustee shall exchange such accountings, receipts and documents as shall be reasonably required by either of them.

If the settlor's spouse changes residence to another state, then, unless such spouse elects to have any such corporate trustee continue in office, the corporate trustee of any trust of which such spouse is an income beneficiary (either outright or in the discretion of the trustee) shall, within a reasonable time, resign and appoint a successor corporate trustee with its principal place of business in the state of the new residence of such spouse and with a combined capital and surplus of not less than Five Million Dollars.

ARTICLE 19. NO GUARDIAN AD LITEM

No guardian ad litem or similar proceedings shall be required, and the trustee shall be released from liability for acts occurring during a period for which it has received written approval of the then adult beneficiaries or for which it has furnished a report and accounting to the adult beneficiaries if no such beneficiaries notify the trustee in writing of disapproval of such report and accounting within ninety days thereof.

ARTICLE 20. INSURANCE PROCEEDS

If the proceeds of insurance on the settlor's life are payable to this trust or to the trustees of testamentary trusts as set forth in the settlor's Will, without specifically designating the trust to which payable, and if such proceeds qualify for the federal estate tax marital deduction, the trustee shall, unless and to the extent it is determined that such deduction should be funded in whole or in part with probate assets, first allocate such proceeds to the marital bequest to satisfy or to be applied toward such marital bequest and the balance of such proceeds, if any, shall be allocated to the Family Trust.

ARTICLE 21. TERMINATION OF SMALL TRUST

If a trust, fund or share of any trust shall, in the judgment of the trustee, be or become reduced in size, so that the administration thereof is not in the best interest of the beneficiaries, the trustee may, but need not, terminate such trust, fund or share; provided, however, the trustee shall not terminate the Marital Trust or any other trust, share or fund if such termination could defeat any federal estate tax deduction allowable with respect thereto or if any portion thereof would be distributed to or for the benefit of the trustee.

If the trustee terminates the Marital Trust during the life of the settlor's spouse, all income and principal shall be distributed to such spouse. If the trustee terminates any other trust, fund or share, the property held therein shall be distributed to the person then living who is then entitled to the income or to have it applied for his or her benefit. If there is more than one such beneficiary, the trust, fund or share shall be distributed only among those beneficiaries and in the following proportions:

(a) If their income interests are definite, then in proportion to their income interests;

(b) If their income interests are indefinite, among the settlor's spouse, if such a beneficiary, and among those beneficiaries, per stirpes, as are descendants of the settlor (with the share of the settlor's spouse to equal the share of any then living child of the settlor or the then living descendants of any deceased child of the settlor, or the entire trust, fund or share if there is no then living descendant of the settlor), or if no beneficiary is a descendant of the settlor or is the settlor's spouse, to those beneficiaries in equal shares.

ARTICLE 22. PRIORITY OF TRUST INVASION FOR SPOUSE

The trustee shall require the settlor's spouse to resort to and exhaust the Marital Trust (unless there are assets which it deems advisable to retain therein) before it applies the net income or invades the principal of the Family Trust for such spouse.

ARTICLE 23. USE OF TERMS

The provisions of this instrument, including the provisions of this Article, shall be supplemented by and when necessary shall be subject to the following:

(a) Each singular expression shall include the plural, and plural expressions shall include the singular, and the context of this instrument shall be read accordingly when the facts require it.

(b) "Trustee" shall refer to the trustee or trustees in office and shall include a successor trustee or trustees, whether so expressed or not.

(c) Whenever the word "property" is used, such term shall include cash.

(d) Whenever the phrase "per stirpes" is used, such phrase shall mean "per stirpes and not per capita."

(e) Whenever this instrument provides for a distribution to or a division into shares or trusts for a person or persons described as "then living," such phrase shall mean those persons living at the termination of the immediately preceding interest in trust.

(f) Whenever this instrument provides for the maximum federal estate tax marital deduction, such term shall not be construed as a direction to exercise any tax election only in a manner which will result in a larger allowable estate tax marital deduction than if the contrary election had been made.

(g) Whenever the phrase "brother and sister" or "brothers and sisters" is used, such phrase shall include a half-brother or half-sister only if the common parent of such half-brother or half-sister is a descendant of the settlor or of an ancestor of the settlor; provided, however, if property passes to an heir of the settlor's spouse under the Article entitled "Absence of Takers," then, with respect to such property, such phrase shall include a half-brother or half-sister only if the common parent of such half-brother or half-sister is a descendant of the settlor's spouse or of an ancestor of the settlor's spouse.

(h) Whenever the term "parent," "child," "grandchild," "descendant" or "ancestor" is used, then for purposes of determining whether a person is a parent, child, grandchild, descendant or ancestor:

(1) An individual (including individuals other than such person) who has been adopted shall be deemed a child of the adoptive parent or parents.

(2) Except as provided in clause (4) below, an individual (including individuals other than such person) shall be deemed a child of his or her natural mother.

(3) Except as provided in clause (4) below, an individual (including individuals other than such person) shall be deemed a child of his or her natural father if his or her natural parents were at any time married to each other at law or at common law or if the paternity of the natural father was proven during the father's lifetime, or if the child was recognized by the

father as his child if such recognition was either general and notorious or in writing.

(4) Notwithstanding the foregoing, an individual (including individuals other than such person) shall not be deemed a child of a natural parent: (A) If adopted during the life of that natural parent and if the parental rights of that natural parent were terminated in connection with such adoption proceedings; or (B) If adopted after the death of that natural parent unless, prior to the relevant division or distribution, the adoptive identity of such individual and such natural parenthood are actually known by the trustee or by any person (or by his or her guardian) whose share or beneficial interest in such division or distribution would be affected by such determination.

IN WITNESS WHEREOF, the parties hereto have executed this instrument the day and year first above written.

                              _____
                              Jane L. Smith, Settlor

                              _____
                              Jane L. Smith, Trustee

                              _____
                              John L. Smith, Trustee

STATE OF _____   )

)ss:

COUNTY OF_____)

On this _____ day of _____, 19 ____, before me, a Notary Public, personally appeared _____, to me known to be the person named in and who executed the foregoing instrument, and acknowledged that _____ executed the same as _____ voluntary act and deed.

                              _____
                            Notary Public in the State of Iowa

STATE OF _____)

) ss:

COUNTY OF _____)

On this _____ day of _____, 19 ____, before me, a Notary Public, personally appeared _____, to me known to be the person named in and who executed the foregoing instrument, and acknowledged that _____ executed the same as _____ voluntary act and deed.

                                        _____

                                 Notary Public in the State of Iowa

Appendix D

Example of a Pour-Over Will for a Living Trust

Last Will and Testament
of
Jane L. Smith

Executed the _____day of _____, 19 ___

Table of Contents

Last Will and Testament
of
Jane L. Smith

The sample Will for the fictitious person named "Jane L. Smith" is a "pour-over" Will which assumes that there is in effect a living trust.

Article 2 covers any items of personal property and any home that may have not already been conveyed to the trust and leaves this to a surviving spouse, if any, or if none, to children.

Article 3 leaves the residue of the estate to the living trust.

Article 4 gives the executor flexible powers, including the power to distribute property to the legal or natural guardian of any beneficiary under legal age. The powers also include the power to buy and sell property, including any real estate that might not have been already conveyed to the living trust.

I, Jane L. Smith, of _____ County, Iowa, being of sound mind and memory, declare this my Last Will and Testament, and revoke all my former Wills or testamentary instruments.

ARTICLE 1. DEFINITIONS AND APPOINTMENTS

The provisions of this Will shall be supplemented by and, when necessary, subject to this Article.

1(a) Spouse.

John L. Smith.

1(b) Executor.

I hereby appoint my spouse, John L. Smith, and XYZ Bank as executors. If my spouse is unable or unwilling to serve, XYZ Bank shall serve alone.

1(c) Living Trust.

All references herein to the "Living Trust" shall refer to the Jane L. Smith Living Trust executed on the _____ day of _____, 19 ____, by and between Jane L. Smith as settlor and Jane L. Smith and John L. Smith as trustee.

ARTICLE 2. SPECIFIC BEQUESTS

2(a) Personal Property.

If my spouse survives me, and there is personal property that has not already been transferred to the Living Trust, I bequeath to my spouse all personal automobiles, household furniture and furnishings, and other articles of domestic use or ornament which I own at my death. If my spouse does not survive me, such property shall be distributed equally to my then living children. If any of my children are not then living, the then living children of each such deceased child shall take the share of their parent.

If my spouse does not survive me, and if the then living children and/or the then living children of a deceased child or children are unable to agree upon division of the above property, the executor shall place a value on each item thereof. Thereafter, each child shall alternately select the items he or she desires (except that if any child of mine shall not then be living and shall leave children surviving, any spouse of said deceased child may select on behalf of said children, or if the spouse of a deceased child is not competent or living, the guardian of said children shall make the choice, or the children themselves, collectively, may make the choice if they are all adults), and when a child has selected items having an aggregate value of one share, the child shall have no further right of selection. The order of selection shall be determined by lot.

The items not selected by the above method shall be sold and the net proceeds shall be divided so that the cash plus the items selected by a child will total in value one equal share. The executor shall have authority to group a number of related items and thus determine what shall constitute a single selection.

2(b) Memorandum of Disposition.

Notwithstanding the preceding section I direct that my executor and beneficiaries abide by any dated memorandum in my handwriting or signed by me which I leave indicating that a certain person should receive a specific article or articles of tangible personal property.

2(c) Homestead.

I devise to my spouse, if my spouse survives me, any homestead or interest therein which I own at my death, including any lands adjacent thereto and used as a part thereof in the event it is not already a part of the Living Trust.

ARTICLE 3. RESIDUE OF MY ESTATE

I bequeath all of the rest, residue and remainder of my estate not effectively disposed of by other provisions of this Will to the Living Trust, such property to be held, administered and distributed in accordance with all of the provisions of that trust as though the property had been a part of that trust at its inception.

ARTICLE 4. POWERS OF EXECUTOR

The executor may do any act advisable in a fiduciary capacity for the administration of my estate. In extension of any power, right or discretion otherwise possessed said executor shall have, without notice to or approval of any court or person, the following powers:

(a) To retain any asset which I own, even though it leaves a disproportionately large part of my assets invested in one type of property, and to sell, exchange, mortgage, lease or otherwise dispose of any asset, real or personal, upon such terms as the executor deems advisable.

(b) To acquire, invest, reinvest, exchange, sell and manage estate assets, exercising the judgment and care which persons of prudence, discretion and intelligence exercise in the management of their own affairs, not in regard to speculation but in regard to the permanent disposition of their funds, considering the probable income and safety of their capital.

(c) To borrow money from the commercial department of any corporate executor, or elsewhere, for the protection, preservation or improvement of any asset.

(d) To collect, receive and receipt for principal or income and to enforce, defend against, prosecute, compromise or settle any claim by or against the estate.

(e) To vote, execute proxies to vote and any other rights incident to the ownership of estate properties.

(f) To hold assets in bearer form or in the name of the executor, or executor's nominee, without disclosing any fiduciary relationship; provided, however, that all estate assets shall so appear on the books of the executor.

(g) To make division or distribution in whole or in part in money, securities or other property, and in undivided interests therein, and to hold any remaining undivided interest. In any division or distribution, the executor's judgment concerning the propriety thereof and the valuation of the properties concerned shall be binding and conclusive on all persons.

(h) To make payments (including distributions of personal property, if any) to or for the benefit of any beneficiary (including any beneficiary under any legal disability) either: (1) directly to the beneficiary; or (2) to the legal or natural guardian of the beneficiary; or (3) to anyone who has custody and care of the beneficiary. The executor need not see to the application of the funds so paid, but the receipt of the person to whom paid shall be full acquittance to the executor.

(i) To pay all expenses, taxes and charges incurred in administration of the estate, and to determine as a fiduciary what is principal and income.

(j) To employ attorneys, accountants and other agents whose services may be required.

(k) To continue, either as a going concern or for purposes of liquidation, without liability for errors in judgment, any business which I own or in which I am financially interested, for as long as executor deems advisable and for any legal purpose and to exercise with respect to the management, sale or liquidation of any such business or business interest all powers which I could have exercised during my lifetime.

(l) To designate, in writing, any member of my family to actively participate in the management of any farm owned by me, to secure qualification of the same for any election or benefits under the Internal Revenue Code or to prevent disqualification for such benefits. The executor may delegate any authority or responsibility to such person advisable to obtain such benefits, and is exonerated from liability for such delegation. The executor may change or substitute such designee from time to time.

(m) My executor may join in filing joint income and gift tax returns for any period prior to my death and may claim expenses as either income or estate tax deductions when an election is permitted by law, or make such other elections, including any special lien procedures, under the tax laws as my executor deems advisable without regard to the relative interests of the beneficiaries. My executor may disclaim, in its sole discretion, all or any portion of any interest in property, including any interest passing from my spouse. Generally, I would anticipate that in making any disclaimer of any interest in property passing from my spouse that my executor exercise such discretion so as to reduce the total death taxes payable in my estate and the estate of my spouse. No adjustment shall be made between such interests to compensate for the effect of such elections or disclaimer and the determination of my executor shall be conclusive upon all affected persons.

(n) My executor may agree with my spouse or my spouse's legal representative (1) as to how federal income tax or gift tax arising out of a joint return shall be borne, and (2) as to who shall be entitled (A) to the benefit of any refund of any such tax, (B) to any refund or credit on account of any joint declaration of estimated federal income tax, and (C) to the benefit of any payment made on such declaration.

No executor named in this Will need post bond.

ARTICLE 5. USE OF TERMS

The provisions of this Will, including the provisions of this Article, shall be supplemented by and when necessary shall be subject to the following:

(a) Each singular expression shall include the plural, and plural expressions shall include the singular, and the context of this instrument shall be read accordingly when the facts require it.

(b) Whenever this Will provides for a distribution or division of my estate to a person or persons described as "then living," the phrase "then living" shall refer to those persons living at the time of my death.

(c) Outright bequests to my spouse in Article 2 shall be made to my spouse's Living Trust, if there is one.

IN WITNESS WHEREOF, I have signed before the undersigned witnesses and declare this instrument consisting of _____ pages to be my Last Will and Testament.

Dated this _____ day of _____, 19 ____.

_____
Jane L. Smith

On this _____ day of _____, 19 ____, the above-named testator of the aforesaid County and State of Iowa, first exhibiting and declaring the foregoing instrument consisting of _____ pages, inclusive of this witness clause, to be such testator's Last Will and Testament and asking us to witness the execution thereof signed such testator's initials and numbered the pages on the margin of the first to the last page, both inclusive of said instrument, in our presence, and signed such testator's name as it appears above at the end of said foregoing instrument in our presence; and as witnesses thereof, the undersigned do now, at such testator's request, in the presence of such testator and in the presence of each other, hereunto subscribe our names and addresses, this clause having been first read to or by us, and we having noted and hereby certifying that the matters herein stated took place in fact and in the order herein stated.

NAME   ADDRESS

_____   _____

_____   _____

Index

About the Author

DAVID W. BELIN is a senior partner of the Des Moines, Iowa, law firm of Belin Harris Helmick Lamson McCormick. His work has primarily been in the areas of corporate matters, business and personal planning, and litigation, including constitutional cases. He has a broad spectrum of public service, having served as counsel to the Warren Commission investigating the assassination of President Kennedy and as executive director of the Commission on CIA Activities Within the United States (Rockefeller Commission). Belin has been particularly active in support of education and the arts and was instrumental in the development of the Connie Belin National Center for Gifted Education at the University of Iowa. From 1984 to 1990 he served on the President's Committee on the Arts and the Humanities.

Belin worked his way through the University of Michigan, where in six years he earned undergraduate, master of business administration, and Juris Doctor degrees—all with high distinction. From the University of Michigan Law School, he received the Henry M. Bates Memorial Award made "to each of the two most outstanding seniors in the Law School." He is a member of many honorary societies, including Phi Beta Kappa and Order of the Coif.

The *National Law Journal* has included Belin in its list of the one hundred "most powerful and influential lawyers in the United States." He serves as a trustee of the twenty Kemper Mutual Funds and on the boards of a number of corporations.